for the Soul

A famous novelist retells classic stories with passion and spirit

FIRST EDITION
First Impression … September 2000

Published and Distributed by
MESORAH PUBLICATIONS, LTD.
4401 Second Avenue / Brooklyn, N.Y 11232

Distributed in Europe by
LEHMANNS
Unit E, Viking Industrial Park
Rolling Mill Road
Jarrow, Tyne & Wear, NE32 3DP
England

Distributed in Australia and New Zealand by
GOLDS WORLD OF JUDAICA
3-13 William Street
Balaclava, Melbourne 3183
Victoria Australia

Distributed in Israel by
SIFRIATI / A. GITLER
10 Hashomer Street
Bnei Brak 51361

Distributed in South Africa by
KOLLEL BOOKSHOP
Shop 8A Norwood Hypermarket
Norwood 2196, Johannesburg, South Africa

ARTSCROLL SERIES®
MORE TALES FOR THE SOUL
© *Copyright 2000, by* MESORAH PUBLICATIONS, Ltd.
4401 Second Avenue / Brooklyn, N.Y. 11232 / (718) 921-9000 / www.artscroll.com

---

ISBN:
1-57819-569-1 (hard cover)
1-57819-570-5 (paperback)

Typography by CompuScribe at ArtScroll Studios, Ltd.
Printed in the United States of America by Noble Book Press Corp.
Bound by Sefercraft, Quality Bookbinders, Ltd., Brooklyn N.Y. 11232

Table of Contents

A Forgotten Story

DARKNESS AND LIGHT, HOLIDAY JOY INTERWOVEN WITH melancholy: all was confusion on that Shavuos of the year 5520 (1760) in Mezibuzh. R' Yisrael *Baal Shem Tov* lay on his sickbed. It was a few days ago that he'd collapsed, and his holy body grew more and more emaciated by the day. He lay on his bed in solitude, lost in celestial thoughts, preparing himself for the transition to the world of the eternal.

In truth, the members of his group knew from the *Besht's* words that the matter of his death was nothing to him; "like leaving one room and entering another." It wasn't for his sake that they walked around with faces dark as cast iron pots. They knew well that he had always looked forward to leaving this world with a storm, as Eliyahu *HaNavi* had in his time. When the *Besht's* wife died, and they saw him grieving terribly, he explained that he was mourning for "the bones that are forced to lie in the earth." He himself had hoped to go up as Eliyahu had, and now, lying here with his body weakening, he knew that it was not to be.

But his students' sorrow was for themselves, for their guide who was leaving them, for the eternal flame that warmed them and their hearts in G-d's service — for their great and holy rebbe, so beloved by them.

And now the awesome time had come upon him. All of his students gathered together in his room. The *Besht* lay on his bed, his face shining with purity. He bade farewell to his students, blessing each with appropriate words, from the greatest among them to the youngest. He showed them the path they should follow after his passing, told them what they should do. There were those to whom he revealed what would happen to them in the future, what would befall them in days and years to come. Others were told how they should provide sustenance for their families.

And now one of his devoted servants, the youngest of his students, R' Yaakov by name, approached the bed. He crouched down to hear what his master, his rebbe, would tell him.

This is what the *Besht* told him before his death: "You, R' Yaakov, shall travel to all the places that have heard of my reputation. In each and every region where I have become known and where they recognize me — you shall speak of me, tell my stories, what I did, and what I accomplished. That will be your livelihood."

R' Yaakov, hearing these words, grew very upset. "My teacher, my rebbe," he cried, from the bottom of his heart, "and is this, then, the purpose of my life here on earth? To wander from place to place and tell stories?"

"Do not fear, my servant Yaakov," the *Besht* replied. "In the future you shall grow very wealthy from this."

On that very day the soul of the *Besht* returned to heaven. His large community had been struck a blow and wept copiously for the light that had been extinguished.

2: The News

After the death of the *Besht,* each of his students began to fulfill what he'd been commanded before his teacher's death. The student R' Yaakov, too, began to travel from city to city, telling miraculous stories of what the *Baal Shem Tov* had done and accomplished.

R' Yaakov was soon hailed as a superb orator and storyteller, and whenever he came to a place, there was great excitement and joy, with many gathering around him waiting anxiously for his words. R' Yaakov had been very close to the *Besht,* and as a result he'd seen much, heard much, and had an endless treasure house of stories. The listeners would treat him kindly and reward him for his tales. But because most of the Jews in those lands were impoverished, they would only give him a few coins, whatever little they could afford.

As the *Besht* had declared, so it was: His sustenance came from the stories he told. It was a scanty living, generally, certainly not one that led to great wealth. R' Yaakov remembered his rebbe's promise, and waited and watched to see how it would be fulfilled.

In the month of Cheshvan, in the year 5523 (1763), two and a half years after the passing of the *Besht,* one of R' Yaakov's friends brought him startling news. "Have you heard? In Italy, in the city of Rome, there is a Jew who is prepared to pay a full gold coin for every true story told about our master."

R' Yaakov was astonished and excited. "Can it be?" he said in wonder. "A golden coin for every tale of the *Besht*?"

The friend repeated the conditions. "Only if the story is true."

"And am I a liar?" R' Yaakov retorted good-naturedly. "If I collect all the stories that I know firsthand about my teacher and master, stories that I myself saw, not some stranger, and add to them some of the tales that I've heard from my colleagues, they will add up to several hundred."

"It's worth your while," his friend said with honest joy. "A few hundred golden coins! You will be able to stay in the same place for years, and won't have to wander around."

R' Yaakov didn t spend much time preparing for the trip to Italy. In the next few days he bought a fine horse and a strong carriage that could undergo the rigors of the journey. He also hired an attendant at a high salary. He realized, after investigating the matter, that the trip was a long and very arduous one, and he was afraid that his strength wasn't up to a solitary journey, and so he heeded the advice of the wisest of men: Two are better than one.

3: The Journey

The journey to Italy lasted seven months. When he left his city he had only a few coins that he'd managed to borrow. R' Yaakov, in his great faith, went on his way, and in each city through which he passed he would stay for a short while, scattering some tiny bits from his storehouse of tales. Merciful Jews helped him by giving him contributions that were enough to get him to the next city.

After seven months he stood at the gates of Rome.

4: The Wealthy Man

Upon his arrival in Rome R' Yaakov didn't waste a minute: He immediately traveled to the Jewish Quarter and began asking about the identity of the richest man in town.

"The wealthy R' Tzadok?" The Jews of the city rubbed their hands in elation. "Ah, that's an interesting man. Ten years ago he came here, and immediately bought the palace of one of the top government ministers. It's a beautiful palace, the likes of which you've never seen in your life, with a marvelous garden full of lush fruit trees, verdant grass, and cool springs of water bubbling out of the earth. He's enormously rich, with quite an army of servants to take care of his complex business interests, and yet he's not at all proud. He learns Torah, *davens* morning and night, and comports himself with great piety. Every day the men of the city *daven* in the *beis midrash* he's built in his large house."

R' Yaakov was impressed. But how did he know this was the man whom he was seeking?

"How does he behave on Shabbos?" he asked.

"Very strangely. Every Shabbos he welcomes large numbers of guests, serves them a meal fit for a king's table, and begs them to tell him tales of the *Baal Shem Tov.* He does this at all three of the meals. Besides the guests, after dinner many of the Jews of the city gather at his home to hear enthralling stories. If we're lucky and one of the guests manages to tell a true story of the *Besht,* we all enjoy it — and the guest enjoys it doubly. After Shabbos R' Tzadok gives him his reward, a gold coin!"

"That's the man I meant to find," R' Yaakov whispered joyfully. He turned to his faithful servant. "We've reached the end of all our hardships."

R' Yaakov and his servant found out where R' Tzadok lived, and quickly turned their carriage there. Even from a distance they could see that the townspeople had not been exaggerating. A beautiful palace loomed before them, its walls intricately engraved, decorated turrets guarding its corners. The gate had a heavy metal door, and armed sentries circled its walls.

R' Yaakov, astonished by the vision before him, began to wonder if there hadn't been some kind of mistake, heaven forbid. Perhaps he'd reached the palace of one of the high officials of the kingdom. His faithful servant approached one of the guards. Nervously, he asked, "Who lives here?"

The guards, seeing the figure of a Jew, one of their own people, answered, "R' Tzadok."

"Please tell your master that one of the disciples of the *Besht* is here, one who knows many tales about him, stories that he saw with his own eyes."

The sentry disappeared into the doorway of the palace. R' Yaakov and his servant didn't have long to wait; R' Tzadok hastily sent the guard to escort them in, giving them a wing of their own and treating them like royalty.

5: The First Meal

On Friday night the entire Jewish community gathered in R' Tzadok's house. The news had been borne on wings: one of the disciples of the *Besht* is in R' Tzadok's house, a man whose bag is full of firsthand stories of the *tzaddik*. Until now, the Jews of Rome had had to make do with second- and third-hand tales. Expectations ran high, almost reaching the heavens.

The large antechamber was jammed; the crowding was unprecedented. The younger visitors pushed and climbed onto the bars of the windows in order to better see R' Yaakov, sitting at the head of the table with R' Tzadok.

The servants cleaned the last of the food off the table. The sound of *zemiros* dwindled; the suspense grew.

"Open your mouth and illuminate us with your words," R' Tzadok commanded in a heartfelt voice. "The crowd can wait no longer."

R' Yaakov cleared his throat, straightened his back, and looked steadily at the large group staring at him. He had hundreds of stories, replete with light and holiness, to take out of his storehouse and make public property. He had only to choose one of them, whichever he wished. With which story should he begin?

"And so," he said, after a prolonged hesitation, "a true story, one that really happened."

Again he fell silent, while the crowd waited with surging excitement. R' Yaakov continued. "The tale is one of the holy *Besht,* when he was going to... going to... where was he going? *Nu,* it was with ... with... that is... What did happen to him?"

He'd forgotten everything.

Nothing. All that he'd seen, all that he'd known and heard, everything flew out of his brain as if it had never existed.

R' Yaakov rubbed his forehead, in a despairing effort to pull out one story at the very least. He nodded his head back and forth, up and down, and to the sides: maybe that would dislodge some tale from the hidden recesses of his brain and pry it out of his memory.

He tried to visualize the image of the *Besht's* holy visage, hoping that would bring the lost stories back to him. To his horror, he realized that not only could he not remember the shining countenance of his teacher and rebbe, he couldn't even visualize the faces of his fellow disciples and students. Even the streets of Mezibuzh itself had vanished from his memory. Every tactic he devised to try and remember even one story proved to be useless. All was erased from his brain: R' Yaakov was like a newborn infant.

The large, expectant crowd didn't remain indifferent towards the storyteller who'd lied. At first the people held their peace, assuming that the disciple had forgotten only because of his great excitement and emotion. Then the children started to whisper among themselves; finally, even the adults lost their patience.

"A swindler and scoundrel has arrived here," one person said. "He's never met the *Besht*. He heard that R' Tzadok pays a golden coin for each story about the *Besht,* and so he's made up a few."

"So what has happened now?" another man asked out loud.

"Now, G-d has repaid him as he deserves, and made him forget his lies."

A burst of laughter flooded the crowded room, packed to capacity. R' Yaakov had become a laughingstock; he didn't know where to turn in his vast humiliation. In a short while the disappointed crowd would have been upon him, but his host, R' Tzadok, rose to his rescue.

"What's the matter with you?" he roared in fury at the mob. "Is that how our merciful brothers conduct themselves? Leave our guest alone. Surely tomorrow he will remember something."

6: The Second and Third Meals

After all the guests had left the palace, R' Yaakov made his way to his room and wept bitterly all night. Occasionally he would try to excavate the figure of the *Besht* and his disciples from his memory, to no avail. He tried telling himself stories of anything that happened to flit through his imagination, hoping that this might bring some true stories back to him, but that didn't work either. In his terrible straits he *davened* to Hashem for mercy but the heavy, oppressive feeling that fell upon him after his prayers showed him clearly that his words had been flung back into his face.

The next day many of the locals again gathered together to see what would happen with the untruthful guest.

Today R' Yaakov again sat across from his host who asked him, at the meal's end, if he'd managed to remember some tale, since he, R' Tzadok, had a tradition of listening to a story of the *Besht* at every Shabbos meal...

R' Yaakov paled. "I remember nothing. Believe me, sir, this has never before happened. It can't just be a coincidence."

"Let's wait for *seudah shelishis*," R' Tzadok answered, a cloud darkening his brow. "Maybe there'll be a miracle, and your memory. will be restored."

The dozens of Jews who had come to R' Tzadok's home left the way they'd come. This time, before the inflexible look of their host, they kept their comments to themselves.

R' Yaakov did nothing all Shabbos, just worked and toiled and racked his memory in a stupendous effort of recall. All for nothing: his brain seemed to all but crack under the effort, but his memory did not return.

At *seudah shelishis,* too, he sat, mortified. Like a drowning man grasping at straws, he tried to grab any thread of memory that would help him to remember a story. Nothing.

After *havdalah,* R' Tzadok left the *beis midrash* located in his house. The large crowd closed in on R' Yaakov. The guest was like ripe fruit in their grasping hands. Not only did the townspeople berate him mercilessly, but R' Tzakok's household, too, felt themselves badly used by a swindling trickster, and poured out their grievances upon him.

"Do you know a story of the *Besht*?" they taunted him. "Here it is: The *Besht* went. Where did he go? Ah, um, well... What happened?"

A long parade of insults followed him until the very doorway of his room...

The pious and saintly R' Yaakov bent his head and accepted his pain with love. "It would seem that my teacher, the *Besht,* is angry at me for having wanted to sell his stories in the impure city of Rome, where the people don't merit hearing them. Or perhaps Heaven just doesn't want me to become wealthy."

At the *melaveh malkah* meal, too, R' Tzadok tried to pull out one fact, one tiny detail. R' Yaakov begged his host to leave him alone. His hopes of becoming rich had disappeared; he had not even made up his travel expenses. He wanted only one thing: to saddle up his horses and leave.

R' Tzadok wouldn't hear of it. "Stay with me until Tuesday. Try with all your might. Maybe Hashem will have mercy."

Nothing. R' Yaakov scratched around in his memory for two full days, but came up empty. On Tuesday, after *Shacharis,* he bid his host farewell, apologizing profusely for the perplexing occurrence.

"You are the one who has suffered, spending seven months on the road," the rich man protested. "But you will not leave my house empty-handed." As he spoke he placed several gold coins into R' Yaakov's hands.

R' Yaakov sat in his carriage. His throat was tight with unshed tears. He raised his eyes to heaven and recited, "G-d is just, for I have rebelled against Him."

The servant sat in his place, and picked up the whip to urge the horse on.

R' Yaakov could feel his senses, frozen all through that Shabbos, begin to thaw. Suddenly his heaviness of memory lifted; from moment to moment his head grew clearer. "Stop!" he cried to his servant. "Don't go. We're going back to R' Tzakok's palace."

"Haven't you been humiliated enough?" his astonished servant asked.

"Go back," R' Yaakov insisted.

They returned to the palace, and R' Yaakov demanded an urgent meeting with R' Tzadok.

"I've just remembered a story that happened to me, together with the holy *Besht,*" R' Yaakov said with gathering excitement.

The rich man's eyes lit up. Clearly, he had been waiting all the while for this moment. "Take everyone out," he commanded. Thus, he and R' Yaakov were all alone as he told the tale...

8: A Strange Journey

It happened ten years ago, on a Shabbos before the Christian spring festival. The *Besht* spent all of Shabbos closeted in his room, pacing back and forth restlessly. On *Motzaei Shabbos,* right after *havdalah,* he asked three men — one of them was me — to come with him. He ordered the horses saddled, and we went on our way.

All that night the carriage traveled. With dawn, we reached a large city. We stopped not far from the city square, at the entrance of a house whose shutters were down, windows dark. When we knocked at the door, on the orders of the *Besht,* an old woman came out and said, in a voice full of lamentation, "Why have you come? Today is the Christian festival, and any Jew found in the street may be stabbed. We were warned yesterday, and no one left the house. The cursed ones then made a lottery to decide whom they would kill in his home. Our rav was one of those selected. They tore him from his house, stabbed him mercilessly with their knives, his blood flowing like water in the streets. Don't come in here, or they'll kill all of us. Run for your lives!"

The *Besht* paid her no heed. He told us to go into the house with our possessions, and to put the horses into her barn.

The members of the household lay paralyzed on their beds, the bitterness of death in their eyes. They could hardly speak for fright. The elderly woman sobbed and screamed in a terrible voice. Nevertheless, the *Besht* stood by the table and opened the closed shutters, despite her pleas. He then stood up and stared out the window at the city square.

In the center of the square stood a large wooden platform. Thirty steps led from the ground to the top. Around it stood a large group of Christians anxiously awaiting the Bishop's arrival. The man of the cloth, we were told, was to give a speech inciting hatred against the Jewish nation; at its conclusion, a pogrom was to begin against all the Jews of the city. Now we understood why the household members were cringing in their beds, their eyes wide with fear and utter despair. These were eyes that were beholding death.

The tolling of dozens of bells brought the ominous news: the Bishop had arrived.

"Yaakov," the *Besht* commanded me, "go to the square and tell the priest that I am waiting for him."

I prepared to leave and suddenly all the house's inhabitants were roused from their stupor and began to speak. "Don't go," they screamed in panic. "The *goyim* are already incensed; before you put a foot in the square they'll cut you into pieces."

"Do not fear, my servant, Yaakov," quoted the *Besht* softly. "Go now."

Despite his words I went out with a heavy heart, terrified of the rabble. And a miracle occurred: I passed by hundreds of bloodthirsty thugs, I saw the hatred on their faces and their bunched fists, shining knives, and heavy sticks, the swords and axes they had prepared for the planned pogrom. And yet not one of them touched a hair on my head.

Without any difficulty I managed to reach the center of the square. I went up the stairs and approached the Bishop, who was speaking to the mob. Everyone stopped and stared, aghast, at the Jew who whispered into the Bishop's ear.

"At a house nearby R' Yisrael *Baal Shem Tov* of Mezibuzh is waiting," I told him quietly. "He is calling you."

I knew that the *Besht* never spoke needlessly, and still I didn't expect to see the spark in the eyes of that evil priest as he heard the name that made angels and *seraphim* tremble. "I know that he is here," he whispered back to me. "Tell him that I will come to him after the speech."

The people in the house where the *Besht* was visiting stared in increasing amazement through tiny cracks in the shutters, watching how I had entered the lion's den in order to speak with the Bishop, the Jew-hater, and was now returning safely home. Hundreds of eyes watched my progress, with looks that boded ill, but no one harmed me at all.

I came in and told the *Besht* what the Bishop had said.

"Yaakov, go back to the square and tell him not to be a

fool, and to come immediately," he commanded. I rushed off to fulfill this second mission. I could see how the others in the house were staring at me. They said nothing; things were happening that were too much for human comprehension.

When I told the Bishop the *Besht's* words, I saw how his face changed. Without a word he left the platform — from where he d been spewing his hate-filled invective against the Jews — and followed me as meekly as a sheep. None of the Christians in the mob dared move. Their wonder was boundless, but it was as if their limbs had been paralyzed.

The *Besht* took the Bishop alone into a room, and spoke secretly to him. After about two hours he came out to us and commanded us to prepare the carriage and return to Mezibuzh. Until today I don't know what happened in there, who the Bishop was, and what the *Besht* wanted from him. Even the name of the city escapes me.

R' Yaakov ended his narrative. He stared at R' Tzadok, as if to ask, "Have I satisfied you?"

10: R' Tzadok

"You've earned your gold coin," R' Tzakok said with satisfaction. "The entire story is true, from start to finish. I recognized you as soon as you came; I identified you and knew you were a disciple of the *Besht*. I knew you weren't lying. Now I, too, want to tell you a true story:

A learned Jew, of good family, a scholar and grandson of holy men, began to swerve off the proper path. Not all in one day, but step by step down the slippery slope to the chasm below. He began by reading works of apostasy, continued by participating in church services, and ended — appointed to be a bishop, a terrible hater of Jews.

His pious ancestors, disturbed in their rest in *Gan Eden,* approached the *Besht* and begged him to intercede and return their wandering descendant's soul to his people. The *Besht* came to the

Bishop in his dreams night after night, speaking to him of repentance. The Bishop was terrified of the radiant Jew who disturbed his sleep each night; from the contents of the dreams he realized that these were real. In the last dream, the night before their spring festival, the Bishop promised the *Besht* that he would run away from the city.

The next day the Bishop wanted to fulfill his promise, but when he heard the church bells announcing the start of his lecture, his heart was filled with pride. "Those bells are ringing in my honor; shall I flee?" He went to the square and began to incite the mob, even though he knew quite clearly that at the end of his speech the rabble would fall upon the ghetto and mercilessly slaughter the Jews.

"I was that Bishop," said R' Tzadok, trembling. "When you came to me that second time in the square and said those words, my heart was transformed and I became like another man. I went to the *Besht* and he gave me a procedure for *tikkun* that I followed until I had become a complete *baal teshuvah*. I was as rich as Korach; I took half my money and gave it to the poor, and bribed the king with one-quarter of my fortune so that he would let me leave the country. The last quarter I took with me to Rome, having changed my name and appearance, and bought this palace.

"When I saw you I felt a great wave of joy, for the *Besht* had given me a clear sign. 'When one of my disciples comes to you and tells you a tale about me, you will know that your repentance has been accepted in Heaven' therefore I began to give away a gold coin for every story of the *Besht;* I was waiting for his disciple to come. Until now there were only those who'd heard the stories from someone else, secondhand.

"When you came I thought I was saved, but when you forgot everything I realized that I was the one who was guilty; my repentance was not complete. All that Shabbos I prayed and begged the Creator to accept me as one of His children. I was afraid that the gates of repentance had been shut before me. On Sunday and Monday I fasted and prayed — and still, I was not helped. When I saw you climb into your carriage, my heart was broken, shattered into bits. I fell to the floor in bitter weeping; I felt lower than the lowest creature on this earth. I realized that the blood of my brothers that had been shed because of me was crying from the ground, keeping me from my Father in Heaven.

"Those tears were honest! There was not a trace of falsity or ulterior motives within them. And those tears burned a hole within the metal barrier that had been built between me and my Father in Heaven, making a path for all of my repentance to reach its proper place. At that moment your memory came back."

It is said that R' Tzadok insisted that R' Yaakov accept one thousand gold coins. He became a wealthy man, as the *Besht* had promised before his passing on the holiday of Shavuos in 5520 (1760).

Buried Alive

THE HOLY *ADMOR,* R' YAAKOV ABUCHATZEIRA, HAD A yeshivah in his city of Dimanhour in Egypt. Many students gravitated there in order to learn Torah from the rav. R' Yaakov Abuchatzeira's reputation spread first in his hometown, and from there he was hailed throughout many lands, with people coming from all over to receive blessings from him. His blessings would come true completely; his words were never unfulfilled.

Not only the Jews appreciated his greatness; even the Moslems trembled before him. The mere mention of his name was enough to set them shivering. At first only the common people, the simple Arabs who heard stories of his miracles, were awestruck. Slowly, though, more tales were told, of how anyone who tried to harm him was punished, and even the toughs, the robbers and swindlers who preyed upon unwary travelers and held them up for all their money, even these hardened criminals began to fear him. From mouth to ear, from Jew to Arab, the hair-raising stories were passed. Still, there were those who refused to believe, until the following tale became public. From that moment on, there wasn't a person in the land who doubted the greatness of this man of G-d.

Once every few months R' Yaakov Abuchatzeira would leave Dimanhour and travel the roads between cities and towns, raising funds for his yeshivah students, who were able to learn in tranquility because R' Yaakov saw to all their needs. But he didn't concern himself only with scholars; he took care of all the poor of Dimanhour, acting as a father and patron to them.

R' Yaakov hired an Arab guide to escort him and do what was needed on the difficult journey.

Several arduous weeks passed, blessed with much success. R' Yaakov managed to collect a large amount of money and decided to return home. "Prepare the animals and luggage for the way back," he instructed the Arab. "We're returning to Dimanhour."

The hired man quickly gave water and feed to the donkeys, tightened the saddles, tied the bundles to the animals sides, and prepared them for the long return trip. R' Yaakov sat on the side and learned Mishnayos by heart; he was extraordinarily diligent and never allowed himself to waste even one moment.

"Everything's ready," the guide said with satisfaction.

R' Yaakov opened his shut eyes. "Everything?"

"That's right."

R' Yaakov looked at the donkeys standing in their places facing north. "Why do you say everything is ready?" he remonstrated. "The donkeys are not ready yet!"

"But they are!" the man declared.

"No! They are facing northward. Turn them around to the south."

"Aren't we going north?"

"No."

The Arab nodded his head in bewilderment, his *kaffiyeh* almost falling off his head. "But aren't we going to Dimanhour?"

"Of course we are. But I know an old shortcut that I learned about long ago, and I want to travel that way."

The Arab stood frozen in place. "I, too, know that shortcut. But it's a very difficult road. Doesn't the respected rabbi know that it s dangerous, and is full of highwaymen?" he asked, startled and perplexed.

"Certainly."

"And the respected rabbi is not afraid of them?" The Arab tried persuasion. "After all, you have much money in your purse," he said craftily, his eyes darting back and forth.

When he saw that the Jewish wise man wasn't impressed, he began to tell him horrifying stories of huge caravans — not two lonely travelers! — who'd been caught in the area and had their last coins stolen from them by gangs of thieves; murdered, too, by the cruel bandits who were not content with their loot, and who hadn't left a single one alive.

His harsh words made no impression on R' Yaakov. "I said we'll take the shorter route — no matter what."

"If so, the respected rabbi will have to go himself," the Arab said, his eyes moving back and forth in fright. "I'm not prepared to risk my life like that."

"You must come with me," R' Yaakov thundered. "I have paid for your services throughout the journey, no matter what road we take."

"But I 'm afraid," the man whined, his voice trembling.

R' Yaakov smiled. "I promise you that nothing will happen to us. But if you are still afraid that something will happen, call over two men to be witnesses. They can sign a document in which I absolve you of all responsibility, since I forced you to come with me."

The Arab went out to the market and brought back two Jews, who signed as witnesses on the document that R' Yaakov gave him.

The donkeys were turned southward and the travelers went on their way. After a short time they found themselves far from civilization. The caravans, too, thinned out, until there were no more passing. The road became harder and harder to pass; they were now in a barren wasteland. Only the wails of the hyenas could be heard in the distance, a mournful moaning that chilled the blood.

Suddenly they heard the sound of horses' hooves behind them.

The guide grew as white as the desert sands. He squinted towards the horizon, and his face grew even paler. "The bandits! I see dozens of them, all armed with rifles," he screamed in terror. "I warned you," he cried brokenly.

The guide hadn't erred: One of the most dangerous of the robber bands, which had terrorized the entire area and was known throughout the land for its murderous deeds and merciless looting, had been following R' Yaakov from the day he'd left Dimanhour, hoping to steal his money. The bandits' spies had been following him from place to place, and knew that his purse was full.

The guide was stricken with fear: He raced away, panting, screaming, "Don't kill me! I'm just helping the rabbi. I have nothing; he has all the money!"

He fled some distance away. When his strength gave out he stopped and hid behind the trunk of a wide tree to see if they were following him. He took a deep breath; the robbers hadn't bothered pursuing him. Instead, they had spurred their horses toward the Jewish rabbi, an easy and certain prey.

The frightening band reached R' Yaakov in a short time. Several dozen robbers, armed to the teeth, circled R' Yaakov, looking at his bag with greedy eyes. It was a terrifying tableau, one that froze the blood of the Arab guide cringing behind the tree trunk.

But R' Yaakov remained tranquil and unmoved. "Why are you standing around me in a circle? What do you want from me?" he calmly asked the head of the band of robbers.

"What do we want from you?" The robber almost fell off his horse, he was laughing so hard. "What should we want? Nothing, just your money. Give it to us now."

"My money is put down before you; come and get it," R' Yaakov said coolly. He took out his purse and put it down in front of the chief.

"Slow down. It's not so simple," the robber said in a tone that bode ill. "You think we're stupid? If we let you go you will immediately go and complain to the authorities. No, my friend, first we have to kill you; then we take your money."

R' Yaakov didn't lose his serenity. "I put my spirit in Your

Hand," he looked heavenward. "Do with me what you wish," he told them confidently as he began to prepare to give his life.

All the bandits aimed their weapons towards the radiant figure of R' Yaakov standing encircled, his lips moving soundlessly. They waited to hear their leader's command, the sign to fire that would set all their rifles off to spew death upon the Jew.

Suddenly the ground began to shake and shiver. Before they could comprehend what was happening, the earth had opened and all the bandits had fallen in. They were trapped halfway; from the waist up their bodies were like stone. Their loaded rifles fell from their paralyzed hands without having fired a shot.

A terrible silence fell upon the place; the jubilant cries of the greedy bandits, who already had imagined themselves dividing the booty, melted away. Despite their massive efforts, they couldn't make a sound. They stood like statues, looking out from desperate eyes.

R' Yaakov picked up the purse that had been flung to the ground and, without pausing, got on his donkey and left the place, leaving the bandits buried up to the waist.

When he had disappeared over the horizon, a horrified figure crawled out from between the trees. The Arab guide rolled his eyes in disbelief. With hesitant steps he approached the half-buried robbers to see if this was no more than a mirage. He thrust his hand out towards one of them and touched his arm. His breath almost stopped and he gave a yell of fright; this felt like a cold marble slab, not a living arm.

In a frenzy he ran off from the place, panting and screaming, calling upon the demons to protect him, until he reached R' Yaakov Abuchatzeira, who was calmly riding along on his donkey.

"Oh, wise man," he cried in despair, "let the holy man wait for me."

R' Yaakov didn't turn his head. "You've come out from behind your tree?" he said mockingly.

"I was afraid. The holy man understands that," the guide apologized.

"These are the moments when a man is tested," R' Yaakov berated him. "To my great sorrow you have failed. All you had to do was believe in me. I told you no one would hurt us."

"What will happen to the thieves?" the Arab said, turning the conversation around.

"They can stay there forever, so that others will see them and be afraid," R' Yaakov answered coldly.

R' Yaakov was welcomed with joy and song when he returned to Dimanhour. The townspeople came out to show him honor, greeting him with drums and tambourines.

However, there were some who looked at the scene with malicious eyes: the wives of the robbers. They knew of their husbands' plan to follow R' Yaakov and murder him, and they couldn't understand how the wise man, who was supposed to be a corpse, had now returned, while of their own spouses there was no sign.

The women waited all that day, and the next. On the third day they realized that things had gone very wrong. Gathering all their courage they went to the rabbi to ask if he knew what had happened to their husbands.

R' Yaakov didn't answer, and gestured to them to leave his home at once.

Weeping, the Arab women left the house.

Near the Rav's house they noticed the Arab guide. "Let s ask him," they said to each other. "Maybe we can find out something from him."

The Arab first tried to avoid them, but when they pressed some gold coins in his hand he opened his mouth and told them the entire terrible affair. He begged them earnestly to go and pacify the rabbi; perhaps there was still hope for their husbands, if they hadn't yet died of hunger.

"Holy man, forgive the sins of our husbands," the women wailed, upon their return to the rabbi's house.

R' Yaakov didn't throw them out this time; he sat and meditated on the matter. Finally, he said, "Go to this-and-this place, where your husbands are buried. They are all still alive. If they promise you that they will stop their thievery and return to an ethical life, they will be healed; if not, that place will be their grave!"

In a short time the city of Dimanhour was almost empty. The rumors flew of the bandits who had been buried alive, and who would want to miss such a sight? And so a great caravan of people made its way from Dimanhour to the desert.

When the huge group came to the place, the men stood, their hearts pounding, staring at the scene before them. None had ever seen such a thing: dozens of men stuck in the dry sand, with apparently nothing stopping them from getting out. Their eyes were open yet seemed frozen; no sound came from their mouths. Even a blind man could see that they'd been struck by G-d's Hand.

"How great is the rabbi of the Jews," went the whisper from one to the other, and everyone shuddered.

The bandits' relatives recovered first. With hasty steps they approached and tried to pull out the men, who were still breathing. But they stopped almost immediately: it seemed as if it would be easier to dislodge huge boulders. The earth grasped its treasure greedily. The relatives spoke to the men, but got no answer.

"Fools that we are, the rabbi said that only if they promise not to harm anyone will they be able to get out."

They stood and asked the buried men the question the rabbi had put to them. And miraculously — after the question was asked, suddenly these rock-men could speak. They eagerly promised to repent completely and never return to their evil ways.

Another minute and the ground that had held them like pincers loosened its grasp. The men crawled out of their graves, weak and close to death. But all lived, as the *tzaddik* had promised.

For many days hence, they spoke in Dimanhour and in all the region of the great *kiddush Hashem,* of the time when the "buried bandits" came to the rabbi, fell on their faces, weeping, and asked his forgiveness. And from that day forward the rabbi was greatly honored, even among the gentiles, who had seen that there was indeed a G-d among the Jews.

A Holy Guest in the Bar

THE CITY OF POSEN LAY ENVELOPED IN DARKNESS. THE skies above were covered with black clouds and a heavy snow fell upon the earth. At this hour, long after midnight, not a living creature could be seen outside. Only in the home of R' Akiva Eiger did a small light flicker in a window. Near a table sat a father and son. The father was the great leader of Israel, the *gaon* R' Akiva Eiger. The son was the genius R' Shlomo Eiger. The two voraciously swallowed up page after page of *Gemara,* hardly noticing the cold and the passing hours. Occasionally they stopped to meditate upon some particularly difficult concept, giving it their complete concentration.

Suddenly there was a loud knocking on the door. R' Shlomo was startled out of his learning. Who could it be, so late at night and in such bad weather? A fear rose in his breast: it could only be a gentile, a hostile gentile, an anti-Semite who found this the best time for his evil plots and schemes. Who knew if some new misfortune was not going to befall the townspeople?

In his anxiety, R' Shlomo didn't dare approach the door. He waited, looking respectfully at his father, who was still deeply engrossed in his learning, completely unaware of the heavy knocking. The banging grew louder. R' Akiva Eiger picked his head up from the *sefer.* "I think someone is knocking at the door," he told his son. "Maybe it's a Jew in trouble. Who else would come so late?"

R' Shlomo went to the door. He'd just opened it when two sobbing women burst in. "Please, holy rabbi, help us," they wailed brokenly.

R' Akiva trembled. "What has happened?" he asked gently.

The two calmed down slightly, and the younger one began to speak. "This is my mother-in-law, my husband's mother. We've come because of my husband. The *poritz*..." Her voice broke and she began to cry once again.

"Try to tell the story," R' Akiva Eiger beseeched her kindly. "One thing at a time."

The young woman controlled her sobbing with an effort and began the tale. "We live in a small village not far from Posen. The *poritz,* the local landowner, has many large holdings. One of these he rented to my husband, who is very diligent and who built an inn on it, and from this we get our livelihood. It was not easy, but, thank G-d, we were not dying of hunger. For a long while we lived fairly well, but for the past few years the wheel has turned. The business has been getting worse and worse until we have almost nothing to live on, and certainly not enough to pay the rental fees. The debt has grown and grown. When the *poritz* saw that his Jewish renter wasn't paying up, he sent several warnings. If the debt wouldn't be paid — the Jew's lot would be bitter!

"My husband went to the *poritz* and begged him. He said, 'I'm not a thief, I'm not trying to avoid paying. But my luck has been bad, and I can't pay you right now.'

"'So what is it you want?' asked the *poritz.*

"'Just a little time,' my husband said humbly, 'a little time for me to get the money together.'

"The *poritz* gave in. 'You can have an extension of three months, but not one day more!'

"But bad luck remained bad luck. The situation didn't improve at all, and in the extra time we haven't managed to get together even a small portion of the debt. The *poritz's* patience ran out. He owns the entire village, and he does what he wants there. Without a trial, he grabbed my husband and threw him into prison, where the *poritz's* servants are torturing him mercilessly.

"Today," the young woman concluded, "the *poritz* himself came to see the tortures. When he'd had enough of that pleasure he told my husband that if in two days he hadn't repaid the debt, his doom was sealed. He would breathe his last, after the most cruel torments imaginable."

The woman finished her terrible story and she and her mother-in-law again burst into tears, begging the holy rabbi for help.

R' Akiva's heart was a merciful one, and he suffered terribly. He longed to help them on this life-and-death matter. But what could he do? Did he have anyone he could turn to at this late hour? He could wait until tomorrow and then try to approach the wealthy men of Posen, but there was a good possibility that he wouldn't be able to raise such a large sum in time. The people had many needs, and he would often come to them and ask for this or that charitable cause. Now they might say: 'The poor of your own city have precedence over the poor of another city.'

R' Akiva Eiger sat deep in thought, looking for a way out of the labyrinth. Suddenly he had a brilliant idea — a true "*chiddush* of R' Akiva Eiger."

He stood up, determination written on his face. He put on his rabbinic garb and prepared to leave.

"Father, where are you going?" R' Shlomo asked.

"First we'll go, then we'll see," R' Akiva answered.

R' Shlomo had vast respect for his saintly father. He asked no more questions, and just walked quietly beside him. The two trudged on frozen feet through the thick snow that covered the streets of Posen, until they had left the city's main center. Now they slid through snowdrifts in the narrow streets on the edges of the city. R' Shlomo's wonder increased; they were now approaching the criminal areas, where the underworld figures roamed about. This shady neighborhood was dangerous to wander through even in the light of day; how much more so in the blackness of the night — and how much more so for the Jewish leader of his generation! Could salvation truly come from this place?

R' Shlomo, though, was completely subservient to his father's will. He knew that his father wouldn't say the slightest thing without first having gone through his entire storehouse of Talmudic wisdom; certainly he wouldn't act without first having thought the deed out from all sides. His father surely knew what he was doing, R' Shlomo realized, even if he, the son, couldn't follow his deep logic and insight.

After trudging through snow and mud for some time, they reached a dark, frightening alley. This was one of the worst areas in town, home to the saloons and illegal gambling houses, where men played cards and other games of chance. R' Akiva Eiger stopped for a moment, then climbed the steps to one of those dens of darkness and knocked on the locked door.

The door opened just a crack and a hairy face peered out. This was one of the town bullies, a Jew who spent his days with the scum of the city. When he saw who the guest was, a shout of surprise escaped him. He quickly slammed the door shut and ran inside in wild excitement.

"Hey, gang, guess which important guest has come to us?"

A number of hirsute heads looked up for a moment from their bottles and their cards. "Who?" they asked, interested.

"The *rabbiner* of the city, R' Akiva," the ruffian laughed. "It seems that he, too, wants some time to enjoy himself and stretch his aching bones..."

"Quiet," his colleagues growled at him. "A little courtesy! R' Akiva is an important rabbi. It will be interesting to hear what he wants from us."

The head of the gang approached the door to respectfully greet his two guests.

The whole lot of them sat, expectantly, around the tables heaped with large piles of coins that were used for betting. Inebriated laughter and wild, hysterical shouts of drunken revelers filled the foul air of the musty saloon. Clouds of stagnant tobacco smoke from dozens of cigarettes and cigars hung heavily in the atmosphere; the scent of alcohol, too, wafted through the air, contributing to the suffocating feeling.

And into this viper's nest strode calmly a giant of the spirit, R' Akiva Eiger.

Suddenly the smoke seemed to dissipate, the scent of wine and beer melted away, and the unpleasant cackling laughter grew silent. The two shining figures seemed so different, so out of place, like a thousand suns shining out of a mud pile.

A sudden seriousness came over the vacuous, frivolous atmosphere. Dozens of flippant, irresponsible men, unused to such a sight, surrounded the two rabbis. Their faces showed their curiosity and wonder: what could this rabbi want? Was he going to scold them for their reckless ways? Most likely he was going to stand up and rebuke them, as if today were Yom Kippur and this were a synagogue...

One particularly brazen young man stood up and said, laughing, "Perhaps Rabbiner Eiger would like to take part in our games of chance? We'll be happy to see if he's got talent that way, to see if, where there is Torah, there is wisdom as well..."

Before the cocksure lad could finish his words, strong hands had reached around him and pulled him away, like a tree being pushed down in a storm. "Idiot, you should be ashamed of yourself, speaking that way to the holy Rabbi Eiger."

The young man fled to a corner and stood motionless, frightened. His friends approached R' Akiva and spoke with complete humility. "It is a great honor for us, and a day of pleasure, when the rabbi has troubled to come and join us here. We understand that Rabbiner Eiger is a holy man, and doesn't waste his time like we do. If he has come here, it means that he has something important to tell us. Let the rabbi speak."

At the same time, the nagging doubt refused to leave them: perhaps the rabbi was going to hit them squarely over the head with a lecture, whipping them with a tongue-lashing over their daily deeds.

R' Eiger took his measured steps towards the large table that stood in the middle of the saloon and began to speak in front of his unusual audience. In short words he told them of the bitter lot of the Jewish renter, the terrible plight of the two women who were standing at that very moment in his, Rabbi Akiva's, house, awaiting his help. In strong words he described the greatness of the *mitzvah*. "You have the ability to obtain your World in one hour," he ended emotionally.

His holy words, coming straight out of his pure heart, carved a path through the stone hearts of these apostates, whom one would think had been completely hardened by their many sins. The walls around them came down; a fresh breeze began to blow through them. The revelers searched through their purses, and the money prepared for betting started to roll towards R' Akiva Eiger. No one stood indifferent; the fate of one unknown Jew suddenly touched all hearts, and all gave and gave.

The charity drive was over. One man there carefully counted the coins. A wonder: the sum was identical to that which the renter owed the *poritz*! The amount they'd raised was exactly what they needed to free the captive!

R' Akiva Eiger didn't conceal his delight and strong feelings, and even the most reckless among them could see G-d's Hand, how Providence had managed the matter so that they had collected the exact amount of money that was needed. The purse was placed into R' Akiva's holy hands. The participants then awaited his thanks, certain that the visit would come to an end now that it had reached its successful conclusion.

Strangely, the visitor stayed in his place. "I would like to say a few words to you, if you are willing to listen."

A quiet grumbling, like the sound of angry bees, filled the room. "What does the holy rabbi want now... we've given all we can... there's no money left even for gambling..."

"Heaven forbid, I don't want to take another penny from you," R' Akiva explained. "I want to speak to you of your deeds. You have done enough and more than enough! You are all standing at the entranceway to *Gehinnom*. If you repent now — good; if, heaven forbid, you don't, you are all lost, drowning in the deep abyss!"

A stranger walking in at this moment would have wondered if these were men or merely stone statues. All stood still, paralyzed by the piercing, harsh words of rebuke that they'd never heard before.

After a moment of panic the men recovered, and the sound of angry voices could be heard. "What chutzpah!" "Very nice, first he takes our money and then he insults us. Why didn't he do the opposite: first lash out at us and then ask for our cash? Because the *rabbiner* knew full well that we would show him the door. So first he takes the gold and then pays us back like this! What gratitude!"

R' Akiva's pure countenance wore a serious look, and hot tears poured out of his eyes. He turned to the assembled and said, in a voice breaking with emotion, "Gentlemen, you must know that I, the rabbi of the city, feel responsible for the situation and lot of each and every one of you. Do you know how many times a day I think of you? Can you imagine? A rabbi is not there only to make decisions in Jewish law; he must give his opinion on the spiritual situation of each one of the people in his city.

"When I see your degraded spiritual lot," R' Akiva continued, his voice shaking, "how close you are to certain destruction, can I be silent? My job is to return you to the proper path.

"You've asked why I didn't do the opposite, why I didn't rebuke you immediately when I came here. A good question, one that deserves an answer. Our Sages have said, 'Just as it is a *mitzvah* to say something that will be accepted, so it is a *mitzvah* not to say something that will not be accepted, I didn't want to speak to you of this at the beginning, knowing that your hearts were as stone and your evil inclinations would never allow you to repent. For that reason I held myself back from speaking to you.

"But now you have merited to save another Jew. Our Sages have promised us that when one saves a Jew, it is as if he has saved an entire world. The *mitzvah* has gone to work upon your hardened hearts and made a large crack in the stone. Now, I knew, the time was right, and you could repent. Again, I couldn't stop myself from issuing the stern warning: return, wayward sons, return before it is too late and you miss your chance. You can still repent, but later, who knows?"

R' Akiva burst out into stormy tears. "Repent before it's too late, repent, erring sons, repent, my sons!"

And those sobs and tears of R' Akiva Eiger did not remain alone. Suddenly many other tears joined them, the tears of many of the revelers who were suddenly thinking of repentance. Broken cries could be heard throughout the saloon. After that night some of those faces were not seen in the bars; instead, they could be found in the synagogues.

One *mitzvah,* indeed, brings another.

Listed for Life

THE LIST OF THE NAMES OF THE *CHASSIDIM* WHO WOULD come and visit the holy R' Pinchas of Koritz was large, almost overflowing. Hundreds upon hundreds made their way to him, from near and from far. His wise eye rested on each and every one, not only when they were in his court, but at all times, as this story shows.

As accepted in many Chassidic groups, the *Chassidim* used to give money at certain intervals, in order to help support the rebbe and his family in a material way, so that he wouldn't be forced to spend his time earning a livelihood and instead could use all his efforts to serve his Creator.

That was the simple explanation for the custom. The more complex reason: as much as the giver does for the poor man, the poor man does for the giver. That is, the *Chassid* was not the one "giving" to his rebbe, but the one who gained from him; his livelihood would be blessed and he would find his sustenance with greater ease.

All the *Chassidim,* without exception, saw it as a privilege to give the rebbe this money. One gave more, another less; the main thing for each one was to remain on the list, so that his name and the names of his family members were under the carefully scrutinizing eye of the rebbe, like sheep being guarded by a shepherd, and that they be remembered by him for good.

Once a year R' Pinchas of Koritz would write the list over again. As the Days of Judgment approached, the rebbe would sit and copy all the names of his *Chassidim* onto a piece of paper. The *Chassidim* knew that whoever was listed by the rebbe would be granted long life on the Day of Judgment.

Therefore the *Chassidim* carefully watched all of the rebbe's movements during that time, when the list was being rewritten. These were moments of tension and suspense for the large crowd that waited, each in his own place, to find his name on the list of contributors.

That year, too, when the rebbe sat at his desk dipping his goose quill deep into his inkwell, every one of the *Chassidim* waited for him to leave his room, for the opportunity to hear from the *gabbaim* if his name was included on the list.

And that was how the large crowd waiting in the courtyard found out the staggering news: the name of R' Alexander Ziskind of Glina had been erased.

"R' Sender? Why, I just saw him a month ago," one of the *Chassidim* cried, an older man with a long grey beard. "When he was going to his grandson's wedding he passed my village, came to my house, and took a hot drink. I can't imagine what has happened to him."

"The rebbe didn't only put a line through his name, but he put his son's name, R' Chanoch, beneath it," the *gabbai* said, throwing a bit more oil onto the fire of the crowd's imagination. Most of the people guessed that R' Alexander Ziskind surely must have gone to a better world, with his son, R' Chanoch, now donating money to the rebbe. But no one had heard a single word about it.

Heavy-hearted, their curiosity unsatisfied, the crowd dispersed.

The news didn't take long to arrive; the day after Rosh Hashanah, on the Fast of Gedaliah, one of the *Chassidim* brought the bitter tidings of the death of their friend and colleague, R' Sender of Glina.

The rebbe, as has been said, would write the list once a year, and when a name was erased from it, it was a portent of things to come.

Many days hadn't passed since R' Sender's death, and the *Chassidim* were thunderstruck by the news brought to them by a *gabbai* sharing the inside story: the rebbe had put a line through R' Chanoch's name!

"He's such a young man!" The agitated *Chassidim* shared one heavy thought: if the rebbe had erased him, this must mean that R' Chanoch would have an uninvited guest, a deadly guest that no one looked for and everyone wished to avoid...

But the days passed and no one heard bad news of R' Chanoch. At first they assumed it was because he lived in a small, faraway village, a village whose long name was almost unpronounceable. But travelers soon brought the news back that R' Chanoch was alive. He had left his village and no one knew where he had gone.

At the end of the year, the community heard startling news: the rebbe had again restored R' Chanoch's name to the list of "the living."

The mystery deepened. If he was alive, why had he been erased? And if, heaven forbid, he was dead, why had his name been rewritten?

Some activists among the *Chassidim* decided not to wait anymore, but to take some decisive action and try to find where R' Chanoch was now living. When they found his new address they immediately traveled to see him. The story he told them surpassed anything they d ever imagined.

R' Alexander Ziskind was a G-d-fearing man, and he gave his son, R' Chanoch, a Jewish education rooted in Torah and tradition. Chanoch outwardly behaved liked a good Jew, but in his heart he fed brutish passions. When his father died he stood with one foot out of the Jewish world. He was a man of substance, a successful merchant, and his business was with the nobles and government authorities. At first theirs was a simple business relationship, but as their financial ties deepened, Chanoch found himself more and more involved in their profligate company. He left the small village and went to live in a large city, in a wholly gentile neighborhood. Little by little he gave up the *mitzvos* until, all too soon, he was completely estranged from his religious belief, and had become an apostate.

On the very day that Chanoch had flung away his Jewish clothing and identity, calling himself Mark, R' Pinchas of Koritz had deleted him from the list of *Chassidim.*

Close to a year passed, with Chanoch living the life of a gentile. He began to feel that his Jewish background was nothing more than a passing episode, a piece of forgotten history that was long dead.

The telegram that reached Mark brought a sigh of satisfaction and contentment to his face. He'd been called by one of his friends, a nobleman from a neighboring city, in order to discuss a large business deal that promised great profits in the future. Mark's eyes sparkled in excitement and his palms grew sweaty. "Hey, Mark, you're going to be a rich man!"

Later, as he sat with his noble friend in the non-kosher restaurant of the gentile hotel where he was staying, replete with *treif* meat and heavy dessert wine, he realized the vast scope of the business of which his friend was now willing to make him a partner.

"I would love to sign the contract right now," Mark said, "but I've suddenly gotten so tired, and my head is feeling very heavy. I'll go up to my room in the hotel, take a quick nap, and then I can go through all the details with you."

The long journey, the heavy meal, and the alcohol had done their work: he felt as if his eyelids were being clamped shut.

Mark was surprised; he'd just finished a heavy meat meal and yet felt ravenous once again. "Waiter," he tapped his silverware together to get the attention of the waiter in his sparkling uniform, "please bring me something to eat; I'm dying of hunger."

"What would you like?" asked the waiter, pulling a pad out of his pocket.

"A chicken fried in butter."

The order was written down on the pad and the waiter disappeared somewhere into the kitchen.

Mark waited impatiently, his stomach rumbling, but the waiter didn't come back. "Look at this," he said, turning to his friend, the nobleman. "Poor service. How long do I have to wait?"

Much to his consternation his friend had disappeared. Instead, on the chair next to him, sat a highly respectable man with a long grey beard.

"What are you doing here?" Mark asked, startled.

"I have something to say to you. I've come to call you to judgment."

"Me? I've never seen you before."

"Come with me right now," the old man commanded. Frightened, Mark accompanied him. From the corner of his eye Mark regretfully noticed the jacket of the waiter as he approached his table, his hands full of a fragrant dish.

"Can't you wait a little, until I've finished my meal?" Mark asked the old man, but he didn't seem to hear him. Mark recovered some of his composure. "How can you take me to judgment?" he asked angrily. "You haven't shown me even one piece of paper, not a bit of evidence that confirms my having taken a loan from you, for example."

"Nevertheless, if I told you I have a judgment against you, you can believe me."

Mark followed behind the old man through the streets of the city as one being pulled by a ghost. They reached an old building and the man asked a servant to announce that they'd arrived. The servant told them that the court was busy with another case and they would have to wait.

Mark took advantage of the break. "I'm going to finish my lunch until the court is ready," he told the old man, racing back to the restaurant to get to the chicken before it became stone cold and inedible.

To his relief, his place had been kept for him, and no one had touched the platter where the chicken gave off its succulent smell. He sat on his chair and wrapped the napkin around his neck. Now no one would disturb his meal.

Not exactly... The tines of his fork had just touched the soft, delectable meat when he felt a light tap on his shoulder. He picked up his eyes in anger, and saw the solemn-faced old man standing over him. "The court is ready; come with me right now."

"Wicked man," Mark screamed furiously. "Why do you keep bothering me? I don't know you. Now let me eat in peace."

"Come with me," the old man commanded once again. "The chicken is already dead; she won't run away."

And Mark once again followed the old man to the same building. No one stopped them this time. They went into the courtroom. Mark felt his knees grow weak.

Several rabbis, noble of countenance, sat around a table. Mark didn't recognize any of them. He stood, frightened, waiting for them to speak.

"You are Chanoch, son of R' Alexander Ziskind of Glina?" one saintly-looking man asked. Mark could hardly remember his Jewish name, but he nodded his head in assent.

"In the next room is the man who has brought you to court. Please go in."

The same old man who had brought him there was standing in the room. He stood before the judges and pointed at Mark.

"This man, standing before you, did such-and-such..."

To Mark's horror, the man began to list, one by one, all of the sins that Mark had committed from the day he'd become a man until this very moment.

"What's to be done with this man?" the old man asked. Mark realized that he was the prosecutor.

"Is there any doubt?" the head of the court answered. "One who has sinned so much shall stay here with us."

Mark now understood: this was the heavenly court that was now sentencing him to death. Tears began to flow from his eyes. He lay down on the floor and started to beg for mercy.

"I'm so young, and I want to repent and do better."

The court was about to reject his appeal, but suddenly one of the judges stood up. Mark immediately recognized him; it was his rebbe, R' Pinchas of Koritz, whom he'd visited together with his father, and to whom he'd occasionally sent donations.

"If Chanoch says that he wants to repent, he should be shown mercy and given new life," R' Pinchas argued.

To Mark's relief, his interceder's words were accepted without dispute. The heavenly court decided to return him to the world of deeds, where things could be mended.

Mark awoke in his room in the gentile hotel, his face bathed in cold sweat. "It was all a dream," he groaned in fright. But what a dream! It had changed him completely, left him awestruck and terrified. For a long while he sat, he head drooping between his knees, his thoughts on repentance. Finally, he decided to do it. He quickly packed his things, raced outside, and returned to his former home and business.

The stunned *Chassidim* calculated the dates. "On that same day that Chanoch dreamed his dream there in the hotel, our rebbe had once again restored his name to the list."

Even to a Gentile

R' ELIYAHU CHAIM MEISEL, THE RABBI OF LODZ, POLAND'S famed industrial city, was known throughout the city and the region as a great and particularly clever rabbi. His position as head of the *beis din,* as well as his unusual verdicts, enhanced his reputation not only among the Jews, who would have naturally accepted him by dint of his piety and phenomenal genius, but even among the gentiles. These non-Jews were amazed by the G-dly spirit that seemed to speak from his mouth, and the vast wisdom that could be seen in every legal decision. Often non-Jewish litigants would come to him, when they had despaired of their own justice system, seeking the verdict of the wise Jewish rabbi. In the vast majority of cases, his rulings were accepted without a murmur; the defendant and the prosecutor — even though they were not of the Jewish faith — accepting the verdict with satisfaction. With the passing of time his reputation grew, until many of the gentiles saw in him a redeeming angel.

One of these gentiles was Stachek Latzki, a respected elder who resided in a neighborhood together with Jews, living with them in peace all his life. When the Polish revolution against the Russians began, in the year 5591 (1831), Stachek was one of the rebels. His high position and personal integrity gained him the position of treasurer of the Lodz region. The monies of the noblemen passed through his hands before being used to fund the rebels' activities.

The rebellion was put down with an iron fist; the Russian Czarist regime again ruled Poland for many years. The rebels went underground, destroying any evidence of their involvement in anti-Czarist activity. The punishment for anyone caught having taken part in the revolt was stern and unyielding: the hangman's noose awaited him after a too-short appearance before a tribunal.

No wonder, then, that Stachek Latzki didn't waste any time. He still possessed some tens of thousands of rubles, a goodly treasure that would have testified to his high position in the rebellion. He secreted the rubles in a sealed aluminum barrel, covered it over with old wooden boards, and hid it in the basement of his house. He was running some slight risk here, since the basement belonged to all the building's inhabitants, but Stachek assumed that no one would pay attention to a forlorn old barrel.

Stachek watched his treasure for some years. Occasionally he would go down to his hiding place at some late hour, a lit candle in his hand, and sift through the old barrel. The rubles, as always, twinkled in the yellowing light, setting his imagination on fire. He would play with the thought of how he could finally get the money out without calling upon himself the attention of the regime, which still scrupulously searched for any remnants of rebellion.

One night Stachek, as was his wont, went down to the basement. The candle's light sparkled in the dark basement. He tiptoed carefully towards the barrel, taking care not to make any suspicious noise. Dust and filth clung to his clothing, as always, but Stachek paid no attention; he always kept tattered clothing just to wear on these nocturnal visits.

Already from a distance he sensed that something had changed: the barrel was not standing in its usual spot. As he pulled it towards him he could feel how light it had become. His heart seemed to stop beating. When he pulled the wooden cover off and saw only the emptiness of the barrel, a shout escaped him, a scream that could be clearly heard outside the basement walls.

The building's residents raced downstairs, and were shocked to see their respected neighbor coming out of the cellar, his clothes in tatters, and on his face a look of utter agony and shock. But their questions received no answer: Stachek would not, of course, reveal his secret, and instead merely groaned from the depths of his broken heart.

For several weeks Stachek was like a sleepwalker, a somnambulist who knew nothing in his melancholy. Then he had an idea: perhaps the wise Jewish rabbi could help him in this difficult time.

"Do you suspect someone?" R' Eliyahu Chaim Meisel asked.

The gentile hesitated. Clearly some inner struggle was going on. Finally he gasped, "Yes, I suspect my Jewish neighbor, Baruch the carpenter. For many years he was completely impoverished; suddenly he and his family are wearing elegant clothing. His wife and daughters now appear in society decked out in fine jewelry: gold and silver necklaces, giant ones laced with diamonds, earrings sparkling with gold — and before this they never had even a simple bracelet."

"And what does the neighbor say?" the rabbi pressed. "How does he explain his sudden wealth?"

Stachek laughed bitterly. "He claims he had a relative, a wealthy and childless man who lived in London, who just died and left him his entire estate. None of the neighbors believe him, but there's no way to prove it's a lie."

The rabbi knew what he had to do. "Tell your neighbor the carpenter that I want to see him in my house quickly. Don't tell him why."

After a few hours, Baruch the carpenter appeared in the rabbi's home. He was excited by the honor, and incessantly smoothed down his elegant coat. The rabbi gave him a few minutes to calm down, asking him about his welfare and that of his family. When the carpenter's breath had slowed down somewhat, the rabbi got to the point.

"I have heard that lately you've gotten quite wealthy."

"That's right, Rabbi," the carpenter smiled happily.

R' Eliyahu's face grew stern. "If so, why haven't you come to me to give *tzedakah,* as all the wealthy of the town do? Don't you know that I am responsible for the sustenance of numerous widows and orphans?"

The rich man paled. "You're right, Rabbi. I didn't think of it. Tomorrow I'll come to give a large sum for *tzedakah.*"

The rabbi gazed at him with wise eyes. "Where did you get your riches?"

"I had a wealthy relative in England," the carpenter breathed heavily as he spoke. "He had no children and left me everything."

"And he had no other relatives at all?" the rabbi continued his questioning. At the sight of the carpenter, who was trembling in his boots, the rabbi knew without a doubt that Stachek had been telling the truth.

The rabbi leaned over towards Baruch and whispered, "I called you because I am concerned for you. The news is going around the city that you're passing forged cash. You know that the government is very strict with forgers."

Baruch's eyes seemed to jump out of their sockets. For a few seconds he couldn't say a word. Finally, he whispered to the rabbi, "The story of the inheritance — I made it up. I found the money in a barrel in the basement."

"And the coins are forgeries," the wise rabbi said. "For your own sake, bring them to me."

Baruch raced out of the rabbi's house. In a short while he was back with the treasure.

"Now you can go back to your house in peace," the rabbi said. His voice suddenly grew stern with rebuke. "These coins are not forgeries after all — but you've stolen them! You're not allowed to take money that doesn't belong to you; since when did you think that this was allowed?"

And on that day the rabbi returned the money to its rightful owner.

All Whom I Have Saved

I T HAPPENED DURING *SHIUR*. THE WELL-KNOWN *TZADDIK*, R' Eliyahu Guttmacher of Greiditz, sat with his students, who were listening intently to the flowing voice of their teacher. The complex *sugya* became clearer and clearer in light of his words; another *kushya* was explained, and still another foundation laid. The students challenged and the rabbi explained; the lecture hall seemed to glow with the combination of fear of G-d and the joy of learning.

Strong knocks on the door cut off the flow of words. The door was flung open and a weeping woman burst into the room. "Holy rebbe, help me!"

"Why are you crying?" the rabbi asked, evincing no surprise or chagrin at the interruption. The woman, between sobs, said, "My husband lies on his sickbed, and he begs the rabbi to come to him."

R' Eliyahu jumped from his place. Murmuring no word about *bitul Torah,* he went immediately to the home of the sick man, escorted by several of his select students.

The walk through the streets of the German city of Greiditz, not far from the Polish border, took some time. Finally they reached the end of the city. "Here is my house," the woman said, pointing to an old building. The rabbi and his students entered. The woman walked into the sick man's room, returning almost immediately, her face woebegone. "His condition is critical, Rabbi. Please come in."

R' Eliyahu opened the door, and almost immediately jumped back out, shocked. He quickly shut the door behind him and waited outside the room for several minutes, lost in thought. His students stood mutely; despite their curiosity and wonder, they dared not ask their rav about his actions.

R' Eliyahu shook himself out of his reverie and went back into the sickroom, his faithful students making a semicircle around him as he walked with measured steps towards the bed in the corner of the room.

The ailing man, an elderly Jew called Hershel, appeared to belong to the lower classes. It was clear that the Angel of Death was hovering nearby. The man's yellow face was like parchment, his eyes half closed.

"Holy rabbi," Hershel whispered weakly, "I ask pardon for having dared to bother His Honor by having him come to my house."

"It's nothing," R' Eliyahu hastened to pacify the dying man. "What is it you want?"

A choked sob came out of the sick man's throat. "I feel that my hours are numbered; in a short while I will go the way of all flesh."

Hershel's sobs grew louder. His wife hastened to give him a cup of water; he drank it down with difficulty.

"I am a simple man," he continued, "uneducated. I never read and I never learned. Good deeds, too, will not stand by me in the World of Truth. I am terrified that in a little while I will stand before the Heavenly Court and they will find me empty of Torah and good deeds, overflowing only with sins. Woe to my soul — where will they send it?" The sick man wept bitterly. "I beg His Honor to have mercy on my soul and to remember me for good after my death."

Several of the students surreptitiously wiped tears from their eyes upon hearing Hershel's simple words, words that came directly from the heart.

"Impossible that you have nothing! If you haven't learned Torah, you must certainly have done good deeds." The rabbi wouldn't let the sick man be. "Think, perhaps, and you will remember one good thing that you have done. It's important to me, and it will serve you well when you stand before the Heavenly Court."

"I wish it were so, Rabbi, but what can I do? I have nothing. I am a simple peasant; I didn't even know how to *daven* properly," the sick man sighed weakly. "All my life I worked for my living; heavy work that didn't bring me any respect. From my youth onwards I flayed hides. Every day I would go to the slaughterhouse and there I worked from dawn until twilight, flaying the skins off the slaughtered animals, sheep and cattle, large animals and small. I only managed to get a few minutes off my work in order to put on *tefillin* and say *Shema*. At night when I got home I fell onto my bed, exhausted; it was only with difficulty that I managed to murmur *Minchah* and *Maariv*. All week I waited for Shabbos, like one waits for *Mashiach,* and I would spend most of Shabbos in deep sleep. When, then, did I have a chance to do good deeds or give *tzedakah*? And so I ask the rav, let him take care of my soul after it has left my body!"

The rabbi and his students stood, deeply moved, before the sick man. It was a heart-rending scene, and even the hardiest among them was moved to repentance in front of this simple soul laying itself bare before the *tzaddik.* It was truly a living lesson in ethics. Here he was, a Jew who had toiled all his life to sustain himself and his household, without a moment to spend alone with his Creator, without the time to stop the mad rush of life and meditate upon his obligations in the world. No chance to set himself times for learning, even a few minutes a day. Now he was about to depart this world, empty, stripped of any garments of Torah or *mitzvos* — arriving in the other world naked and barefoot!

But R' Eliyahu was not the sort to spend his time in bitter thoughts and recriminations. His face alight with pity, he turned to the man lying in front of him. "And yet, it is clear to me that at some time you fulfilled a great *mitzvah.* Tell me what good thing you have done."

Silence fell upon the room. Hershel lay, lost in thought, his brow wrinkled with the effort of memory.

"I remember something," he finally blurted out quietly. "I just thought of a story, worthless and simple, but for the honor of the rav I will tell it."

The rabbi put his ear near the sick man, who began to speak.

"As I said before, I used to get up and set out to work while it was still dark..."

Dawn on that winter's day was no different from the many dawns that had preceded it, nor from the dawns to come. Hershel, the flayer of skins, walked heavily down the hill towards the slaughterhouse in the valley, his hands clenched within the pockets of his coat against the freezing cold. His brain was still fuzzy with sleep. It wasn't easy for him, this business of waking up while it was still dark. He had to leave his warm bed and walk into the frigid air at an hour when most of humanity was still reposing on its pillows in sweet slumber.

From a distance came the sound of an approaching carriage. It seemed to be far away, and he wondered if it was his imagination playing tricks upon him: surely this was no time for travelers to be taking to the roads. A few minutes passed and doubt turned to reality; the sound of galloping horses grew louder. Worried, Hershel turned around, and his blood froze in his veins.

A large carriage hitched to two pairs of horses was making its swift way down the road towards him. The driver was throroughly drunk, and made no effort to stop the stampeding animals. The carriage was jammed with dozens of men, women, and children returning to their homes in the valley from a wedding that had taken place on the top of the mountain. They were crying in fright, begging the driver to stop the mad race before a terrible accident took place. The drunken man sang a merry song and ignored them. In their panic, the horses left the paved road and began to gallop down the hill. Another minute and the carriage with all its passengers would go right down into the looming abyss beneath them.

"Stop!" Hershel screamed in a loud voice. "Stop!" he screamed again. The startled driver grabbed at the reins with all his strength, and the horses slowed their frenzied dash. At the same time Hershel managed to steady the carriage with his sturdy arms, fighting with clenched teeth against the frantic horses, who rose up on their back legs in an effort to continue. He used the last of his strength to stop their efforts to drag him into the chasm. "Jump out, if you value your lives!" he screamed at the terrified passengers. They obeyed the command and flew out of the carriage, rolling to the side of the road onto the dew-moistened grass. The entire incident took less than a minute; the horses overpowered Hershel, who hastily jumped to one side, and they galloped down into the deep ravine.

The awful cries and sounds of destruction that came from below caused the people to look around in horror, to see if, heaven forbid, someone had stayed inside that carriage of death. They let out a sigh of relief when they discovered that no one had been missed; even the drunken carriage driver had managed to recover from him alcoholic haze at the very last moment, and had jumped out.

"Maybe that's what you meant," Hershel ended. "I don't know if this was worth anything, but except for that there is certainly nothing to accompany me and protect me in the world of truth."

R' Eliyahu Guttmacher's face lit up. "Go in peace," he said to the dying man. "I will *daven* for your soul. But then promise me that after the Heavenly Court gives its verdict, you will come and tell me what it is." The dying man nodded with the last of his strength and soon his soul departed, in the presence of R' Eliyahu and his students, who said *Krias Shema* with him.

When they returned to yeshivah, after having attended to all the needs of the dead man and his funeral, the students, deeply moved, surrounded their rabbi, one question on all their lips: "Why was the rav so startled when he opened the door; why did he stop and think about it before going in?"

R' Eliyahu was silent for a moment, as if wondering just how much to reveal. Finally he nodded and said, "I was certain, as you were, that I was going to the home of a simple man, one of the peasantry. But when I opened the door I was shocked to see above the sick man's head a menorah of fire, with seven lit candles.

"From that I understood that this Jew, who was so ready to speak badly of himself, was no simple man, if he had merited such a thing. I stopped to think how I could find out from him what he had done, what merit he had. And you yourselves heard his story of how he risked himself to save dozens of Jews."

It was still during the days of the *shivah* that Hershel the flayer of skins appeared to R' Eliyahu in a dream, and said, "When I came to judgment for my deeds, they put my merits and my obligations onto a scale, and I don't have to tell you which side came out heavier... You already know that I had few *mitzvos* and abundant sins. Suddenly a carriage arrived, weighted down with men, women, and children, a heavy burden — all the souls that I'd saved. The scale immediately righted itself and the other side went down. Even the mud on the carriage's wheels was weighed on the side of merits. At that moment the verdict was given: I was to enter *Gan Eden*. But when I wanted to enjoy the Holy Presence, I was not allowed to, for a thin thread still tied me to the world of falsehood — my promise that I'd made to you. That is why I have made the effort to come down. Except for my promise, I wouldn't have left my place for even a bare second."

He finished speaking and disappeared. R' Eliyahu related the man's words to his students, in order to teach them just how deep the Heavenly justice reaches, and to confirm how great are the words of our Sages: "Anyone who saves one Jewish soul..."

The Six-Year-Old Father

"**H**E PURSUES CHARITY AND LOVINGKINDNESS." "HE gives charity at all times." These were just two of the descriptions of R' Shlomo of Karlin. And not in vain: He would give away all his money to charity, up to the last penny. Things came to such a head that the members of his household had to set up a special person at his door to thin out the crowds that would assemble there day and night, in order to ensure that something remained for the family's needs.

One of those who turned to him was an impoverished Jew whose daughter's wedding was quickly approaching, though he had absolutely nothing to give. At a certain point he understood that the *gabbai* was determined not to let anyone else in, no matter what. Desperately looking for help, the poor man somehow managed to sneak into the rebbe's room.

"Holy rebbe," he gasped between bitter sobs, "the time for my daughter's wedding has come and I have nothing. I'm afraid that the match will be broken, heaven forbid!"

R' Shlomo, whose heart felt the troubles of every Jew, immediately stood up and searched through his house for money. Much to his anguish, not even one coin turned up. The weeping of the bride's father touched his heart deeply. Hastily, the rebbe put on his overcoat. "Come with me," he cried to the surprised pauper. "If Shlomo has nothing, Shlomo will go to ask someone else."

The two walked quite a long way until they reached the beautiful and ornate home of one of the area's richest men. R' Shlomo knocked on the door and said to the servant who answered, "Please call your master outside." The servant, who recognized the rebbe's holiness, turned wordlessly back and in a few moments the rich man was there with them.

"This Jew needs 6,000 rubles for a dowry for his daughter, the bride." R' Shlomo pointed towards the man. "I am asking you to give him the entire sum."

The rich man's eyes opened wide in shock. "What is he to me?" he stammered. "I can give him 100 rubles, as is my custom. And that's all."

R' Shlomo wouldn't let up. "You are obligated to give him 6,000 rubles."

A spark of anger lit up the rich man's eye. "Obligated? I don't even know him!"

"Let me tell you why you are obligated," the rebbe said. "As you know, after the passing of the holy rebbe, R' Aharon the Great of Karlin, the members of the community begged me to take his place and become their rebbe. I refused. Even after some great men from the higher worlds appeared to me and asked me to take on the mantle of leadership, I didn't change my mind. The *Baal Shem Tov* and the *Ari HaKadosh* both pleaded with me, but still I stuck to my decision.

"Until the word came to me from *HaKadosh Baruch Hu* Himself: Shlomo, my son, it is the will of Providence that you become the leader of the generation, and in the merit of this, whatever you pray will come to be. And in addition, you will have eyes that can see from one end of the world to the other!

"I was young and foolish," the rebbe continued to relate to his enthralled listeners, the poor man and the rich one, "and so I agreed to accept such gifts… and thus I became a rebbe in Israel."

Immediately upon assuming the mantle of leadership, R' Shlomo learned just what it meant to see "from one end of the world to the other." As soon as he agreed to take on the job of rebbe, people began knocking on his door, clamoring for help.

One day, the children of the richest man in town came to him sobbing. "Father is critically ill," they cried. They put their hands out with a "*kvittel*" that bore the name of the sick man and his mother, together with a sum of money as a means of atonement for the ill man.

The rebbe had just begun to speak with them when suddenly a few frantic men burst into the room. "A poor woman who is having a difficult childbirth is already lying for a few days in the city's poorhouse, the *hekdesh*. Her condition is very serious and her life is in danger."

R' Shlomo immediately saw, with his holy spirit, what others could not perceive: the soul of the rich man who was hovering between life and death was destined to be incarnated once again in the body of the infant son who was to be born to the poor woman in the *hekdesh*. One was contingent upon the other; all the time that the wealthy man lived — the baby couldn't be born!

With a heavy heart, R' Shlomo was forced to accept the sentence of death that had been placed upon the rich man. Not only did he not pray for his health, but he actually strengthened the hand of the one which was to implement the verdict. Not long afterwards one could hear the broken cries coming from the palace of the rich man; on the other side of the city, at the exact same moment, came the shouts of "mazel tov!"

When the men came to him from the poorhouse with the good news, they brought with them a request as well. "We need money to buy firewood for the *hekdesh;* the cold is dangerous for both the mother and the newborn." The rebbe took the funds from the money left by the dead man's family.

"It's all connected," he said to himself. "The soul of the rich man is now in the *hekdesh,* and somehow it was arranged that he would enjoy his own money and not need the money of others." For that reason, the rest of the *"pidyon"* money went for the expenses of the *bris* and other necessities.

When the son of the poor woman began to grow up, he started to help his mother in her "job": wandering with her from village to village, town to town, begging. For several years he learned the art of beggary from her. Now he was a big boy, already six years old, and there was a celebration in the city. In the home of the wealthy man who had died six years before, they were about to celebrate the bar mitzvah of the *"ben zekunim,"* the son born to him in his old age. The bar mitzvah of the 13-year-old orphan was to be marked with due pomp and luxury. All the poor of the town had been invited to the kingly feast as well, among them — who else? — the poor woman and her six-year-old son.

On the appointed day, the masses made their way to the rich family's mansion. Though six years had passed since the wealthy father's death, his memory had not faded. Certainly not at a time when the huge kitchen had been bustling for days, with chefs working on the most wonderful delicacies, the fragrant aroma of the foods wafting on the winds, tempting the townspeople constantly.

When the invited guests entered the luxurious salons they were struck with wonder. Whatever they had imagined seemed to pale next to the fabulous wealth that was set before them.

They had just begun to recline in the luxuriously upholstered chairs and set their glances on the mountains of delicacies laid out beautifully and set on trays of silver and gold, on tables, when the elegant atmosphere was rent by the sudden terrible cry of the poor woman's child.

No one could understand or explain how that youngster, child of a pauper, who in his entire life had not seen a fraction of such wealth, could have the gall to stand up and demand, with the determination of a grown man, to sit at the head table, next to the bar mitzvah boy.

"Go, little boy, to your brothers, the paupers," one of the bar mitzvah boy's brothers jeered at him. "That is your place."

But the boy wouldn't back down. He gave the angry young man a loving smile, an inexplicable smile, and again demanded to be seated at the head table. When the bar mitzvah boy's brothers tried to hit him, he gave off a shriek that echoed through the hall.

"Who is that child?" the word went around the palace. "Let his mother come and take him away."

When the embarrassed mother appeared, the servants and the family of the bar mitzvah boy attacked her verbally for the terrible education she'd given her child. She explained that this was the first time she'd ever seen him behave so; he d never done anything like this before. Minutes hadn't passed and the youngster again returned to the head table, pulling one of the brothers up and taking his seat. In another minute a resounding blow would fall upon his cheek.

Now R' Shlomo hastened to the spot. How he wanted to explain what was happening: their father simply wanted to take part in their celebration, in his celebration — and anyone who hit him fell into the category of one who struck a parent. But he was forced to hold his peace, and not to reveal G-d's secret that had been shown to him in His mercy.

"Stop that," he grabbed the upraised arm of the bar mitzvah boy's brother. "Why should you destroy your party? He's only a boy. He wants to sit with you. So let him sit!"

Out of respect for the rebbe, the family acceded to the request. With haunted looks they sat with the youngster, listening to the cease-less prattle of the boy who'd forced his way among them, the six-year-old who demanded the very best portions of food. If not for R' Shlomo, who came from time to time to protect him, he would have been thrown out with the garbage. Finally, the boy went too far: when they were giving out money for charity, he demanded a much larger sum than any of the other poor people were getting. Their patience at an end, the family grabbed him and forcibly threw him out.

And R' Shlomo of Karlin, heartsick, watched the unbearable scene. "Who adds knowledge, adds pain." He *davened* to G-d, praying that his eyes would no longer see from one end of the world to the other — and the request was answered.

"But some of the power remained," R' Shlomo ended his story, with the rich man and the poor man still listening, open-mouthed, in the wealthy man's courtyard. "Do you remember that you once had a business partner, who died before you could repay a debt that you owed to him a 6,000 ruble debt? This man," here he pointed at the pauper, "is the son of that partner, and needs the entire sum to marry off his daughter."

And the rich man paid off his debt, as he counted out 6,000 rubles into the waiting hands of the man who needed a dowry.

The Hidden Light

"The secret of Shabbos, that is Shabbos."
Raz (secret) is, in gematria, ohr (light):
the secret of Shabbos is its light.
[R' Mordechai Melkovitz]

A JUMBLE OF HOUSES SHOULDERING ONE ANOTHER STOOD in the corner of the Jewish ghetto of Lublin — ungainly houses, with sharp tiled roofs burnt by the summer sun and frozen by winter chill, houses covered with tin sheets, as if seeking protection from the winds and the rains.

Among these crowded houses incongruosly stood one lovely building, one that kept its distance from its neighbors. This was the *beis midrash* of the holy rebbe, R' Yaakov Yitzchak, the *Chozeh* of Lublin.

It was an ordinary weekday, a day when the rebbe would meet with people in his room. A long line awaited him, each person impatient for the moment when he could unburden himself of whatever lay in his heart.

The door opened; a man who had been inside walked out, and now the next in the line asked to enter.

But no: the door was closed. The *gabbai* came out and announced to the large crowd, "Take a break."

The assembled already knew of this custom. Occasionally the rebbe of Lublin would stop in the middle of receiving people, lock himself into his room for a short period of time, and then once again open the door and continue his meetings. Later there would be another break, and then his audiences would resume.

The students of the *Chozeh* longed to know what their rebbe was doing during those mysterious moments. One of them, who would later gain fame as R' Naftali of Rupshitz, was more daring than the rest, and he took action. At a time when the *Chozeh* was not in his room, R' Naftali snuck inside and hid himself inside a closet, leaving the door open a crack. From within he carefully watched what was going on.

When the *Chozeh* began to receive the public, R' Naftali grew even more alert. The rebbe sat with five different men, heard their troubles, gave them advice, and dispensed blessings.

After the fifth one had left, the door was closed.

R' Naftali struggled to see exactly what his rebbe was doing during this secret moment.

The *Chozeh* serenely opened the *Gemara* that lay before him on his desk and learned from it, like any student in a *beis midrash,* with deep emotion and enjoyment.

Was that all? R' Naftali could hardly believe what he was seeing. No esoteric books of Kabbalah, no visitations of angels, no heavenly messengers sent from above?

He continued to scrutinize his rebbe's behavior all through the evening. The mystery was solved: from time to time, between one man and the next, the rebbe would learn Torah.

R' Naftali couldn't hold himself back any longer. He left his hiding place and revealed himself to the *Chozeh*. "It is Torah, and I must learn, and therefore I hid myself here," he confessed to his rebbe. "Please let the Rebbe teach me, what is the significance of studying Torah in between receiving petitioners?"

The *Chozeh* answered his wise student, R' Naftali: "When *HaKadosh Baruch Hu* created His world He created the spiritual light first, and then He hid it. Where was it hidden? We are told — in the holy Torah. That was where the Creator concealed the light of the Creation. And from this light I find the wisdom, insight, and knowledge to answer each person with an answer that satisfies his situation. But after a long while the impression of the light weakens, and again I don't know what to advise those who look to me. Therefore I take a short break, learn a little bit, and again fill myself with the hidden, G-dly light."

R' Naftali told his colleagues the words of their rebbe and all were thunderstruck. And yet they hadn't completely understood the depth of his words. A few years passed and in Lublin an awesome event took place, one that revealed just a little about the character of this hidden light.

Shabbos, before evening.

The dimness of twilight falls, spreading upon the face of Lublin, conquering the streets that had until now been drenched in sunshine, sending the light scurrying before it. Piece by piece the city gives way to the darkness, until night falls entirely. The blackness covers the land, sweeping away the retreating rays of sun.

Minchah prayers have ended. The students are hurrying to wash their hands for the third meal of Shabbos. They sit around creaky wooden tables and bite into their *challah*.

The *Chozeh* tarries, as is his custom. After *Minchah* he would always go from the *beis midrash* to the attic of his house, climbing

13 steps and locking the door behind him. After a short while he would descend and join his students for *seudah shelishis.*

The students knew that to this place, to this attic, no man dare come; no one would climb those 13 holy steps. A mysterious secret could be found there, shrouded and concealed within that dusky, narrow room where the rebbe would sit in solitude during the holiest hour of the week. There was no lack of students and *Chassidim* who would have given a fortune to know what their rebbe was doing there during those few minutes, but no one dared penetrate this sanctuary, this holy of holies.

But every rule has its exception. One of the *Chassidim* longed to see his rebbe in the attic; his heart actually burned with a fever of desire to know what was happening within. He didn't reveal his thoughts to anyone. One Shabbos, before *Minchah,* he climbed the 13 steps and snuck into the dim room.

His heart pounded wildly. He knew that what he was doing was unspeakable, and yet he couldn't contain his growing curiosity any longer. He hid himself in a niche in the wall, relying on the thick darkness to keep his rebbe from seeing him.

The minutes passed, each one an eternity; it seemed that much time had gone by. Perhaps this was the week that the rebbe wouldn't come up? But there it was: the sound of footsteps climbing up, stair after stair, 13 times. The door opened and in the beam of light from the outside, the familiar countenance of his rebbe could be seen.

The *Chassid* held his breath. He moved only slightly, in order to see what his rebbe would do now.

The rebbe of Lublin sat down by his desk, pulled the *Sefer Yad HaChazakah* of the *Rambam* towards him, and opened the *sefer* to the laws of Shabbos.

At that moment a blinding flash of lightning came out of the book. An awesome, great light exploded within the darkness; thousands of suns seemed to shine, illuminating the room all at once. The hidden *Chassid* covered his eyes, incapable of gazing at the great light.

After the flash of illumination the room seemed to grow even blacker than before. The *Chassid* was astounded at the sudden fall of night, but at the same time breathed a sigh of relief: he had feared that in the brilliance his rebbe would find his place of concealment.

The rebbe studied the *halachos* of the *Rambam* for a few minutes, then left the attic and descended to eat with his students.

The *Chassid* left the recess in the wall and began to feel his way towards the door. Though he knew the attic was dark, when he left it and still found blackness around him, he was astonished.

"What's going on?" he thought. "I don't recall ever seeing darkness so thick, darkness you can almost feel, like that of Egypt. It must be that the light that came out of the *sefer* has blinded me temporarily; soon, my vision will be restored and I'll be able to see again."

He felt his way along the walls until he reached the *beis midrash,* joining his friends at *seudah shelishis* and waiting for *Maariv.* After prayers, candles were lit, bringing light to the *beis midrash.* It was time to go from darkness to light.

But the *Chassid* saw nothing. A horrifying, profound fear fell upon him. Had he, then, gone blind?

All that bitter night he tossed and turned on his bed awaiting the next day, hoping that the clear light of dawn would brighten his darkened vision. At dawn he stood by the window, his face to the east, eagerly waiting for the rising sun.

But when the rays of the sun hit his face, warming him, and yet he saw nothing, the *Chassid* began to cry and wail, "Woe is me! I'm blind; I can't see!"

Sadly, he went to the *beis midrash,* his hands outstretched before him, feeling his way like a blind man in a maze.

"What's the matter?" his friends asked, shocked. "Are you mad?"

The man burst into tears. "Yes, I was mad, insane. Yesterday, on Shabbos, I did something terrible, something unthinkable."

And he told his friends just what had happened when the *Chozeh* had opened his *sefer.*

His friends surrounded him, trying to give him comfort. "You will be healed. Whoever blinded you has the power to open your eyes. Don't be embarrassed: go to the rebbe and tell him the truth, how you hid yourself in his attic yesterday. Beg him to heal your eyes."

The man followed their advice, but the rebbe of Lublin told him, "I don't have the power to help you."

The *Chassid* burst into tears and, brokenhearted, begged the *Chozeh*: "Please! A blind man is considered dead. I want to see again."

"Do you know our R' Berish?" the *Chozeh* asked. "He has the power to help you. He has many precious and effective remedies, *segulos,* and he has helped many blind and deaf people. Go to him."

R' Berish, who was later to gain fame as the *Saba Kadisha,* R' Dov Ber of Radoshitz, heard the weeping of the *Chassid* who had gone blind.

R' Berish's heart was filled with pity for him. He gave the *Chassid* a *segulah* that had been used dozens of times with great success, and commanded the man to do certain actions in his house for several days.

The man did everything exactly as R' Berish had instructed, followed the remedy in every tiny detail, and waited tensely to see (literally, as well as metaphorically) what would happen.

The days passed, the remedies were taken, and the eyes remained darkened.

The man came to R' Berish a second time. "My dear rebbe, the *segulah* didn't work."

The rebbe of Radoshitz was very surprised, but thought that perhaps it was a coincidence. He gave the *Chassid* a second remedy, also tested and tried, a *segulah* that had opened many a blind eye. He cautioned him severely to follow the instructions to the letter.

After a few days the man appeared again. "I did everything you told me to do. I didn't change even a hairsbreadth, but I am still blind."

The Radoshitzer stood still, frozen in shock, for some time. "Impossible," he said in anguish. "Whoever has received this *segulah* has had his sight restored."

R' Berish searched through his secrets, and gave the unfortunate *Chassid* the strongest of his remedies, a holy and heavenly *segulah* for opening closed eyes, one which he'd carefully kept concealed, using only rarely, for the most difficult cases. "I am giving
you the greatest of my *segulos,* a remedy that will turn around the
laws of nature," he told him. "People who were blind from birth
began to see after using this remedy! But be very careful not to discuss this with anyone."

"I won't say a word," the blind man promised. "I just want to
see again."

The man followed the third *segulah,* but it seemed to do nothing. His two eyes stayed useless, and he remained completely blind.

On his fourth visit to R' Berish he cried hopelessly.

The *Saba Kadisha* of Radoshitz looked at him and said, "You
must know that this was the last *segulah* I had to give you. It had
the power to bring light even to a stone. And yet you've remained
blind! It's very strange, very shocking. Tell me exactly what happened."

The *Chassid* repeated the story of what he'd done during *seudah shelishis,* how he'd snuck into the attic of the *Chozeh* and how
he'd lost his sight.

The rebbe of Radoshitz clapped his hands together and cried
out loud, "Now I understand! You tried, with your human eyes, to
see the hidden light! Didn't you know that our rebbe, the *Chozeh*
of Lublin, sees the hidden light concealed within the Torah?" R'
Berish added, "Our holy rebbe can give life to the inanimate,
change rain to wind. He purifies his eyes and can see heavenly
scenes, the hidden light of the six days of Creation. This hidden
light, it is said, illuminates from one end of the world to the other,
and so our rebbe's eyes can travel throughout the entire world. But
you?"

And the man remained blind until the end of his days.

The Clothing of a Defender

R' YEKUSIEL YEHUDAH TEITELBAUM, THE *AV BEIS DIN* OF the community of Sighet and author of the *Sefer Yitav Lev,* was the grandson of the *Yismach Moshe* of Ohel; father of the author of *Kedushas Yom Tov,* R' Chananiah Yom Tov Lipa Teitelbaum of Sighet; and grandfather of the Satmar Rebbe, R' Yoel Teitelbaum.

One evening the rebbe turned to his *gabbai* and asked him to bring him his *shtreimel* and *kapatah.*

"What?" the *gabbai* asked, surprised.

"That's right," the author of the *Yitav Lev* repeated his request. "Bring me my Shabbos clothing, my *shtreimel* and *kapatah.*"

The man didn't know what to think: Why did the rebbe need his Shabbos clothing on an ordinary weekday evening? He couldn't have been invited to be the *sandak* at a *bris,* for the sun was on the verge of setting; no "eighth day," this. Nor was there any *chupah* on the horizon. But here was the voice of the *tzaddik* asking him a third time to bring him his clothing.

The *gabbai* waited no longer. He roused himself from his doubtful thoughts and hastily did as the rebbe had bid.

The rebbe donned his Shabbos clothing and sat by his desk. Only a few minutes had passed when knocks could be heard at the door. In the doorway stood a Jew wearing the dress of a German merchant. His dapper, elegant appearance attested to the fact that this was no pauper.

"I have something to say to the rebbe. May I see him?" he whispered to the *gabbai.*

The *gabbai* approached the *Yitav Lev* and asked him if he should bring in "the *Deutscher.*" The rebbe nodded his head.

The *gabbai* immediately called in the wealthy merchant and told him to enter. The man went into the room, and looked at the rebbe sitting by the desk. His face paled and, in the grip of some strong emotion, he whispered, "Yes, that is him...it's him." Then he collapsed and landed, unconscious, on the floor.

The *gabbai* and the members of the rebbe's household labored long trying to restore him to life, rubbing his temples with cold water and alcohol until they'd brought him out of his faint. When his eyes opened they gave him a drink of liquor and honey pastries. Finally, his composure returned. Only then did they approach the *Yitav Lev,* who received the man with a beaming countenance and open delight, as if he was a beloved old acquaintance. "Have you been here before?" the *gabbai* asked, stunned, as he didn't recognize him at all.

"No, I've never been here," the man answered frankly.

The household grew silent, reluctant to press him for an explanation. But the man seemed to feel some internal need to explain what had happened.

And this was his story:

My father was a successful merchant and a G-d-fearing man, one of the respected men of Berlin, whose seat in the *shul* was on the eastern wall, near the seat of the rabbi. Most of his business was in textiles, and his fabric store in Berlin gave him a fine livelihood all his life. When he got old I left my previous occupation and began to help him in managing the store.

My father grew older, and his energies waned. I noticed that he was very disturbed about something; occasionally he would give a heavy sigh.

"Why are you sighing, Father?" I asked him, but in reply he just sighed even more, gave me a mournful glance, and sighed once again.

When Father grew ill with the disease that would ultimately kill him, I stood by his bedside and faithfully took care of him from morning till night. There was no sleep for me; I didn't move from his side. And all that time Father would sigh, terrible sighs that broke the heart of those who heard them.

"I have two questions for you, dear Father," I told him. "Why do you keep on sighing? And what will happen to your textile store?"

These were Father's last days, and he hardly had the strength to speak. I saw that he was making a tremendous effort to gather his energies. He took a deep breath and told me, "The two questions have one answer. I want to leave the business to you, my only son, but I'm afraid that I can't do that. Instead, I must command you to call a lawyer and have him sell the store and divide the profits among the poor."

I was so shocked I was speechless. For quite a while I couldn't utter even one word. "But Father," I finally said, when I'd recovered a bit, "why are you doing this to me?"

"Because I know you, my beloved son, and I know that you won't keep Shabbos. How can I bequeath the business to you, knowing that with my own hands I am causing you to desecrate Shabbos?" Father replied weakly, resuming his bitter sighs.

Now I understood the reason for those awful sighs: he was certain his store would be open on Shabbos. To be perfectly honest, he was right in his suspicions. I was far from a Torah-observant Jew then, though as I served my father in his illness and saw the bitterness of death approaching step by step, many thoughts of repentance flitted through my brain. At that moment I strengthened myself and cried out loud, "Father, I accept upon myself to keep Shabbos completely; I won't desecrate Shabbos, no matter what!"

Father was very moved by my honest words. Still he hesitated, sunk in deep thought. Finally he told me, with his last strength, "If you promise me, with your handshake, that every Friday at noon exactly you will close the store — I will bequeath it to you."

I didn't hesitate at all; the sacrifice seemed easy compared to the great profit that I could look forward to six days a week. We shook on it and I sincerely promised him, "Every Friday at 12 o'clock exactly, the store will be closed."

A smile of contentment passed over his tortured features. Two days later, he was dead.

For several years I successfully kept my promise. Every Friday at noon, not one minute later, the store was closed. From eleven o'clock on, no new customers were admitted, and at 11:30 the salesmen would begin to hurry the people and ask them, politely but firmly, to finish up their purchases quickly and leave.

Until the noontime of that Friday. (A cloud of discontent covered the eyes of the German merchant as he made his confession in the home of the *Yitav Lev,* with all the household listening silently to his words.) A nobleman from a village adjoining Eisenstadt came in to buy a large quantity of my most expensive fabric. You don't get a purchaser like that more than once a year, and the profit from my transaction with him would be enormous. The salesmen who had hurried all the others out didn't dare say a word to him, though I kept glancing at my watch with increasing anxiety. Right before noon I suddenly told the nobleman, "I hope his honor excuses me, but I must stop the business at this point, as I have to close my store."

The *graf* looked at me in astonishment and demanded an explanation of my strange words. I told him about Shabbos and its holiness, and he was even more amazed. "But it's only noon now; we can finish up a lot of business before sunset!"

"I can't. My store is locked up every Friday at noon, and today, also, it will be so," I said determinedly.

The nobleman's face turned scarlet in fury. "Either you continue with me until our business is finished up, or our deal is through."

I was caught between a rock and a hard place. "Don't be a fool, a huge profit will go down the drain in a second," a voice screamed out from the left side of my heart. "You shook hands with Father," another voice answered, this one coming from the right side. But I was taken captive by the "left side," as it says: A fool's heart is on his left. For the first time since my father's death, the store was not closed at noon. I calmed down my anxious soul, assuring it that this was a one-time occurrence that wouldn't make a difference later.

The hours passed, and as Shabbos approached, the nobleman showed no inclination to leave. The opposite: he sat smugly upon an upholstered chair, his legs crossed, occasionally increasing his order by calling out the name of some other luxurious fabric from the list that he'd brought with him.

Shabbos was approaching and I was in dire straits. I found my courage and tried my best to encourage the nobleman, with excruciating politeness, to hurry and finish up the purchase. Finally, right before Shabbos arrived, I managed to close the store. The setting sun painted the streets of Berlin gold and the Jews of the city streamed to the *shuls* in their Shabbos garb at the time that I was racing home. I felt a tremendous sense of shame: I hadn't passed the test! But then I stroked my bulging purse. The nobleman had paid in cash, and in two months of work I hadn't made as much as I had this one Friday!

That night I had a horrifying dream.

My father, may he rest in peace, appeared before me, dressed in his white shrouds. His face was furious. "I've come to call you to a *din Torah*," he said.

"*Din Torah*? Why?"

"You broke the agreement we shook hands upon," my dead father replied, touching my hand. I then flew up with him, higher and higher, until I came to a majestic place. "This is the Heavenly Court," he explained to me. Before I could recover my composure, I was already hearing Father recite his complaints about me and tell of the handshake we had exchanged before his death. The court then weighed the two sides.

My eyes grew dark: the Court had found in favor of my father! Another second and it would deliver its verdict, declaring that I should stay with Father, up there…

Suddenly a fine-looking Jew, dressed in a *shtreimel* and a *kapatah,* appeared, and said to my father: "Leave your son; one is not punished without due warning! He failed once; give him the chance to make good!"

Father, on his side, was firm, and demanded that judgment be cast. But the eminent old man wouldn't give in, trying to persuade him with many different arguments, asking that I be given the chance to repent. Father approached the Heavenly judges and asked them who the man was. They answered that it was the holy rebbe of Sighet, and that his opinion was often listened to Up Above. When Father heard this he immediately agreed to give me another chance to repent.

I awoke drenched in a cold sweat. I understood that I'd been given a second chance to live because of this *tzaddik* whom I'd never before seen. I had never even heard of the name Sighet! That morning I went to *shul* and asked about the city. If there is no such place, I told myself, that is a sign that the dream is nothing more than the fruits of an over-active imagination.

To my shock I was told by those in the know all about Sighet, a city in Hungary. I immediately decided to go there. When I saw the rebbe in his Shabbos clothing my entire body shook, and I fell into a faint, because I immediately recognized the holy visage of the elderly man who had defended me when my father had wanted me to be punished with the law's full severity.

The household of the *Yitav Lev* stood in silent shock, and only the rebbe said calmly to his *gabbai,* "Now you know why I wanted my *shtreimel* and *kapatah.* I wanted the German merchant to recognize me, to see me exactly as I had looked on that Friday evening in the Heavenly Court..."

(I heard this from my uncle, the rav and *gaon* R' Chaim Eliyahu Sternberg, *zt"l,* who was one of the close disciples of the Rebbe of Satmar.)

Out of the Lion's Mouth

AFTER MANY YEARS OF OCCUPATION AND OPPRESSION, THE Polish people rebelled against the tyrannical reign of the Russian Czars. Like a fire raging out of control, the rebellion burned through the borders of the entire kingdom. The Polish farmers lifted their bowed heads and began to collect the shards of their shattered pride. With unequaled courage and spirit they raised the banner of nationalism and reconstructed the national honor that had been trampled beneath the heavy Russian boots.

At its inception the rebellion was wretchedly poor. After many years of cruel Russian exploitation, the granaries of Poland's farmers remained bare. The rebellious farmers were completely impoverished and they were out for much more than just glory.

A barefoot band of soldiers approached the palace of Leibish, the wealthy lord. The sight of the band wasn't impressive; there was something in these soldiers, dressed in a motley of rags, the patches on their clothing forming a kind of colorful mosaic, that aroused derision in the onlooker. There was no order, no careful lines as the group marched. From thick red throats came a buoyant tune.

In a short moment the soldiers had surrounded the castle. One of them, whom the others regarded as an officer, kicked the gate outside the courtyard.

The gentile maid peeked out and flew back inside in a panic.

"The *bossiakim* are coming!" she cried out.

A dark fright fell upon the household. The populace had derisively nicknamed the rebels, these impoverished Cossacks, *bossiakim*, barefoot ones. These *bossiakim* would fall upon the homes of the wealthy like a swarm of locusts, leaving behind them nothing but desolate earth.

"Where is the master of the house?" the soldiers called. "Open this gate immediately if you value your lives!"

Leibish was sitting at that moment crouched over thick ledgers, marking accounts in the cramped lines. His heavyset body was encased in a light silk robe. His face was round and florid, his cheeks well padded. His eyes gave off a light of contentment as he reached the end of another long column marking off income.

At the sound of the shouting, he stood up from his chair and slowly walked towards the gate.

Leibish, a lord among lords, was suspicious of the revolution from the first moment. "No good will come of this rebellion," he declared to his friends and acquaintances. "Why shouldn't we continue to live our lives in tranquility under Russian sovereignty? As Jews, it is preferable to live under the protection of enlightened Russian rulers, rather than be governed by wild Polish farmers." Now, he was coming face to face with some of those wild men.

"What do you want?" he asked carefully.

"Open the gate!" the officer roared in fury.

The tone of his voice cowed Leibish a little. He opened a path for the gang, who burst into the palace like a pack of wild wolves.

"Give us food, bread, and wine!" The soldiers threw covetous glances at the beautiful home, their eyes seeking out the kitchen overflowing with delicacies.

Leibish rose up to his full height. "Insolence!" he hissed furiously, his face growing scarlet. "I will give you nothing!"

The barefoot ones stared at him for a moment, as if they couldn't believe what they were hearing.

"You thugs!" Leibish seemed to take on new courage from the silence, which he mistakenly interpreted as weakness. "Get out of my house now."

The end of the sentence came out choked, as a mighty fist plunged into his belly, knocking the air out of his lungs. Leibish doubled over and fell onto the ground, his face grey with pain.

"Leibish!"

A terrible scream echoed through the vastness of the house, as Leibish's wife staggered towards him in a faint. The household didn't know to whom they should turn first: to their father, rolling in agony on the floor, or their mother, lying unconscious, as the rebels emptied the contents of the larder into their sacks.

When the horde had finished its work they turned to take care of Leibish.

"Here is the rebel; let's take him with us."

After a long moment Leibish was stashed into a carriage, his hands and feet bound behind him like a cow being brought to slaughter.

One of the sons didn't panic; he raced after the swaying carriage to save his father. A whip cracked in the air and left a thin red line across his face. He stopped, his features contorted in pain.

"You'll hear from your father again," came the drunken laughter. "Look for his body in one of the swamps!"

After a few days there came a sign of life from the missing man. A sign of life — and one of death.

"We have sentenced your criminal father to death," was the message that came to Leibish's household, "for the grave crime of refusing to assist the rebels."

Leibish's home was in the region of Radomsk. On that very day his household went to see the holy *admor*, R' Shlomo HaKohen, the rebbe of Radomsk, author of the *Tiferes Shlomo*, who had performed miracles that had startled the entire country. When they stood before him they raised a dreadful cry.

"Why are you screaming?" the *tzaddik* roared at them. "The rebels will not kill him."

Leibish's sons exchanged wondering glances; none knew what to say.

"The entire affair will end with money," the Radomsker explained. "Your father will pay a ransom and be set free. Now this is what you must do," instructed the rebbe. "Go to the head of the band and plead with him. Who knows, perhaps he will have mercy."

Leibish's family did as the rebbe had commanded. They traveled to the rebel encampment and fell at the feet of the rebel chief, begging him to let the prisoner live.

Wonder of wonders, the leader of the thugs didn't kick the faces of those bowing towards him, and didn't even scream at them to go away!

"Stand up," he said quietly. "What do you want?"

Leibish's sons burst into tears. "Have mercy on our father's life!"

"And why not?" the officer said. "Take your father with you and go to life and peace."

The sons' hearts skipped a beat; they seemed almost in a trance.

The officer smiled wickedly, and in a chilled voice added, almost as an afterthought, "If you bring us 30,000 golden coins, as ransom, of course..."

And because Leibish was one of the wealthiest in the land, it wasn't long before the sons had returned with the demanded sum. Leibish was set free, and went from death to life. The family immediately raced to the home of the rebbe of Radmosk.

"How did those murderers let you out alive?" the rebbe asked, as if he didn't know everything about the affair.

Leibish told him all that had occurred, mentioning the money that the head rebel had demanded. Immediately the *tzaddik* shouted, "Can it be? Such greed, to ask for such a great sum?" His holy face gleamed. "This cannot be! Your money will be returned to you, until the very last coin!"

The onlookers were taken aback. What lay behind the *tzaddik's* anger about the ransom money? Hadn't he himself prophesied from the beginning that Leibish's life would be saved only through money?

And furthermore: When had anyone ever heard of the rebels returning money? These hooligans, these swarms of locusts, had never given back anything that had fallen into their greedy hands!

But none of those present dared reveal what he was thinking.

The years passed quickly. Leibish's kidnapping and remarkable liberation were all but forgotten. The Russian regime put down the rebellion with an iron hand. The Polish revolution wasted away, leaving behind it thousands of corpses.

Battalions of Russian soldiers marched in the rebels' footsteps, from encampment to encampment. When they came to the base that had housed Leibish, they discovered a well-sealed box. After they'd broken into it and rummaged through its contents, they found a bag that contained the lordly sum of 30,000 golden coins!

"How did the barefoot ones get their hands on so much money?" the soldiers wondered. They inspected the records kept by the commander and found that the money had been taken from a wealthy Polish Jew by the name of Leibish, from the Radomsk region.

In complete contrast to their usual practice, at the behest of the army chief, they sent an invitation to Leibish to come and get his money — up to the last coin.

Immediately afterwards the entire family traveled to the *tzaddik* of their city to tell him how his words had been fulfilled, to the very last detail.

"Enough!" the rebbe threw Leibish out with a roar. "Have you come to confuse me with talk of miracles? I don't want to hear!"

One of the students of the *Tiferes Shlomo* gathered his courage together and asked, "Can our rebbe teach us why we shouldn't speak of miracles? A blind man could see how this affair goes against nature! Is there something wrong in speaking of the miracles and wonders of *tzaddikim,* how what they say comes true? After all, we know that a *tzaddik* decrees and Hashem fulfills!"

"You've spoken well," the rebbe praised him. "But this particular wonder may simply be a test for me..."

And the *tzaddik* then told them:

"The story is told of one of the students of the holy *Baal Shem Tov*, whose rebbe advised him to take on an honored position in the rabbinate of one of the cities. The student refused. The *Besht* looked at him sternly. 'Can this be? I am giving you a blessing today, the possibility of sitting in serenity, learning Torah and serving G-d — and you refuse this favor?

"Perhaps,' the *Besht* continued, searing him with his rebuke, 'your diligence in Torah learning is lacking, and you don't want to take on the burden?'

"The student lowered his eyes before the remonstrance but wouldn't budge from his refusal. 'I don't want to be a rav.'

"The *Besht's* face then grew radiant with joy, as he told his student, 'You must know that my intention was to test you. I wanted to see if the Torah that you have acquired here has truly become a part of you!'

"This is a sample of what *tzaddikim* must face," R' Shlomo explained. "Sometimes wondrous and remarkable things come through a *tzaddik's* hands; Hashem, as it were, changes all of creation. But the *tzaddik* must always wonder: perhaps the miracle is nothing more than a test to see if he will grow haughty and proud, and fall into the pit of oblivion...

"When *HaKadosh Baruch Hu* told Moshe Rabbeinu 'I will make you into a great nation,' it was an enormous test. Had the greatest prophet of all agreed, he would have been lost, Heaven forbid. But he withstood the test, saying, 'If not, erase me from Your book.'

"And if so," the *tzaddik* sighed, a terrifying sound, "who knows if all these wonders and miracles that you are telling me are nothing more than a test for me..."

Who Built the Church?

W HEN R' AHARON OF KARLIN, AUTHOR OF THE *BEIS Aharon*, passed away, his son R' Asher, known as "the young rebbe," who was still a youthful student, was appointed rebbe. A shining future was predicted for him; his greatness, holiness, and extraordinary asceticism became a byword. But he did not lead for long: after only 14 months he, too, passed away, during a visit to the city of Drohovitch. A cholera epidemic had left many dead there, and R' Asher had traveled there in order to be a sacrifice for the sake of his brethren. And with his death the epidemic came to an end!

Immediately after the passing of the *Beis Aharon* it became clear to his son, R' Asher, that the loss was not only confined to the spiritual sphere. He soon learned that his father had taken on a huge debt, borrowing tremendous sums to give out to charity. The creditors were not prepared to wait long, and immediately after the *shivah* they came to demand payment. Every day more and more people left notes on the table of debts incurred. "Look here," they would wave the papers before the son's face, pointing to his father's signature. R' Asher paid from his savings but soon came to the end of his funds. To R' Asher's great sorrow he was forced to send the creditors away empty-handed, promising them earnestly to repay everything speedily.

But if R' Asher thought the job would be an easy one, he found out quickly that it was not so. The days passed and the pit wouldn't fill. The matter distressed him deeply, and in great bitterness the rebbe called out to his *Chassidim*, telling them that if they knew just what the situation was they would even sell their own *tallis* and *tefillin* in order to repay the debts!

The rebbe's call had enormous repercussions. The *Chassidim* had learned that things had become unbearable, and no one could ignore the dire situation. The Jews began to come to the rebbe's house, sacks of money in their hands, some with more and some with less — and still the sum was far from what was needed for the creditors.

One day, as usual, several Jews who'd answered the rebbe's call for help gathered together. Among the men was one of the creditors, an upstanding and wealthy man who had been one of the foremost *Chassidim* until he'd suddenly been distanced from the rebbe, who had refused to see him without giving any explanation.

Now the man stood among his friends, his hand clutching a promissory note for 1000 gulden, a huge treasure by any measure. He'd lent the money to the *Beis Aharon* a short time before the rebbe's passing.

"Listen," he whispered to the *gabbai,* his tone beseeching. "Tell the rebbe that if he will only see me and make up, I am prepared to tear up this note and wipe out the debt!"

Annulling a debt of 1000 gulden would go a long way in easing the financial burden under which the rebbe was struggling. The *gabbai* didn't waste a moment; he immediately entered the rebbe's room and told him of the beneficent offer.

"Ask him to leave the house immediately," the rebbe told the thunderstruck *gabbai.* "Do we need his thousand golden coins?"

At the time, the *Chassid* R' Yisrael Ber Heller of Teveryah was in the rebbe's house, and the rebbe's reply displeased him greatly. "What can this be?" he thought to himself. "If the situation is as desperate as the rebbe has said, how can he so easily wave away such a generous offer?"

R' Yisrael Ber, like all the *Chassidim,* knew that his thoughts were clear to the rebbe, like an open book. If a *Chassid* wondered about the rebbe's conduct, and particularly if he was disturbed by it, he took care not to stand before the rebbe for some time, lest he raise the *tzaddik's* ire. And so, when the thought flashed through R' Yisrael Ber's mind, he immediately ran away, not daring to show his face in the *beis midrash* for quite a few days.

It didn't help. After a few days had passed the rebbe called to R' Yisrael Ber, who was his regular *shochet,* and commanded him to travel immediately to Trivishova.

The village of Trivishova is located not far from Stolin. Reb Eli, one of the rebbe's closest *Chassidim,* owned a pub there.

"Tell Reb Eli that we are coming to him this evening for dinner.

And be so good as to slaughter a chicken for the meal," the rebbe said. R' Yisrael Ber immediately went on his way.

Reb Eli's joy reached almost up to heaven. On a regular weekday, just like that, the holy rebbe was coming to him! Though he couldn't understand why he merited such an honor, he immediately began to prepare the meal. The drunken gentiles, the usual customers at his pub, were hastily evicted from the place. Shining Shabbos tablecloths were laid on the tables, and soon the air was filled with the fragrance of wonderful foods being prepared.

Towards evening, with the setting of the sun, the sound of horses' hooves could be heard, together with the rattle of carriage wheels, heralding the rebbe's arrival.

Immediately after *Maariv* the rebbe and all those present washed their hands for a meal. The rebbe broke off a piece of bread, and after eating a piece he called to Reb Eli, who was busy in the kitchen among the bubbling pots.

"Sit down, please, Reb Eli," he said pleasantly to his perplexed host, who hastily wiped his greasy hands on a shabby handkerchief. "I want to tell you, and all those sitting here, a story that happened not very long ago."

That winter the building housing the ancient church of Trivishova collapsed. The local priest was horrified: without a church he wasn't worth a counterfeit penny. He immediately sent off several telegrams to Petersburg, the royal city, asking for government help to build a new church. "If you can give us a detailed estimate, you will get all the assistance," came back the generous official offer.

The priest's eyes lit up as he read the telegram. His finely-honed senses immediately caught a whiff of a gold mine. "I will give them an estimate double what I need, and half of the expenses will go into my pocket," he thought.

On second thought, though, his face fell. In order to take some of the money he needed a partner in crime. What clever contractor would give him a doctored list of expenses? What Christian would do it? His thoughts darted here and there. Suddenly he thought of Eli, the Jewish owner of the pub, and his face lit up. "He's a clever man and will understand the matter," he said to himself. That very evening he snuck quietly into Eli's house at a late hour.

"The priest comes to me? In the middle of the night?" Eli said in wonder.

"I've got an incredible deal for you," the priest whispered, his eyes flashing. "You will be the contractor who will build the church. Give me a bill for 5,000 gulden, and since the cost of the building will only be 3,000, we'll find ourselves richer by 2,000 gulden. One thousand for me; one thousand for you."

Reb Eli was in a quandary. The temptation was great: one thousand gulden could pull him out of his difficult financial situation for many years to come. But how could a G-d-fearing Jew build a Christian church?

"Wait a few days," he told the priest in confusion. "I want to think about it."

"What should I do?" he wondered after the priest had left him. Suddenly an idea hit him. "I'll get the rebbe's advice," he thought to himself. "The rebbe will know what to tell me." He quickly prepared the carriage and started on the road. But the carriage hadn't even left the village when Reb Eli suddenly realized the implications of his actions. "Money has blinded me so terribly that I've almost lost my senses entirely." He wiped the sweat off his shining brow. "What am I doing? Going to the rebbe, the *tzaddik,* in order to ask him about building a church?

"I will not build the church, no matter what," he declared, turning the reins in the opposite direction. The next day he gave the priest his determined answer. The priest then turned to another Jew, who didn't hesitate even one second.

"The Jew who built the church is the same one who wanted to write off a debt for 1,000 gulden, just so I should forgive him," R' Asher ended his amazing story, turning to his *shochet*, R' Yisrael

Ber. "Tell me, those 1,000 gulden that our Eli wouldn't sully his pure soul with, should I take them?"

All this time Eli hadn't opened his mouth; he sat, listening to the story being told about him, in absolute silence. Only after the rebbe had taken his heartfelt leave of him did the words come pouring out: "I don't know how a mortal man can have such *ruach hakodesh*. I never told my story to anyone in the world, never revealed a word of it, and yet the rebbe sat here and told over all my thoughts in detail, not missing even one thing! It could only be Hashem's spirit that spoke through him."

(I heard this story from R' Chaim Asher Lederman, *zt"l*.)

The Deposit, the Witnesses, and the Rabbi

I T WAS *EREV* SHABBOS WHEN UZIEL'S CARRIAGE ENTERED Prague. The hour was late and the rays of the sun glistened red on the cobblestones, as if coming to remind the tired merchant of the light of the Shabbos candles.

Occasionally he would pat his moneybag with his hand. Two thousand gold coins lay securely within, the fruits of the past winter's labors.

He began to panic. Where could he go? Shabbos was fast approaching. The coins! What could he do with them?

The clatter of the wheels and the clip-clop of the horses' hooves suddenly came to a stop. The wagon driver turned around and asked in a thunderous voice, "Where to?"

Where to? That's exactly what I'm asking myself, thought the merchant, perplexed. At that very moment a thought flashed through his brain; a Jewish thought.

"Take me to the synagogue."

The driver immediately grabbed the reins and directed the horses to Prague's synagogue. There they found the *shamash*, holding a long wooden stick with a flame at one end. He lifted the stick and lit the dozens of wicks lying in glass globes full of oil that were placed in gold-plated lamps hanging from the high ceiling. The flames of the wicks gave off a clear glow all through the large synagogue. It was dusk, and in the homes of the Jews the hour for candle lighting drew near.

Uziel's eyes darted back and forth. The *shamash* was too busy to pay him any attention. Still, the alert eyes of a dignified Jew sitting near the eastern wall watched him curiously. The man's dress marked him as one of the notables of the community.

"*Shalom aleichem*, Reb Yid," the man approached him. "I can see that you've come from far away. Do you have a place to sleep and eat this Shabbos?"

"No, and no," Uziel replied. For a millisecond he wondered if he could trust this man. Clearly, he was a respected man, a leader. Surely he was known in the community, even if he, Uziel, didn't know who he was.

"If so, please be my guest for Shabbos," the man offered with a generous smile.

Uziel thought it over and accepted. The man introduced himself. "My name is Elimelech Dov, but no one calls me that. Even the children in the community know Meilech Ber."

The man took Uziel to his house and settled him into one of the large rooms. The room had no closet with a lock, and the merchant was afraid to leave his money without adequate protection. He turned to his host with his request. The man once again graciously acceded, placing the moneybag into a metal container in his bedroom, and taking the burden of protecting his things away from his guest.

Uziel spent a lovely Shabbos. His host was very hospitable, offering him the best of foods. He enjoyed a tranquil night's sleep on the sparkling clean linen.

On *Motzaei Shabbos* after *havdalah,* Uziel stood before his host. He thanked him fervently and asked if he could pay for the trouble he'd taken.

"Heaven forbid," Meilech Ber jumped at the suggestion, his face showing great offense. "I should take money for my hospitality?"

Uziel then asked his host to give him his moneybag containing the 2,000 coins.

"I don't know what you re talking about," Meilech turned an honestly bewildered face to him. "What money are you speaking of?"

"You're joking, of course," Uziel grinned. "Have you forgotten that yesterday I gave you, right before candle lighting, a moneybag with 2,000 gold coins in it?"

"What?" his host shouted. "It never happened!"

Uziel heard the words and was struck with a terrible fear. But still he tried to judge his host favorably: perhaps he'd truly forgotten he'd taken the moneybag for safekeeping. But Meilech Ber continued to deny the entire thing, turning on his guest and accusing him of base ingratitude for the hospitality he'd shown him by accusing him falsely. "Ask about me in all of Prague," he roared at Uziel. "Everyone knows me; there's no one more honest than I am in the entire city."

With downtrodden spirit Uziel left the home, despair eating at his heart. He had no idea of what to do, until he thought of the rabbi of Prague, the holy *gaon*, R' Yechezkel Landau, author of the *Noda B'Yehudah*.

With his face drawn, Uziel told the rabbi how his host had cheated him and slyly stolen all his money.

"Do you have any witnesses?" asked the rabbi.

"No witnesses and nothing in writing," Uziel admitted, his voice choked.

"Our Sages, *zt"l,* warned us not to do what you've done," the rabbi rebuked him. "Three shout [in a court] and are not answered, and the first of them is: one who has money and lends it without witnesses [*Bava Metzia* 75]. You've brought this trouble on yourself."

"How could I have done differently?" the merchant justified himself. "It was only a few minutes before Shabbos. Who would have believed him capable of such a terrible swindle?"

"If so, how can I help you?" the *Noda B'Yehudah* asked him, with inexorable logic. "Nothing in writing, no witnesses. Who says that your story is true? Maybe you made the whole thing up."

Uziel left the rabbi, bitter and despairing. For three days he wandered around Prague like one drunk, almost losing his mind in his misery and depression.

On the fourth day he returned to the rabbi. His face had withered, showing terrible stress. "Great rabbi, I am certain that with your incredible wisdom and broad knowledge you will know how to get my stolen money out of the hands of that thug. And if not — I will go up to the roof of your house and jump off it, and my innocent blood will be on the rabbi's head!"

"Honest words can be recognized," R' Yechezkel replied. "Your words, which have come straight from your heart, have gone into mine. I see that you haven't made it up. And I've got an idea. Sit in the next room and wait. I'll call Meilech Ber here. When you hear me shouting, over and over again, the words '300 gold coins,' jump into this room and scream at him as loudly as you can, and demand the 2,000 coins that you gave into his keeping."

The rabbi's aide immediately went to Meilech Ber's house. Only a short time had passed when the community leader sat himself down in front of the great rabbi. The rabbi spoke pleasantly to him on this matter and that, until he got to the point.

"Do you know why I've called you here so urgently?" he asked.

"I haven't the faintest idea," the man admitted.

The rabbi leaned forward, like one sharing a secret. The man, too, leaned his elbows on the desk, his face bent towards the rabbi, his ears ready to hear him.

"The community is in trouble," the rabbi whispered.

"A blood libel?" Meilech Ber trembled.

"No, no. But we've got no money," the rabbi said sadly. "There are some incredibly important charity projects and the coffers are empty. You've got to contribute 500 gold coins."

Meilech Ber shifted in his chair. "I'm sorry, but I'm one of those who doesn't have as much as others think. I'm not a rich man; though G-d has given me for my own needs, He hasn't given me more than that."

The rabbi scrutinized him with wise eyes. "Let's work this out. If that's true, give me 400 coins for the community chest, and you will merit all the blessings."

"What do you want from me?" the rich man complained. "I have just explained to our respected rabbi that it's absolutely impossible for me in my current situation."

The rabbi stood up and began to shout loudly. "At least 300, only 300, just 300!"

At that moment the door opened and Uziel burst into the room, running around as the rabbi had instructed him. He screamed, "Rabbi, save me from the swindlers! This man took my 2,000 golden coins and refuses to return them!"

The rich man was dumbfounded. Uziel approached him, his fists balled. "Rabbi, I warn you, I will kill this thief right here if he doesn't return my money."

"Sit down, please," the rabbi asked him in soft and calming tones. But the man refused to settle down; his anger was absolutely real. He screamed with all his might at the rich man, threatening to beat him to death if he didn't give back the coins.

"Do you recognize him?" the rabbi asked Meilech Ber.

The rich man was startled. "First time I've ever seen him in my life."

"We've got to get rid of him," the rabbi said. "Make him leave. It seems he's mad. Give him 100 gold coins just to get rid of him."

Meilech Ber put his hands into his purse. "If the rabbi commands me, I'm prepared to do it now."

"Am I a beggar?" Uziel screamed furiously. "Am I asking for handouts? Give me all my money, 2,000 gold coins!"

The rabbi and the rich man exchanged glances. "Give him 200, such a nuisance," the rabbi whispered encouragingly.

The man was prepared to do so, but Uziel's shouts deafened him. "What! Can this be? Two hundred instead of 2,000?"

The rabbi seemed baffled. He whispered to the rich man, "This man is endangering your life. Give him 500 coins and get rid of him!"

Meilech Ber agreed. "Five hundred, just so this monster leaves me."

At that moment the rabbi stood up imposingly from his chair and began to thunder at Meilech Ber: "You wicked man! An entire community is asking for 500 gold coins and you don't have it, for your own community, but for this man, whom you claim you don't recognize and have never seen before, you are willing to give 500 immediately? Give him his money back now, up to the very last coin!"

The rich man's face turned as white as the sheets he'd offered his guest. Realizing that he had no choice, he raced home and returned with the money, 2,000 gold coins.

R' Levi Yitzchak of Berditchev's Commission

MATIS MEIKLER WASN'T A LARGE-SCALE BROKER, EVEN though he'd been known by the word "*meikler*," Yiddish for broker, for so long that it had become his official name. He was a small businessman, in today's parlance. Occasionally some business deal would come up and he would hurry to plunge into it, sometimes with success, sometimes not. But even when things went well, his profits never exceeded 20 rubles or so.

Now he stood at the fair in Lemberg, his eyes shining. The deal of a lifetime stood ready before him, and all he had to do was bend over and grab it. The commission would be hundreds of rubles, if not more.

In the course of his business dealings, Matis had developed sharp senses and a keen perception of promising barter possibilities. On his right stood ten wagons in a row filled with fine Italian silk, striking an alien note between the cattle cars, sheep pens, and chicken coops surrounding them. Amid the confusion of the fair he managed to question the owner and hear from him how he'd managed to get stuck in such an inappropriate place.

The bored merchant was thrilled that someone was speaking with him. He explained to Matis that he'd been in a hurry and hadn't bothered finding out where he was to display his merchandise at the fair, and thus he managed to get stuck in this unsuccessful spot, with no potential customers to even inspect his costly wares.

"Why don't you pay a wagon driver or porter to take the silk to the other side of the fair?" Matis wondered.

The merchant answered him frigidly. "I paid enough money to bring the stuff here. If Heaven decrees that I should sell my products, the customer will come to me," he said confidently. "Actually, I'm not looking for money in exchange for the silk. I need a large shipment of wheat for my neighbor, who owns a flour mill in my city. He promised me a generous payment for a goodly amount of wheat, a payment far larger than anything I can get for the silk."

The day before, Matis had inspected the other side of the fair, and he'd met a merchant who had told him he was longing to get rid of a huge shipment of wheat. His competitors to the right and left of him were taking in vast profits, and for some reason he'd been left alone and neglected. Matis had conversed with him, trying to find out why his merchandise alone wasn't selling.

"Because I'm looking for a barter deal. I need Italian silk rather than money. Italian silk is very rare in my region and there is a great demand for it; I will be able to make a lot more money on the silk than on the wheat."

Now Matis put the two conversations together. The fair bustled with life; everyone was busy with trade, and no one but he, Matis, knew of the possible deal that could be put together from two sides of the large fair, a distance of several streets.

"It seems to me that if I make a deal between the silk merchant and the wheat merchant I will get a very high commission," Matis thought happily, his excitement growing from moment to moment.

After a few minutes of sweet fantasies on what awaited him once he'd pocketed the huge profits, he suddenly sobered up. How could he suggest a deal of such huge proportions? What was he, after all: small fry, a tiny, unimportant salesman wearing a patched overcoat and a dusty hat. In his heart of hearts he knew the truth: even if he had something to say, there was no one who would want to listen to him. Because of his bedraggled appearance, the merchants wouldn't bother with him at all.

The more he thought about it, examining the affair from all sides, the more hopeless it seemed.

He stood motionless for some time, flinging his hands up in despair. Then he noticed the well-known salesman, Itchele of Berditchev, strolling through the fair with an air of self-importance, looking carefully around him. Itchele was known as the city's most successful salesman. In his fantasies Matis would dream of being second to Itchele, a dream that could never come true.

With no other choice he approached the important salesman and suggested a deal. Itchele would make the bargain between the wheat and the silk merchants. As a successful merchant, he would be listened to and his word respected. The two of them, Itchele and Matis, would then split the commission equally.

With his sharp senses, Itchele could smell a big deal; he could uncover good business from a vast distance. At first he was loath to believe Matis — the thing sounded too good, a treasure that one merely had to go and pick up. But when he heard all the details, his eyes sparkled with delight. "Of course I'll do it," he told Matis with a broad smile and a firm handshake. "As soon as I get my commission I'll give you half."

Itchele raced from one end of the fair to the other. He told each of the merchants that he was able to furnish him with the merchandise he desired, in exchange for a high rate of commission. The merchants knew him well, and understood that despite the high price it was well worth listening to him.

After a few hours of negotiation the deal was finalized. The loads of wheat and silk had exchanged hands, and Itchele was given six hundred rubles that were immediately placed safely in his wallet.

Matis suddenly appeared at his elbow. "Mazel tov, Itchele. Good business, huh? Let's shake hands."

Itchele stared at him in overt hostility. "We haven't done any business," he said angrily.

"What does that mean?" Matis asked in sudden fear.

Itchele stood for a moment, moving his thumb back and forth in a time-honored gesture of learning. "What it means," he said, his voice using the tune of *Gemara* study, "is that I don't owe you even one kopek."

"But we made a deal!" Matis protested.

"Look, you're a small-time salesman. Even if you had made the suggestion to the two merchants, you would have been talking to the air. They wouldn't have given you a second glance. You never sold anything more important than a coat button. Who made the deal? Me! To whom did they give the money? Me! Go in good health, and don't bother me anymore."

Matis wouldn't give up. "How dare you? What ingratitude!" he shouted in fury, as some curious passersby began gathering around them. "Who gave you all the information? Me! You yourself promised to give me half the commission. It's mine, and don't you cheat me!"

"Leave me alone," Itchele called out, quickening his footsteps. "Are you starting with an expert salesman like me, who after half an hour in the fair would have found the two merchants who needed each other? What do I have to pay you for, for half an hour's work? Take 20 kopeks and leave me," he taunted, looking in open mockery at Matis running beside him, his breath coming in wild gasps.

"Thief!" Matis shouted, trying to get the fairgoers to come to his help. "Return the money to me, the 300 rubles that belong to me!"

"Do you see such chutzpah?" Itchele screamed at the people gazing at them. "Get away from me; if you embarrass me here in the fair I'll take you to a *din Torah*."

"And you're threatening me, too?" Matis gave a hoarse yell. "You're not ashamed! I'll take you to a *din Torah*, you thief!"

Itchele showed him a fist of steel. "Quiet!" he hissed, striking him without mercy. "You won't humiliate me in front of all the customers at the fair!"

After his fury with Matis had abated somewhat, he left the area. He told whoever asked that Matis, the small-time salesman, was eaten up by jealousy at his success and was trying to publicly embarrass him; when he, Itchele, had had enough, he'd given Matis a small beating. Just to teach him a lesson.

Matis wasn't ready to give up without a fight. He called Itchele to a *din Torah* in the court of R' Levi Yitzchak of Berditchev.

They stood before the judges in the courtroom. Matis recited his complaint, telling them the entire story without embellishment. But Itchele, slick and sharp, knew how to present his case well. Matis looked around him, at the room, as Itchele spoke. Ancient books in shabby brown bindings were neatly placed on cracked wooden shelves. A thin ray of light made its way in through the window but soon disappeared into thick drapes, placed there against the stares of the curious.

Though Matis had heard Itchele's arguments before, the blood rushed to his face. "Aren't you ashamed?" he flung the words at him. "Bad enough to lie at the fair, but here? In front of the judges?"

R' Levi Yitzchak gently calmed him. "There's no need for anger. Wait and listen to the verdict as given by our holy Torah."

A tense silence fell upon the room. R' Levi Yitzchak spoke. "Itchele must pay Matis 300 rubles, half of the commission, as they agreed before the deal. The agreement was for half; Matis brought the deal to Itchele's attention, Itchele successfully carried it out. The two should split the money equally."

"Absolutely not!" Itchele cried out brazenly. "Matis beat me by half an hour. He earns 20 kopeks. I'm prepared to give him 50 kopeks, and no more."

He flung 50 kopeks at Matis and left the courtroom in a wild fury.

Matis burst out crying. "Look what he's done, this man. Fifty kopeks! He got rich, 600 rubles, and he gives me 50 kopeks? And I'm a poor man!"

R' Levi Yitzchak was terribly disturbed by the behavior of Itchele the salesman. It was enough that he'd actually raised a hand against Matis, but now he was setting himself up against the court. R' Levi Yitzchak immediately sent a court messenger after him. The man followed Itchele until he caught up with him, and then he sternly warned him to turn back with him. If he refused, the messenger told him, a *kesav seruv* would be issued and he would be excommunicated in all of Berditchev.

Itchele, frightened by the threat, turned back with the messenger and again stood before R' Levi Yitzchak.

The rabbi of Berditchev began to speak.

"As you know, Itchele, you are not the only salesman in the world. I, too, work in the world of sales and agents, and I, too, have received commissions in my time. I have experience in the area."

Itchele opened wondering eyes. The holy rabbi an agent? He'd never heard of such a thing.

R' Levi Yitzchak explained himself. "I am an agent between the Jews and their Father in Heaven. I bring up their merits from the earth to Heaven, and I bring down bounty to them on this earth. And all is done through the means of persuasion and encouragement, just as all the agents work between the seller and the buyer, until everyone is ready to do business. So I, too, am busy persuading the Holy One, blessed be He, bringing Him together with His people.

"Once I looked and saw that the Jews had some merchandise that wasn't worth their keeping; conversely, it would be a good idea to get rid of it. This merchandise was sins, iniquity, and wickedness. Against that, when I was up Above I saw that there were three types of merchandise not needed there: forgiveness, pardon, atonement.

Every rational person knows that these are not needed in Heaven — for can the angels ever sin? They have no evil inclination, as our Sages tell us: In the next world there is no jealousy, no hatred, no competition [*Berachos* 17]. If so, what use have they for *mechilah, selichah,* and *kaparah*?

"I therefore worked hard to arrange a trade: the Jews would send their Creator the three types of unnecessary merchandise: sins, iniquity, and wickedness, and the Holy One, blessed be He, would give the Jews His merchandise: *mechilah, selichah, kaparah.*

"They told me Above, 'Levi Yitzchak, go and see if the Jews want to give up their goods.' I went and I asked. How shocked I was to find that there are people who didn't want to make the trade! The sins were just fine for them, they'd invested a lot of money, a lot of time and effort in obtaining this merchandise. How would they give them up after having gone to so much trouble to obtain them, and for wares that they weren't even sure had value?

"These sinners were so stubborn that it was only with great trouble that they agreed, at the very least, during the Days of Judgment, in the months of Elul and Tishrei, to make the trade. Even then they only agreed if I got them three more pieces of merchandise in exchange: children, life, and sustenance. These things, too, are not necessary in the Heavens, for the angels have no children, no physical being, and no need to eat.

"Before I came down from Above, the Master of the World called to me and asked, 'Levi Yitzchak, My son, you've worked hard on this deal until we could complete it. Will you leave without getting paid, without a commission? Tell Me what you want and I'll give it.'

"I answered and said, 'The Jews are a holy nation and I'm not expecting anything from them; they don't have enough to give me. But from the One Who gives everything I will ask that He give me whatever He wishes.'

"And suddenly came the declaration in the Heavens: 'Levi Yitzchak, because you have worked hard on this, I give you the key to the three types of wares: children, life, and sustenance. They are in your hands. Give them to whom you wish, or take them from those not worthy of them.'"

R' Levi Yitzchak concluded by telling Itchele the salesman: "If you listen to me and give Matis his commission immediately, I'll do my part of the deal as well, and cause you to benefit in these three areas: children, life, and sustenance. But if you persist in refusing to accept the verdict of the court I will take my share — the share of life — away!"

But Itchele maintained his position, stubbornly refusing to pay. Wordlessly, he turned away from R' Levi Yitzchak and went home.

Only a few hours passed and Itchele grew deathly ill. From hour to hour his condition worsened; in a short time he was swaying between life and death.

He wasn't a completely wicked man, and right there in the gateway to *Gehinnom* he repented. He understood well that it was G-d's Hand striking him because he'd refused to listen to the *tzaddik,* and if he didn't give in he was lost. He sent messengers immediately to R' Levi Yitzchak of Berditchev asking forgiveness; at the same time he dispatched 300 rubles to Matis's home, just as they'd agreed upon.

And he recovered completely.

A Flaming Whip

THE MERCHANTS' CARAVAN PLODDED ALONG SLUGGISHLY. The way seemed endless. But finally, after several tiring days, they could see the outskirts of Polana in the distance, a hint of the city they were fast approaching. From the outskirts to the city itself was quite a trip, but just seeing it gave them encouragement.

"But until the bar you also need a drink, " one of the merchants sighed. "A mere drink of water. We've got a journey of several hours before us and what will quench this terrible thirst?"

It was in the midst of the summer, and a harsh sun glared down on them. Sweat poured down from sunburned brows. "Oh, I'm so thirsty," another of the merchants groaned, an elderly man whose white hair attested to his age.

"Me too, me too," others repeated. The thirst was indeed dreadful. They lifted their eyes and looked around them, as if searching for help.

"Here," one of them cried out joyously, as if he'd seen the Messiah. Across from them they saw a broad castle, large and beautiful. The *mezuzos* hanging on the courtyard gates attested to the fact that the owner was a Jew — and, it seemed, a very wealthy Jew, one who, for some reason, preferred to reside out of the city.

"Let's go there; we'll be able to quench our thirst."

The wagoners had almost turned the animals around when one of the merchants, who was somewhat familiar with the place and its residents, stopped them with a loud cry. He turned amused eyes upon them. "Fools, don't you know you'll just turn back in the way that you've come, humiliated and shamed? Don't you know that it's Feivish the Miser who lives here?"

"Feivish the Miser?" The others shuddered, as if hearing the name of Haman from the *Megillah*. "If so, better to stay thirsty and continue on our way to the city. For even if Feivish sees us dying of thirst he wouldn't agree to give us one drop of water!"

An overstatement? If you had asked the residents of Polana, they would have assured you that there wasn't a shred of exaggeration in those hard words.

That Feivish was a G-d-fearing Jew, learned, a scholar, careful and stringent in his observance, was not an issue of debate. But despite this, and in spite of his legendary wealth, the trait of stinginess had clung to him to a most remarkable degree. As a result, he had made his home far from the city, so that beggars should not come to his door and waste his money. Feivish the Miser was so careful of his spending that even when he was forced to give a spare coin here and there, it was as if it had come out of his flesh, a piece of himself.

And as Feivish the Miser and his wealth became one, he was less and less able to bear giving any charity at all, and even showing hospitality to guests became a burden. For weren't the food that guests stuffed themselves with and the drinks they poured down their throats also worth money?

Ultimately, people stayed far away from his beautiful palace and would spit in disgust at the mention of his name. The name Feivish the Miser became a symbol of disgrace and humiliation. Yes, there are people who love their money more than themselves, but to this extent?

And those thirsty merchants dragged their feet into the city of Polana, sighing with their burning thirst, their souls longing for a drink.

So it was for many years before this caravan passed, and so it continued throughout the summer afterwards. Harvest time flew by, summer was over, and the chill of winter descended.

Torrential rain and heavy hail came down that day; the earth was soaked with water. It was a day of endless precipitation, a day that is a blessing and a pleasure to those safely ensconced in a warm home, an icy nightmare for one whose fate sends him outside into the ceaseless flood.

That same caravan of merchants was on a winter's trip on the outskirts of Polana. But instead of crying out for a drop of moisture as they had done the last time, now the men begged for a little dryness. The wheels of their carriages showed an alarming tendency to sink deeply into the thick mud that covered all the roads. The way to Polana seemed longer than ever. The dense hail threatened to break anything that moved on the earth.

"We've got to stop," one of the elders of the group declared. "First, the hail might come down again any minute. Second, even if we continue like this until tomorrow, we'll hardly have progressed." The hail had already broken the wooden roofs of the wagons, and the rain pounded in heavily. Everyone agreed that they would have to do something while they still had the chance, before they would all drown.

"Where can we go for shelter?" was the question on everyone's lips. After a short consultation it was decided that despite everything, they would turn to the palace of Feivish the Miser. Surely he had some kind of outbuilding there where they could find haven.

Secretly — or as secretly as was possible — the merchants fled, hiding beneath a large shed in Feivish's courtyard. They hugged themselves, the water dripping off them like spray from a drainpipe, and shivered with the cold. Occasionally a flash of lightning would split the black sky, and then a terrible roar of thunder would set the earth atremble. The heavy hail began again; another minute and the shed's roof cracked in half beneath the pressure of the deluge. The merchants were again left defenseless, with nothing to shelter them.

Now that they were already in Feivish's courtyard, they found the courage to approach the palace. They quickly found another refuge, this time in his large grain silo. But the silo was within earshot of Feivish's home, and after a few minutes of debate and argument — who was taking the driest place, who was most exposed to the hail — they realized that their loud words would give them away. They immediately decreed absolute silence among them, lest one of the rich man's servants hear them and chase them out into the fury of the weather, prey to the unforgiving flood.

After a minute, perhaps two, the door of the palace opened and Feivish himself, carrying an oil lamp in one hand and a large piece of cloth to protect his head in the other, could be seen approaching the silo.

The merchants felt goose bumps on their flesh, and now it wasn't the cold that caused them to shiver. Their hearts pounded wildly. The old miser would surely drive them out now, far away from his palace gates.

To their vast shock and surprise, the miser invited them in instead. His face glowing, he offered them hot drinks to revive themselves, and graciously asked them to be his guests and satisfy their hunger.

"Feivish likes to make jokes," they thought bitterly. "He's probably going to use this moment to the fullest, and tease us as much as he can."

But Feivish meant business. He didn't let them say a word, and practically pulled them forcibly into his warm home. His servants crowded around them, taking their sodden coats, relieving them of muddy boots, and offering them alcoholic beverages to warm up their frozen bodies. They then invited them to feast at a fully set table.

The guests rolled their eyes in the shock of disbelief. What was he planning, this Feivish the Miser? Could it be that he meant this playacting seriously?

But something in the countenance of their host caused them to wonder a little. It was clear that he was sincere, that his actions were coming from the depths of his soul, that his intentions were pure.

But because they weren't used to such treatment, the guests felt increasingly uncomfortable. They waited for the inevitable outburst, that would be followed by their being thrown out into the rain like stray dogs. But the change that they feared didn't materialize; the opposite, in fact, occurred. Feivish wandered among them, his face soft and gentle, begging them to wash their hands and eat whatever they wished.

"I'll tell you the truth," the head of the group finally said. "Even the most delicious food that you would serve us now would stick in our throats, if we don't know what you are planning. Has Feivish the Miser changed his ways?"

"A valid point," their host agreed, without even a hint of anger or offense at the harsh words. "Let me tell you a short tale, and perhaps afterwards you will understand what has happened to me, and the reason for the complete change that has taken place in my personality."

On that fateful night, Feivish went to bed early. His face glowed with contentment; after checking his books, he had found that there had been some mistakes in the profits column. That is, his wealth had grown even more, by some hundreds of *reinish*.

Absolutely satisfied, Feivish lay his head down upon the pillows, and pulled the warm down blanket up to his neck. Not a minute passed before he had fallen into a refreshing sleep.

And in his sleep he dreamed. He was sick, very sick, on his deathbed. In a few hours he left the world, his soul longing to return to its Creator, to where it had been formed.

But it wouldn't be easy for Feivish to get to the Heavenly Court.

The dead man's sons came to the *chevrah kaddisha* and asked them to take charge of the burial. To their absolute chagrin they were told they would have to pay an enormous sum for the burial plot, a treasure of 1,000 rubles, cash!

And why so much? Everyone else paid 100 or 200 *reinish*! They angrily confronted the members of the *chevrah kaddisha*, who told them stonily, "The choice is yours: either 1,000 rubles, or you can let your father's body rot in your house! Feivish the Miser, the man who hardly gave one coin for charity, should leave the world so easily? The money will go to *tzedakah*, and the dead man will go to his place, happy and rejoicing that he managed to do after his death much more than he could while alive..."

The sons tried to bargain and bring down the price, but the men of the *chevrah kaddisha* were adamant.

The apples hadn't fallen far from the tree: If Feivish was the miser among misers, his sons, too, were not lacking in the trait. In a fury they left the *chevrah kaddisha*, and in the dark of night they left their father's body in the women's section of Polana's main synagogue, hoping that the townspeople would have mercy on the anonymous corpse and bury it in one of the unimportant graves left for beggars.

Feivish's corpse spent an entire night there in the women's section, humiliated and shamed. With morning's light the *shamash* came to the synagogue, a man of great composure who didn't fall in a faint at the sight of a *tallis*-wrapped body lying silently on the earth.

He approached the corpse and pulled the *tallis* to one side. When he saw the grey face of Feivish the Miser, his own face grew scarlet in fury. The *shamash* of the synagogue was also the gravedigger for the *chevrah kaddisha*, and so he understood well all that had happened.

Because he was a man of great strength, he pulled the cold body up, held it under his arms, and walked to the palace of the miser, leaving it there in the courtyard like someone returning a lost piece of merchandise to its owner.

When Feivish's sons saw their father they were forced to accede. They paid 1,000 rubles, and on that very day their father was buried.

Feivish lay in his grave for one day, then two. There was no sound, no voice. Silence. *What has G-d done to me,* he thought in terror. *Has He left me here, unclaimed, without judgment?*

On the third day, a silent angel came and escorted him, worried and anxious, up, higher and higher, until the gates of the Heavenly Court.

"Were you honest in business?" Feivish was asked. "Did you make regular times for Torah study?"

To each question Feivish responded with a joyous "yes." After all, all his life he'd fulfilled many *mitzvos,* had learned Torah with fervor, had prayed with devotion. Nothing was missing in the perfection of his soul. A bit more and the Court would allot him a fine place in *Gan Eden.*

And then, suddenly: "Have you fulfilled the *mitzvah* of giving charity? To open your purse, to give, to let your brother live with you?"

Feivish froze. Here, in the World of Truth, could he possibly lie and deceive? "In the matter of charity I was weak," he confessed in a mutter. "I was born a terrible miser, and I couldn't change my nature."

The Heavenly Court sat on its platform and debated the matter. A G-d-fearing Jew, it seemed, one who fulfilled *mitzvos,* learned Torah, *davened* well. Only one *mitzvah* was lacking, that of charity and lovingkindness.

And the announcement came from the Court: either Feivish would go back to the world in another incarnation, to correct the *mitzvah* of charity that was so lacking, or he would spend three months in *Gehinnom,* and only then take his place among the *tzaddikim* of *Gan Eden.*

Feivish spent some time trying to decide what was preferable.

To go back to the world? And who knew if he would withstand the test this time; perhaps he would fail again and not give *tzedakah*. Seventy more years wasted! But to go to *Gehinnom*? Who knew if he could withstand its terrible tortures?

Finally Feivish decided that he could somehow get through three months. Better that, and get immediate repair of what he'd done wrong; anything not to have to go through the world of deceit a second time, and then, perhaps, still have to face *Gehinnom*.

The words had hardly come out of his mouth, and he was already being escorted by one of the *seraphim* to the place of his punishment.

They traveled for seven days, and still could see no sign of the abyss. "Tell me," he asked the angel, "maybe you're going the wrong way? Maybe they want me to go to *Gan Eden*?"

"Not likely," the angel assured him. "I've escorted more than one there... soon you'll begin to feel the emptiness and the heat."

After a few more days Feivish began to feel a burning heat; the soles of his feet burned. And still they were far away from *Gehinnom* itself...

The more they approached the abyss, the more the heat grew. It was a burning and fiery heat, a flaming pit, and still they were quite a distance away from the entrance to *Gehinnom*!

"I've changed my mind!" Feivish screamed, his heart bitter. "Bring me back to the Court; I'd rather return as a new incarnation into the world of deceit. Anything, but let me flee this inferno!"

"Impossible," the angel told him. "We must abide by your first choice."

"But it was an unfair deal!" Feivish wailed. "I didn't know just how terrible the judgment was, how much it hurt. If I had known — I would never have preferred this *Gehinnom*, even for a second!"

"Even so," the angel returned, "a messenger is forbidden to change his task. If I bring you back to the Court, I will be severely punished."

As he spoke he once again grabbed Feivish by the hand, and continued to pull him to the place.

"Have mercy on me," Feivish sobbed like a newborn child. "Bring me back to the Court. I am prepared to take upon myself your punishment as well; just get me out of this nightmare."

Hearing his despairing cries, the angel felt mercy well up within him, and he turned back. After a few days they reached the place they'd left.

"Can this be?" a voice thundered, rebuking the angel. "How dare you change your mission?"

The angel told them all that had happened, and the verdict was immediately declared: "That's what Feivish wanted? He's agreed to take on the angel's punishment? That is what he will get!"

And before Feivish could move, one of the *seraphim* approached him with, a *pulsa d'nura*, a burning whip, in his hand. He gave Feivish's back a terrible smack that burned and sizzled. Feivish fell down, further and further, the flames of *Gehinnom* burning his body.

With an awful scream Feivish awoke. The members of his household, hearing his cries, raced in. "What's happened to you, Father? Aren't you feeling well?"

Feivish looked around at them in disbelief. Had he returned, then, to this world? Was the whole incident nothing more than a dream?

But if so, what was the explanation for the excruciating pains he was feeling, the burning sensation on his back?

Feivish told his wife and sons what he'd dreamed. He raised his robe and showed them his back.

They looked and were gripped with a paralyzing fear.

Feivish's back, from the neck to the hips, was laced with searing, fiery-red burns! As if he'd been hit — just now — with some kind of hot iron rod...

"Now you understand why I've changed my ways and am no longer worthy of being called Feivish the Miser," their host explained. "From that day on I began to give out my money to charity with no bounds.

"And if you say that perhaps the incident didn't happen, and was a figment of my imagination...

"Here is the proof!"

Feivish removed his winter clothing and turned his back to them.

The guests stood, paralyzed. They'd never in their lives seen such a thing: there was the scar, the scar of a burning whip, along the entire length of his back, raw and searing as the day it had been made!

There is, indeed, a Judge and a judgment.

(I heard this story from my uncle, R' Chaim Eliyahu Sternberg, *zt"l*, of Katamon.)

To Teach Him Torah in Pinsk

"THE GREATEST RABBI IN THE *MINYAN*, THE ONE WHO will guard an orphaned generation, the wisest in the group, the honor of Israel." The *maggid* R' Mordechai of Chernobyl used such language and unique adjectives to describe his son, eldest among eight, his successor and heir, R' Aharon of Chernobyl.

R' Aharon was a being apart from others, and all his interest from morning to night, night to morning, was Torah and G-d's service.

Was it a wonder then that the worthy community of Chernobyl appreciated the *maggid's* oldest son just as much as they did the father? The Jews of Chernobyl recognized their good fortune in having the son of their teacher and rabbi living among them, close by.

To sustain the *maggid*, R' Mordechai of Chernobyl, and his household, the men of the city would go from house to house, from *beis midrash* to *beis midrash*, collecting funds. Every week his father, R' Mordechai, would give a few of those coins to R' Aharon and his family. Thus R' Aharon sat, engrossed in Torah and G-d's service, without the burden of livelihood.

So it continued for several years. The *tzedakah* collectors would gather money for R' Mordechai, and the *maggid* would give some of his meager earnings to his son and his impoverished family. R' Aharon, for his part, constantly thanked his Creator for not having placed the heavy burden of livelihood upon him, and prayed that the situation should continue for many years.

R' Aharon and the *gabbai* who called him to his father, at the express request of R' Mordechai, would never have guessed what the *maggid* planned to say.

"My firstborn son," R' Mordechai turned to him, "from where do you make a living?"

R' Aharon's face registered shock. "Why, you, dear father; you give me money every week!"

"Yes, I support you, that's true, but the question remains: for how long?"

R' Aharon's perturbation increased. What was his holy father trying to tell him?

"My dear father," R' Aharon turned to him, his voice beseeching, "I don't understand what you mean."

R' Mordechai gave his beloved son a mysterious look. "And what is there to understand? Until when can I support you? Haven't you married a woman and raised a family? Until when will I be obligated to support you all? We know of no obligation for a father to support a married son, to give bread to his grandchildren. You are responsible for it yourself!"

R' Aharon stood, astonished and dismayed. Had he not heard his father — his merciful father — speaking to him like this with his own ears, he would never have believed it. All these years his father had supported him so that he, R' Aharon, could devote himself to Torah and the service of G-d without the worry of making a living.

What had happened now? Why was today different from all the others?

R' Aharon gazed fearfully at his father's face. Was his father testing him, trying to see how he would react? Should he accept the yoke of livelihood without a murmur, as if he wasn't truly firm in his service of G-d? Or should he try to refuse.

But when he had looked directly at his father's face he saw that this wasn't the case. R' Mordechai wasn't testing him; he didn't mean anything more than what he'd said. His heart and his lips were acting in unison, as they always did.

"If so, is my father telling me that from now on he will no longer support me?"

R' Mordechai kept a long and meaningful silence.

"I have to take the yoke of livelihood upon myself?"

"Indeed."

R' Aharon was out of ideas. For a few minutes he stood, mute before the terrible shock of this sudden turn of events. Then he recovered.

"What should I do?" he posed the question to his father. "I've never trained for any kind of job; my work has always been the work of Heaven."

"What kind of question is that? You've got the trade of your ancestors at your fingertips. Your ancestors were *maggidim* in the villages and towns; you, too, will do so; you will take a walking stick and go on your way. Preach to the Jews in their synagogues and *batei midrash*, and live from the hands of the Jews, which are generous and forthcoming. After your speech they will give you some coins as a reward; from these coins you can support yourself."

"Where should I go first?"

"To Pinsk."

The city of Pinsk, in those days, was fortified and protected by those who opposed the Chassidic movement. R' Aharon knew that if he traveled there, he wouldn't manage to pick up a single coin; he probably wouldn't even make one ruble.

He couldn't understand his father, who had asked him, R' Aharon, to take care of his own livelihood and who had, at the same time, sent him to Pinsk.

"To Pinsk?"

"Indeed."

R' Aharon put his pack on his shoulders and went on his way, wandering up and down the roads from Chernobyl to Pinsk.

In his great righteousness and his unswerving faith and unlimited goodness, he didn't doubt his father's behavior, didn't wonder why he'd uprooted him from his place to throw him so suddenly into the stormy sea of earning a living. Under the directive of "Honor your father," it was up to him, R' Aharon, to do all that his father had commanded.

When R' Aharon reached Pinsk he went to the city fathers to ask them how one behaved in this holy city. Would he be allowed to preach in any synagogue or *beis midrash* that he chose?

"No!" The city fathers made themselves eminently clear. "There is a rav in the city, the rav of Pinsk, and everything goes by his word. The rav examines every speaker who come to Pinsk, and if he is not impressed by the man, the lecturer must leave the way he came, with purse empty and mouth full of the speech he was not allowed to give!"

R' Aharon wasted no time and immediately turned towards the home of the rav of Pinsk, a man who was one of the most vociferous opponents of the Chassidic movement. He had hardly begun to speak with R' Aharon when the rav wrung his hands.

"Oh! You are the son of the *maggid* of Chernobyl, R' Mordechai, grandson of the well-known *maggid* R' Nachum, a third-generation *Chassid. Oy, oy, oy!*"

R' Aharon kept silent, not answering at all.

"And you want to speak in our city on the holy Shabbos? What will you speak about, the words and tales of your rabbi, the *Besht*?"

R' Aharon, always scrupulously honest, answered in the affirmative.

"You want to know the truth? I'm not very enthusiastic," the rabbi said sincerely. "Pinsk is a city of fervent *misnagdim*, and the Torah of the *Baal Shem Tov* hasn't gained a foothold here. But I am prepared to allow you to give three speeches on this coming Shabbos, but only on one condition."

"And that is—"

"Do you know how to learn?" The rabbi cast a penetrating look upon him. "You're a speaker, and you surely have learned a little *Gemara* and *Tosafos*. For several weeks I've been having trouble with a difficult concept found in a certain *Tosafos*. I've been looking all over, and haven't found a satisfactory explanation. If you manage to resolve my problems with the *Tosafos*, you will be permitted to speak about whatever you choose, the words of the *Besht*, the words of his students. More than that, I commit myself to go with you to the homes of the rich men of Pinsk and to help you to collect something substantial.

"But if not," the rabbi hurried to expand the condition, "you won't be permitted to give even one speech!"

"Let's take a *sefer* and look," R' Aharon said. "Let's examine that difficult *Tosafos*."

The rabbi opened the *Gemara* and pointed to the *Tosafos*. "Do you know what he means to say?"

R' Aharon intently read the words of the *Gemara*, went on to the commentary of *Rashi* on which the *Tosafos* rested, and reviewed the words that were so disturbing the rabbi's serenity.

"What can I say?" R' Aharon said after a short term of study. "I can't work out your problem right here and now. I'll go to my lodgings and there delve into it in peace. Perhaps Hashem will illuminate it and I will be able to understand its meaning."

However, even after R' Aharon went to his lodgings and probed the matter, he couldn't find a satisfactory conclusion. The problem was indeed a weighty one. He studied the words again and again, weighed dozens of possible solutions and rejected them all. None of them seemed good enough to soothe the unyielding rabbi's unrest.

R' Aharon felt a tremendous sorrow; he empathized with the rabbi, whose lack of comprehension of the *Tosafos* was destroying his tranquility. He felt that he shared the burden, was a full partner in the rabbi's misery.

He had, too, another reason to mourn: if he didn't manage to fulfill the rabbi's condition, the rabbi would send him away just as he'd come, with empty hands. And then what would be of his father's words? Had he, R' Aharon, been sent to Pinsk for nothing, just so that he should leave it in shame and humiliation?

In the midst of all this, R' Aharon's tears began to fall, like a spring at its source. A thin, whispered moan came from his lips, slowly growing louder, until he was sobbing bitterly. In the midst of his wailing his head sagged down towards the table, and suddenly a deep drowsiness overtook him.

In his dream he saw his father, R' Mordechai of Chernobyl, coming to meet him with a shining face.

"Why are you crying, my son?"

"Why should I not cry?" R' Aharon answered. "You sent me to Pinsk, and here I am, about to be sent away, humiliated. The rabbi has asked me a very difficult question, and if I can't find the solution he'll send me out like a vagabond. More than that: the pure name of *Chassidus* will be desecrated and shamed, as if *Chassidim* are ignoramuses."

"Why should you cry when the solution is easily worked out?" his father replied. "Here it is." And with that, R' Mordechai explained the words of the *Tosafos*.

"Can you see any other problems with the *Tosafos*?" his father asked when he'd finished his explanation. R' Aharon happily thanked his father, realizing that with this one solution there was not even a shred of a problem left.

"So stop crying, go to the rabbi's house, and tell him the solution. Hashem will send you blessings and success in whatever you do."

R' Aharon didn't waste any time in fulfilling his father's bidding: he awoke, studied the topic — and yes, it was as if the problem had never existed at all!

Without hesitating he raced to the rabbi's home, pulled the *Gemara* off the shelf, and explained the *Tosafos* with a new understanding, his words satisfying the heart as if they'd come straight from Sinai.

The rabbi's eyes glowed with joy. "Now you may rest tranquil, as I can," he said fervently. "If you only knew how many weeks I hadn't slept because of these words, how much anxiety and pain I've undergone this past month."

The rabbi showed R' Aharon great honor, personally attending all three lectures. Paying no heed to his own honor, he accompanied R' Aharon, as he'd promised, to the homes of the city's wealthy men, asking them to contribute to the son of a holy line.

After several days R' Aharon returned to Chernobyl. His father, R' Mordechai, greeted him, his face glowing.

"Now I can reveal to you the reason I sent you to Pinsk. Your support was a mere pretext; there was a different reason.

"You must know that the anguish of the rabbi of Pinsk has been disturbing the entire heavenly host for some weeks. His suffering was acute, and pierced all the heavens. Finally the Celestial Yeshivah decided to send a messenger to him to solve his problem and give him peace. A merit is brought by the meritorious: that is the reason they chose you, my beloved son, to be their messenger and bring the news to the rabbi's home.

"And if you ask why I didn't tell you the reason for your journey: First, it is generally not possible to reveal that which takes place Above. Second, you had to share his pain, feel his anguish, for in order to lift a burden from a Jew one must first be a partner in his distress, as it says, 'One who prays for his friend and he needs the same thing, he is answered first' "

The Heavens in the Forest

THERE WAS LOVE AND FRIENDSHIP, PEACE AND BROTHER-hood, between those two dear friends, R' Yechiel Michel Goldschmidt, a fervent *Chassid* of Kotzk, and R' Zalman Chinkis, a no less devout *Chassid* of Varka. They were the same age, and immediately after marriage settled in the same far-flung Polish town. The two were the only *Chassidim* in the place and so each sought out the other's friendship. Every Thursday night they would learn the *Ohr HaChayim HaKadosh* together; Friday nights after *davening* they would study *Chumash* and *Rashi* and pore over Chassidic works until the hour grew very late. Trips to their rebbes, too, were taken together.

One late night they sat together in the *beis midrash* after they'd finished their studies.

"It's almost Rosh Hashanah," R' Yechiel Michel sighed. "The year has flown by and I have yet to do *teshuvah*."

"That is how I feel, too," R' Zalman replied. "Why should I fool myself: I know the feelings of my heart intimately. How will I stand before my rebbe on Rosh Hashanah? The very thought alone fills me with shame."

"What should I say if you, who are going to your rebbe, R' Mendele of Vorka, known as the silent *tzaddik*, who rebukes only with his gaze, are afraid to stand in his presence? I must stand before my rebbe, the angel of Kotzk, who does not flinch before anyone, as everyone knows."

"First," R' Zalman waved his hand in a gesture of dismissal, "it's not true. Our rebbe, R' Mendele, can tear us apart with his searing words of rebuke. He will often give us a test of our behavior, to see if we are worthy of belonging to his wondrous group of men who serve G-d. And there was once a story of one who didn't deserve to belong..."

"You never told me," Yechiel Michel said, surprised.

"This is the story," Zalman began.

Before the holiday, a large group of *Chassidim* arrived in Vorka, among them great Torah scholars and well-known rabbis. Coming, too, were *Chassidim* who served G-d with fervent devotion. There was also one who had come to infiltrate this illustrious group. He had heard many rumors about them, good stories about heavy drinking during prayers, about the fiery liquor imbibed...

On the day of the holiday, in the early morning, the *beis midrash* was jammed. All the tables were surrounded by people learning; everything seemed wonderful. But the guest felt that something was wrong. He began to look around him and realized that the small, elite group that was always with R' Mendele was missing from the *beis midrash*.

In a side room he found the members of the group *davening Shacharis*, and he immediately joined them. After prayers they descended into the basement, together with the rebbe, made *Kiddush* on wine, and drank copiously. Liquor and mead, a honey-based wine, were also poured with a generous hand.

"All the rumors were correct: it's a gang of revelers," the man mocked them in his heart. He, too, managed to down a good few cups, so that no one would suspect him of spying.

Immediately afterwards R' Mendele said a *d'var Torah* — a small number of words whose depth penetrated the soul. The group of *Chassidim* suddenly cast away the mask of party-goers, and were whisked up to the celestial heights in their great effort to understand the profundity of the words.

After the meeting, the group went up to the *beis midrash*. The congregation had reached the Torah reading. The guest, who was a learned man, was honored with an *aliyah*. On his way up he walked with unsteady gait, an effect of the hard drink within him.

When he came down from before the Torah, R' Mendele approached him.

"You are not one of us..." he roared.

Yechiel Michel was impressed; he'd never heard such a story before. Zalman continued, in a tone of triumph: "Do you see, our rebbe doesn't spoil his *Chassidim*. Besides, it's actually his silence that hurts the most. Sometimes we'd prefer to face his anger, rather than stand before his penetrating gaze."

So the years passed, with amity and good will between them, each explaining to the other the unique philosophy of his rebbe. The debate lasted for years without a final outcome. In any case, each man learned to respect the path of his friend's rebbe, a fact that had consequences many years later, in another world.

The years passed. R' Yechiel Michel Goldschmidt, the *Chassid* of Kotzk, suddenly grew seriously ill, and after his death was buried in his town's cemetery. His old friend, R' Zalman Chinkis, felt as if his world had ended. He mourned his comrade's passing, refusing all comfort.

The next week, in the middle of the night, as Zalman lay asleep, he was suddenly gripped by terror. In his dream, he saw Yechiel Michel coming to greet him. His friend was wrapped in shrouds, and his face was gloomy.

"Yechiel Michel," Zalman shouted in the dream, "why so melancholy? Is there some kind of problem?"

"Woe is me, for the trait of strict judgment," Yechiel Michel burst into a wailing that sent goose bumps up Zalman's entire body. "Humans haven't even the shadow of an idea of how deep the judgment goes, how careful they are of even the smallest of sins that a man leaves behind!"

"Woe!" Zalman joined his friend's lamentation. "Who would ever have believed that you, Michel, wouldn't come out acquitted by the Heavenly Court! All your life you were as careful with all *mitzvos*, easy and difficult, and what is your lot? They haven't sent you to *Gehinnom*?"

Yechiel Michel didn't give him a direct answer. "Zalman, one thing I can tell you: My situation is not good... More than that I am not permitted to say. But I have one great request of you: speak of me to my teacher and rebbe, the *seraph* of Kotzk; he can work for the sake of my soul."

But even in a dream Zalman didn't forget to whom he belonged: "I can't promise you that. I have a great rebbe, R' Mendele of Vorka, and he, too, has influence on high. If you want, I can speak of you to him; I have no doubt he can bring your soul back to its roots."

"But why can't you go to Kotzk?" Yechiel Michel complained.

As we have said, it was a debate that had no resolution, and it continued even in the heavens.

Yechiel Michel saw that his friend was determined and conceded defeat. "Okay, speak of me to your rebbe, the rebbe of Vorka. It is true that his opinion is heard in the Heavenly Yeshivah."

Zalman awoke and, yes, it was a dream! His body was covered with cold sweat, and he was trembling. The sound of Yechiel Michel's voice rang in his ears for hour after hour; that night he slept no more.

At the first opportunity Zalman traveled to Vorka. He was indeed a devoted *Chassid* and never let more than three months go by without visiting his rebbe's court. He never used the long distance to Vorka as an excuse to miss a trip. The weather conditions, too, never kept Zalman away from his rebbe, R' Mendele, whether it was a cold, snowy winter, with the thermometer plunging to well below zero, or a hot summer with temperatures above the nineties.

Zalman sat in his rebbe's shadow for two full weeks, satisfying his thirsty soul with the abundance of holiness. Frequently, though, he would stop, feeling something buzzing in his brain, disturbing his serenity.

"What can it be?" he wondered. "Why am I so restless? What's bothering me?"

He made an intense effort to remember. Perhaps one of the children hadn't been quite healthy when he'd left? Maybe it was that soon his oldest son, Chaim Yehudah, would have to present himself to the hated Polish draft board? Or maybe... But as much as he pondered the matter, he didn't manage to pierce the mystery — what was giving him this terrible feeling of suffocation?

When he left the rebbe, he asked for a blessing for all that was bothering him, but still his tormented soul knew no rest.

He sat in his carriage, constantly turning around to look back. He'd wanted to tell the rebbe something, but he'd forgotten what it was. What could it have been?

The carriage, jolting up and down among the trees in the forest grew further and further from Vorka.

And suddenly he remembered.

"Stop!" he cried to the wagon driver. The man turned towards him in surprise.

"Turn the carriage around to Vorka," Zalman said. "I've forgotten to discuss a certain matter with the rebbe."

"If I didn't know you well I would think you'd lost your mind," the wagon driver said angrily. "What's wrong with you, Zalman? You want to make everyone else travel two hours to Vorka? Two hours that will be four — two to go there and two to return to this spot. And how much time do we have to wait until you've finished with the rebbe?"

"Have mercy; the matter just can't wait," Zalman begged.

"If it's that important, how could you have forgotten it in Vorka?" the wagon driver taunted him. "There's an old saying: One who has no head, has legs. You are welcome to walk to Vorka..."

Zalman didn't hesitate for even one moment; he descended from the wagon and began to walk the long road to Vorka. As the wagon rolled away, the other passengers stared out at him pityingly from the window, shaking their heads.

Zalman walked quickly, his pack on his shoulders and a stick in his hand, hurrying to Vorka to ask his rebbe to remember his friend, the *Chassid* of Kotzk.

When he grew weary he sat down to rest, astonished at how the path that had seemed so quick and easy for horses' hooves to pass should have turned into an endless journey. Before he hadn't noticed the passing scenery at all, hadn't paid attention to the many hills and valleys, forests and woods through which the wagon had passed.

He got up and continued the long trek.

Suddenly he stopped. It seemed to him that in the distance he could see his rebbe's wagon, a special wagon kept by the rebbe for trips out of the city. Now it was passing by him, Zalman, with great speed.

"Perhaps the Rebbe is coming to me?" Zalman thought hopefully. But the speed of the oncoming wagon didn't leave him the leisure for wonder. He stood at the side of the road and began to wave his stick and scream that the rebbe's assistants should stop the carriage, because he had something of great urgency to tell the rebbe. To his chagrin he saw the rebbe gesture to his aides not to stop. The wagon surged on.

For a few moments he felt as if the breath had gone out of his body. His heart bled; he had seen, with his own eyes, how the rebbe had looked at him and had refused to stop. Why?

Not far away was a bare strip of woodland. The stunted trees told their own silent story of a forest cut down in the fullness of its growth, some trees to be used for firewood and others for furniture.

The wagon stopped in the middle of this bare area. R' Mendele descended and began to circle the stumps with a countenance that spoke of deep secrets. Zalman raced towards the rebbe, and found him leaning, lost in thought, on the remains of a cut tree.

"What's the matter, Zalman?" the rebbe asked. "How did you get here? Hadn't you gone in a wagon?"

Zalman stood, his head bent, his cheeks burning with shame. In a low voice he told the rebbe of his good friend Yechiel Michel, who, after death, had appeared in a dream. R' Mendele asked him about his friend's behavior during his life, discussed Yechiel Michel's Torah learning and fear of G-d. Then he wished him farewell.

Zalman didn't understand very much, but his heart told him that the rebbe had made things better for his deceased friend. He was satisfied.

Zalman continued on his way, walking. That night he found lodging in an inn owned by a Jew. While he was asleep, his friend Yechiel Michel once again appeared to him. This time his face was shining joyfully.

"Good for you, my dear friend," he told him happily. "The prayers of your rebbe helped me immediately. My poor soul has immediately found its *tikkun*."

"Forgive me, Michel, for having forgotten you in Vorka," Zalman apologized.

"It wasn't you who forgot, and it didn't happen by coincidence," Michel explained. "It was right next to that stump of a tree, right there, that the demonic angels were endlessly chasing me, tormenting me. R' Mendele knew this, and wanted to help my soul in that exact place. He intentionally reached that place, but he didn't let you in on the secret, for G-d's secret is kept by those who fear Him... Your rebbe knows how to manage very well between the crooked pathways of the world of deceit; he particularly can navigate the roads of the heavens..."

From Ponovezh to Ostrova

WHEN THE YOUNG MAN CAME INTO THE *BEIS MIDRASH* OF Yeshivas Ponovezh, the impression that most of the students got was of a tourist who'd come to see the world's most famous yeshivah. He was dressed in modern garb, very different from the usual yeshivah look. He stood and looked in wonder at the *beis midrash*, vibrant with the sound of Torah. For a long while his eyes took in the scene; then he bashfully asked what the procedure was for one who wanted to be accepted into the yeshivah. The students grinned and explained that he'd made a slight mistake. The guest took a paper out of his bag, read it, and asked, "Where does R' Kahaneman live?"

A few students, very curious, offered to show him the way to the home of R' Yosef Shlomo Kahaneman, the rav of Ponovezh.

The young man rapped hesitantly on the door. It was opened immediately, and the glowing face of the rav met him there. "Oh, *shalom aleichem, ver zent ihr* — who are you?" the rav asked in Yiddish.

The young man introduced himself. The rabbi's forehead wrinkled, and then he called out happily, "Oh, of course, I remember. I was once a guest in your parents' home in South Africa. Thank you for coming to visit. How are you?"

"I haven't come to visit. I want to be accepted in the yeshivah," the young man said. "I've just finished my studies in the high school in Capetown."

The rabbi gently explained that the path between high school and Ponovezh was a long one.

"But the rav promised me," the young man said, close to tears. He pulled out the paper once again.

"What's that?" the rabbi asked.

The boy told the story:

"I was a boy, and the rav was a guest in my parents' home for several days. My father explained to me that our guest was a great *rosh yeshivah* from *Eretz Yisrael* and I — a young boy, full of enthusiasm — decided then and there to be the rav's assistant. I followed our guest around everywhere, made his bed, served his food, raced to bring his hat and overcoat when he was going out, and so on. The rav enjoyed my devoted service and before he left he asked me, 'How can I repay you, my dear boy? Do you want me to give you a priestly blessing?'

"'No,' I answered. 'I want a promise that the rav will accept me into the yeshivah when I will be a young man.'

"The rav of Ponovezh laughed merrily and promised the sweet boy — that was me — that he would accept him in his yeshivah. But I was a good businessman and I demanded a promise in writing, and the rav gave it to me...

"And here it is," the guest pointed at the paper.

R' Yosef Shlomo's face grew serious. He read the note penned so many years ago, and then said, "*HaKadosh Baruch Hu* turns the world; it appears that things had to be this way."

The young guest was accepted into Yeshivas Ponovezh as a student among the others. The rav made certain he would get private tutoring from the other students. In the course of years the boy flourished and became a noted Torah scholar and a G-d-fearing Jew.

One of the boys who learned with him during the entire process in which he became a noted scholar, who now serves as a *rosh yeshivah* in a well-known institution, told this story at a gathering in which several rabbis and teachers participated. One of those listening replied, "These things have happened before..."

The best students came from all over to the top yeshivah in Ostrova — the yeshivah headed by the *gadol hador*, the *gaon* R' Shmuel Eliezer Aidels, known as the *Maharsha*. More and more chairs were brought into the *beis midrash*, until there was hardly an inch of room left. The philanthropists and activists of the Ostrova community, men fiercely devoted to Torah study, called an emergency meeting in light of the situation. At the conclusion it was decided to build a new *beis midrash* for the yeshivah.

"From where do we get the money?" one of the participants asked.

"As always," another answered, "from the generous hearts of the Jewish people. We'll have to sell the honor of laying the cornerstone to whoever contributes the most; from that money we can put in an infrastructure and foundation."

And so it was: the various communities in Ostrova were told of the decision, and a day was chosen for the public auction of the honor of laying the cornerstone.

A day before the sale, Reb Leizke, one of the residents of the community, came to the home of the *gabbai*, the man who was to stand on the raised wooden podium in the square near the *beis midrash* and announce the price as it climbed higher and higher. "I have something confidential to say to you," Reb Leizke whispered to him.

The *gabbai* brought him into his house and shooed away the flock of children which surrounded them, telling them to go out and play. When the two were alone, he seated his guest in a wooden chair near the table, poured him a hot drink, and asked, "What's the matter?"

"The laying of the cornerstone," the man replied. "I want to make a confidential deal with you. How much do you think it will go for?"

The *gabbai* thought for a moment. "No more than 200 rubles," he said. "That should be the highest we can get."

Reb Leizke pulled out a bulging moneybag from his pocket. "Here are 500 rubles, cash," he told the startled *gabbai*. "I'm asking that tomorrow you should hold the auction only outwardly. Start with a low price, let it get higher quickly, and finally announce that it's been sold for 500 rubles."

"That's certainly a fine sum," the *gabbai* said joyfully. "Of course I"ll do it!"

The next day the public auction went just as the *gabbai* had predicted. The main bidding was between two notables. "Thirty-five rubles," one announced. "Forty," his friend answered. The price climbed, reaching 100 rubles. The *gabbai* let the two exhaust themselves, until it reached a record level: 160 rublesz. He was silent for a short while and then he announced, "One of the community members, who prefers to remain anonymous, has approached me with his bid: 500 rubles."

The shock struck the crowd dumb. The *gabbai* asked, "Does anyone have a higher bid? No? Five hundred rubles going once, going twice, going three times... The winner is the one who asked to remain anonymous."

The community of Ostrova was all agog. Had such a thing been heard of before? There were two unusual aspects: the ultra-high price, and the request for anonymity. The two together offered the townspeople something to talk about.

But the donor hadn't finished yet. A day before the cornerstone was to be laid he came to the *gabbai's* home once again and ordered, "When you lay the cornerstone, don't show me any special honor."

"So whom should I honor?" the *gabbai* blurted out.

"Our teacher and rabbi, the *gaon* R' Shmuel Eliezer. I am as dust beneath his feet."

The *gabbai* was amazed by the nobility that was being revealed to him. To buy the *mitzvah*, at twice the cost at least, under the mantle of anonymity; not to derive any honor from such a wonderful act of charity; and, finally, to give the honor that is rightfully his to the rav? It was too lofty for him to comprehend.

The *gabbai* went to the *Maharsha* and told him what had happened. The *Maharsha's* eyes lit up and he said happily, "Lucky are you, Ostrova, that you have such Jews among you!

"I want to meet this *tzaddik*," the *Maharsha* added. "Tell this respected contributor that it will be worth his while to come to me, and I will meet him face to face."

The *gabbai* was baffled: Reb Leizke had commanded him again and again not to reveal his identity to anyone. "That is impossible," he said hesitantly. "The contributor asked me, begged me, not to even hint at his identity, so that his charity be whole and perfect, without the trace of reward in this world — and honor, too, is a reward."

"Go to him and tell him that it is I who wish to know, and promise him that from my mouth no living creature will ever hear of it," the *Maharsha* said.

"I didn't expect this," Reb Leizke said to the *gabbai*. "If our rabbi, the greatest among our shepherds, has asked to know my identity, I can't say no."

The *gabbai*, released from the bonds of his vow, returned to his illustrious master and revealed the name of the philanthropist.

When the *Maharsha* heard who it was, he cried out in surprise, "Reb Leizke? He's not one of the wealthy men of our community! What can this mean?" He turned to the *gabbai*. "Go back to Reb Leizke and tell him to come to me immediately, without delay."

Not much time passed before Reb Leizke entered the rabbi's study, his knees weak and shaky. Impressed and overawed, he scanned the huge number of *sefarim* neatly arranged in rows on shelves. Such a library was very rare in those days.

The *Maharsha* lifted his head from his studies and turned to Reb Leizke. With glowing face and soft voice he said, "Welcome, Reb Leizke. You've had the opportunity for great merit, to beautify and lift up the house of G-d; and another great merit, that it will be done modestly. But I want to hear your secret; surely you are not a rich man."

Embarrassed, Reb Leizke stood there, his cheeks turning scarlet. He tried to speak several times, stopped, and finally gathered together all his courage. "That's true, I'm not a rich man. I'm a simple laborer, who works with his hands. I've been married for 20 years, and I have been saving every penny, denying myself even food, in order to save up so that I can pay the men who will teach my children Torah. But much to my sorrow I have no children, none at all. When I heard about the problem of the yeshivah I told myself, 'I've saved 500 rubles over many years. Why should the money just sit in my home? Better that I should donate it for the Torah study of others; the only thing that matters is that Hashem's Name be honored.'"

The *Maharsha* was moved by these honest and simple words. He pumped Reb Leizke's hand and said, "Reb Leizke, I promise you that in the merit of this great *mitzvah* you will be answered, and next year at this time you and your wife will be holding a son!"

Ostrova was all abuzz. The talk began with the great miracle that had occurred: after 21 childless years Reb Leizke and his wife had a baby! They were still talking about it when more news came, lightning-swift, through the streets of the Jewish quarter: "Our teacher, our rabbi, R' Shmuel Eliezer, will be the *sandak*!"

Men stood in every corner, trying to understand the exciting news. What an honor! The *gadol hador* would be the *sandak* for the son of a simple Jew! Only a few lone men from among the notables of Ostrova had ever merited such a thing. Everyone talked, everyone guessed, but the matter remained a dark mystery.

A crowd of Jews from the community gathered at the *shul* during the *bris*. Who would stay home and miss such a thing? Afterwards, the *Maharsha* called to the father of the boy, who was overcome with emotion, and blessed him with beaming countenance. "May you merit to raise your son to Torah, *chupah*, and good deeds, and when he grows up, with G-d's help, I will accept him, *bli neder*, into my yeshivah."

Reb Leizke carefully guarded the *Maharsha's* promise within his heart.

Their only child grew up, sprouting like a rare flower. His parents watched over him carefully, guarding his every step. A child gifted from Heaven, he was quick-witted and brilliant, handsome and beloved, possessor of a kind and merciful heart and fine character.

When the boy reached the age of *mitzvos,* Reb Leizke celebrated his bar mitzvah with deep rejoicing, calling to his friends and relatives to join him for a meal in honor of the event. And the very next day he turned to the lofty yeshivah of the *Maharsha*.

The yeshivah administration opened their eyes wide in surprise. "You want your young son to enroll in yeshivah?"

"He's a special boy, with unusual talents and capabilities. Ask any of his tutors and they will tell you," Reb Leizke said with paternal pride.

The administrators would have none of this. "Even if he is a genius, we can't accept him. He's too young. Everyone knows that only the top students learn in our rabbi's yeshivah, only the elite among the elite, those who have learned much Torah in their younger days and prepared themselves to accept our leader's deep Torah knowledge, knowledge vast as the sea. The yeshivah is geared for young men ages 16 and over. Go and look in the *beis midrash*; the vast majority of the students are bearded, and even the youngest among them have begun to sprout hairs on their chin. A bar mitzvah boy? Absolutely not!"

"But our rabbi promised me on the day of his *bris* that he would accept my son as a student in the yeshivah," Reb Leizke cried, his eyes moist. Hardly aware of what he was doing, he was on the verge of revealing his secret. But the administration sent him out, refusing to consider his son. "Let him learn Torah for some years, put a few *masechtos* in his pocket. When he's skilled in *Seder Nashim* and *Seder Nezikin,* learned with *Rishonim,* he can come back here and we will take him in."

After much hesitation Reb Leizke went to the home of the *Maharsha,* and begged to be allowed to see the great man for a short while.

"I've come to get repayment for an old debt," Reb Leizke said, gathering his courage as he walked into the *Maharsha's* room. "Our rabbi promised me that my son would be accepted into his yeshivah. The time has come: I can't wait even one more day."

The *Maharsha* didn't refuse him the way the others did; he took the youngster under his wing, helped raise him as one would a beloved child, and took care of him until the boy had grown into a great Torah scholar.

The second blessing that our rabbi gave him — "that he will grow to Torah" — was even greater than the first — "in a year you will be holding a son" — said the Jews of Ostrova — for to make the second come true, the *Maharsha* himself put in many years of work and toil.

A Faithful Spirit Conceals the Matter

(Mishlei 11:13)

THE HOLY *TZADDIK,* R' TZVI HIRSCH, WHO LATER BECAME the *maggid* in Nadvorna and authored the *Sefer Tzemach Hashem L'Tzvi,* yearned to visit the saintly R' Yechiel Michel of Zlotchov. He wanted to visit him, but could not. He was very poor and didn't have the funds for the trip. His eyes grew forlorn with longing, and he tried again and again to figure out a solution to no avail. But his pleas rose to Heaven.

At that time, one of the wealthy men of the town made a match with someone of equal riches, a man who lived in Zlotchov. The wedding was set to be in that town. Before the affair the rich man turned to R' Tzvi and asked him if he would like to accompany him to Zlotchov.

"Of course!"

R' Tzvi Hirsch was exultant. The gates of heaven were open before him: his prayer had been answered.

For many days R' Tzvi Hirsch drank from the clear wellsprings of the *maggid* of Zlotchov, but his thirst remained unquenched. R' Yechiel Michel of Zlotchov saw in him a wise and understanding pupil and behaved generously to him, denying him nothing, opening before him the treasure houses of his mighty spirit and goodness.

As R' Yechiel Michel saw more and more of his amazing student he grew increasingly impressed, until he said, "I merited 60 valiant men of arms around me, my pious students. And the greatest of all of them is the *maggid* of Nadvorna, R' Tzvi Hirsch, whose presence is enjoyed by Eliyahu *HaNavi* himself!"

Even before he'd passed over the threshold of the *maggid* of Zlotchov, R' Tzvi Hirsch was already one of a very special group of G-d-fearing men, but after the *maggid* opened before him the study of *Chassidus,* R' Tzvi Hirsch knew with complete certainty that up until now he hadn't reached even a tiny sliver of G-d's service.

Now he remembered that his father had told him that during R' Tzvi Hirsch's childhood, his father had taken him to the holy *Baal Shem Tov.* The *Besht* looked at the precocious youngster with satisfaction, took him in his arms, and played with him for some time.

"This little one will be great, great in Torah, in revealed and hidden wisdom," the *Besht* gave his blessing in the hearing of the father, who was overcome by emotion. Then he added, "He will lead a community in the midst of the Jews!"

And the time had come — R' Tzvi Hirsch did, indeed, lead a large congregation. He began in the village of Dulina, then moved to Nadvorna, where he had many exceptional students. Some were great scholars, others astonishing in the fear of G-d; some students were versed in the study of hidden wisdom, while some possessed unusually refined characters. The common denominator was that all were beloved, all were straightforward and honest. Students such as the author of the *Aishel Avraham*, R' Avraham David, *av beis din* of Butshatesh, and R' Menachem Mendel of Kosov, author of *Ahavas Shalom*, basked in his presence. R' Tzvi Hirsch of Ziditchov, who learned Kabbalah from him, said, "My first understanding of service of G-d came from him."

But there was one among all those who came to the *beis midrash* who was not sincere, a man with a pernicious fault that gnawed at his vitals. With an appearance as beautiful as that of a peacock, the onlooker would have said, "One of the group." But he would have been wrong...

It was not unusual for such a letter to reach Nadvorna. The great rebbe, R' Yechiel Michel of Zlotchov, had not forgotten his illustrious student, and once every few months a missive would reach Nadvorna from Zlotchov. But when he read the contents of this particular letter, R' Tzvi Hirsch's face grew radiant with joy and celebration. His eyes danced and he almost jumped from his seat.

"The rebbe is coming to visit here in Nadvorna!"

From that day on Nadvorna wore its holiday best; the city got a thorough cleaning and was decorated in honor of the arrival of that giant among great men, the *maggid* of Zlotchov.

On the day set aside for the visit, all of Nadvorna gathered together at the outskirts of the city — old and young, women and children all waited impatiently on the road.

A thin boy, almost emaciated, climbed onto the shoulders of a tall, robust young man, who himself stood upon the sturdy shoulders of yet another, this one owner of a body reminiscent of a wild bull. This human ladder served as a watchtower for all those surrounding it. The boy — highest among the three — cupped his hands over his eyes and peered, squinting, into the distance.

Finally he saw a small dot moving, growing larger and larger within a cloud of dust. He controlled his mounting excitement, and stared again.

"Folks, a carriage is approaching. The *tzaddik* of the generation is coming!" he called excitedly. There was a surge of noise from the joyful crowd. When the carriage finally came within viewing distance, the people of the town raced to meet it. They unstrapped the sweating horses and themselves pulled the carriage, greeting R' Yechiel Michel like royalty, their music and song accompanying him until the entrance to the place where he was staying — the home of R' Tzvi Hirsch himself.

If R' Tzvi Hirsch's home was normally full of people, on the day that R' Yechiel Michel of Zlotchov arrived in Nadvorna, it was jammed. From all the city, from the outlying villages, from near and far, all came to greet the *maggid*. A long row of people snaked their way towards the entrance to the house. Only a few managed to push their way in. The *tzaddik* met the public for many hours but finally the crowd dispersed and the great man could rest.

Early the next morning R' Tzvi Hirsch's *beis midrash* was jam-packed with townspeople: the news spread quickly that the holy visitor would be *davening* there.

When the *maggid* entered the *beis midrash* wrapped in his *tallis* and crowned with his *tefillin,* the crowd fell back in a gesture of respect and awe. But almost immediately the pushing began again, a mass of people surrounding the guest. Everyone wanted to take advantage of the rare opportunity to see the *maggid's* pure and holy countenance from up close, to examine the face that shone like the noontime sun.

But the celebration ended almost at once. Something was wrong.

The *gabbai* hastened to the *maggid's* side, ready to escort him to his place. But the *maggid* didn't move. He stopped short and looked around him in disbelief. His holy face grew pale; a cloud of sorrow seemed to settle upon it. His features seemed to grow contorted for a moment in distress, like one suddenly confronted with a horrible smell. An awful fear fell upon the congregation. The *tzaddik* began to walk from bench to bench, staring intently at the face of each man, examining and probing everyone's darkest secrets, until he'd passed through the entire room.

The people were riveted, almost paralyzed with shock and fear. The *maggid* of Zlotchov had left their *beis midrash*, had refused to pray within its walls! R' Yechiel Michel hurried to the home of his host, R' Tzvi Hirsch, and shut himself up in his room.

The peoples' faces were dark with dismay; their eyes looked stunned. They had no idea of what wrongdoing their guest had found among them, so terrible that it had sent him racing away from their presence like one avoiding some filthy bog.

R' Tzvi Hirsch, too, had disappeared, together with the *maggid* of Zlotchov. He escorted the *maggid* to his room and waited while he entered. The two didn't exchange a single word between them, just exchanged looks like men who understand each other well without the necessity for verbal communication.

When R' Tzvi Hirsch returned, he found an atmosphere of mourning within the *beis midrash*, a Tishah B'Av feeling. All eyes turned to him, an unasked question within them.

"Gentlemen," R' Tzvi Hirsch stood before his congregation, his voice beseeching, tears in his eyes, "The complaint of my teacher and rebbe, the *maggid* of Zlotchov, may he live long, is not against us."

The puzzlement and surprise grew even greater; the atmosphere was leaden. The words not spoken seemed to dance around them: "His anger was not upon us? Why, then, did the rebbe leave us, running away like one fleeing from fire?"

The answer was not long in coming: "There is one here, a young man with dry rot in his heart, a man with bitter roots: one who, deep within him, feels a pull towards Christianity! From the outside he seems like one of us; he shows himself off, he says, 'I am pure.' Know, then, that it is because of him that this terrible thing has happened. The *maggid* cannot pray with us because of his presence; it disturbs all that is holy. He will not return here until you have cut away the evil from among you!"

A murmur rose within the *beis midrash*. "Who is it? We'll tear him limb from limb!" some of the more hotheaded cried in furious voices. Their faces grew red with anger that threatened to explode like lava flowing out of a live volcano.

"Not like this, this is not our way!" R' Tzvi Hirsch threw water on the flames of their wrath. "I know who this young man is... but I cannot reveal his name. But here is a sign: this young man is giving out copies of the *Sefer Zohar* that are nothing more than apostasy. This young man has dared, with unprecedented brazenness, to draw in his *Zohar,* in many places, the forms of an impure sign. He lends his book out to others in the desire to have them fall, as he has done; he hopes that, in their naivete, they will not know the significance of the cross and will fall into his trap. Before they know what has happened to them, a strange fire will burn within them, the fire of impurity!"

Not another word was necessary. That young man was known as a generous, open-hearted person always willing to lend out his *Sefer Zohar* to others. His identity was well known.

The people grabbed him and pulled out the incriminating book. If not for R' Tzvi Hirsch's intervention, there wouldn't have remained a trace of the man.

"This young man is fundamentally kosher. It is only because of the influence of several friends who have cast away all decency that he has done this. If you speak to him, you can easily put him back on the right path," R' Tzvi Hirsch explained when the man, pale-faced, his eyes open wide with fear, was brought before him. "Open your mouth and tell us who you are."

In a thin whisper the young man told his story: he had been an upstanding man, but at some point he'd veered off the correct path and grown close with a group of apostates who'd been persuading him to convert.

When rebuked for his terrible error, the young man broke out in dreadful sobs of regret and repentance. It was said that he did not leave that place until he was a complete *baal teshuvah.*

And after the young man had repented, the *maggid* of Zlotchov returned to pray with the congregation.

"Tell us, rebbe," R' Tzvi Hirsch's students asked him, after the holy *maggid* had left to return to Zlotchov, "did you know the identity of that young man even before the *maggid's* visit?"

"On the first day that he came to pray with us, I recognized his type," R' Tzvi Hirsch admitted.

"So why were you silent until today? Why didn't you protest, as our visitor did?"

R' Tzvi Hirsch explained. "The *maggid* of Zlotchov is so pure, so holy, that he is above certain rules; he cannot tolerate even the faintest smell of something impure. But when a *tzaddik* is sent down to the lower world, he is made to promise that he will not reveal the secrets of the celestial, things that he finds out through *ruach hakodesh*. Revealing such secrets can take away man's free choice. Hashem created mankind able to choose between good and evil, and the *tzaddikim* are not permitted to pull him in one direction or the other; even if we see that a person is easily deceived, our lips are sealed!

"It can be compared to a craftsman who makes barrels, who fastens iron hoops around them in order to make certain that no wine leaks out. That's how we must fasten our lips together, so that we do not reveal what we see and what we hear. Only infrequently are we permitted to reveal things that are hidden from human eyes...

"And that is the meaning of the words said of Moshe *Rabbeinu*, 'In all My house he is faithful...' These words are interpreted to mean that the *tzaddik* knows many secrets, much that he sees with *ruach hakodesh*, but he seals his lips and holds his peace even though it may go against his own nature. 'A faithful spirit conceals the matter'" (*Mishlei* 11:13).

A Question of Gratitude

EVEN WHEN YOUNG, BEFORE HIS NAME WAS RENOWNED throughout the land, R' Nosson Nota — known as Reb Nottele of Chelem — author of the *Neta Sha'ashuim*, knew of no limits in his service of his Creator. He afflicted his body with many kinds of torments in order to break down the physical form. His days were dedicated to learning, his nights to weeping and prayer and complete identification with the anguish of the *Shechinah*, which from the day of the Temple's destruction has found no sanctuary in this world.

In order to mortify his body even more, so that he would feel to the very marrow of his bones the sorrow of the *Shechinah*, he chose for himself a life of exile. He would walk along the roads, wandering between villages and towns. He would stay in some small hamlet for a few days, a few weeks, but before he would have the chance to take part in the life of the place and set down roots, he would arise and leave for the next town, where, again, he would not stay long.

R' Nota took it upon himself to continue his self-imposed exile until Heaven would send him a sign that he should end such behavior and settle down in one place.

A sign? Not that the angel Michael should come down from the sky and tell him, "Do it." Not that; true *tzaddikim* can hear the voice of their Creator from within natural causes, unlike most of humanity, who see only those causes. In their profound connection with the Creator of the universe, they know that behind everything that happens to a person, there is a cause emanating from the Prime Cause — G-d.

When Chaim Mendel, an innkeeper in one of the far-flung villages to which R' Nota wandered, set his gaze upon R' Nota's glowing face and shining eyes, he realized immediately that this young man was no mere vagabond, nor even a simple, average man. After a few days he asked R' Nota if he would serve as a tutor for his two sons. They were grown boys, the elder close to bar mitzvah but — if one is permitted to admit it — neither knew a single Hebrew letter. R' Nota agreed on the spot; this was the sign that he'd been waiting for, the sign from Heaven that the time had come for him to stop his wandering and settle down in one place.

The countryman called to his sons, introduced them to R' Nota, and told them, "This is your rebbe. From now on he will learn with you every day. From the beginning, from *alef*. The *alef-beis* first, then *Chumash*, *Mishnah*, and up to *Gemara*. Oh, how I hope that you will be able to say a proper *Kaddish,* without breaking your teeth."

He pushed a *Chumash* into their hands and pulled them forcibly to the table. "You do your job," he told R' Nota. "Feed them with learning until they have no more strength, make sure they don't wander around with the fowl and the animals in the courtyard. And if they don't want to learn — grab a stick and give them a whack!"

He left the room, his eyes flashing a silent warning, wordlessly letting them understand the bitterness of their fate should they tease their new teacher.

The boys looked suspiciously at R' Nota, as if to say: Who are you, and what are you to us? Then they got up and swiftly raced to the barn, lightly slapping the sleepy cows on their flanks — but there was Father and his stick...

And so the new students were forced back to their room. R' Nota began with the letters of the *alef-beis,* speaking gently and with endless patience.

Chaim Mendel was not one of your lazy countrymen. He'd leased the huge forest near the village, as well as an inn and pub, from the local *poritz* who owned the entire region. Chaim Mendel would chop down the trees and sell them, and, in order to prevent theft, he hired a non-Jewish guard who lived in a hut in the heart of the forest. The guard was feared by all: more than once he'd put gangs of thieves to flight. But that week, Chaim Mendel fired his gentile guard. Why should he pay two salaries, to hire a teacher and a guard, when the young rebbe could also serve as a caretaker?

R' Nota therefore went to live in the forest, and in the gentile world of the area the word went out: tonight the forest is ours!

And the young, emaciated Jewish man? No one gave him a second thought.

Several shadowy figures snuck through the deep darkness of night, axes and shovels in hand. They were prepared to cut down as many trees as they could, until daylight would end their work.

But just as they passed deep into the forest their blood froze in their veins.

From inside the blackness they could hear chilling screams, frightening shouts that set their hearts thumping madly. They were certain that the owner had set a trap for them, passing around a rumor of a weakling guard and, instead, filling the woods with tough, armed men!

The gang dispersed in all directions.

The next day they subtly tried to discover details of the gang of strongmen whom Chaim Mendel had hired, and when the true facts came out they laughed at themselves for their stupidity of the previous night.

Not ten armed guards, not five bullies brandishing weapons, not even one mysterious watchman...

Only the lone young man!

But who had made those horrifying noises in the middle of the night? they wondered. No matter. Their fears melted away as if they'd never existed. They decided to try their luck on this coming night and watch events unfold.

The same thing happened: the deeper they penetrated into the forest, the louder the terrifying noises became. But this time they found the courage to approach the source of the noise, which somehow seemed less threatening, and which seemed, actually, to resemble the sound of a wailing sob.

To their surprise, they discovered that the noise was coming from the guard's hut. Quietly they tiptoed towards it.

"What is that bright light shining out of the hut?" they asked each other. They snuck closer and peered into the window.

And what did they see?

The source of the light was the thin Jewish man who by day served as the rebbe of the innkeeper Chaim Mendel's children and at night as the guard of his forest properties. The face of the guard shone with a luminous light; his features seemed like a gigantic lantern. He was rolling on the floor, ashes on his forehead, crying bitterly and screaming.

They stood, thunderstruck, before the blinding glow, trying to understand why the man was crying and what was going on.

"I know," one of the gang spoke up, a Jew from the village who had joined the other thugs in their nocturnal doings. "He's saying *Tikkun Chatzos*. That's the prayer of lamentation for the Temple that was destroyed."

He explained to his non-Jewish cronies the meaning of *Tikkun Chatzos*. The others heard his words and were gripped by fear.

"Here is such a holy man, and we're busy with theft?"

That night no trees were cut down... For a long while they stood and watched, like men entranced, at the young man rolling on the floor in tears. Afterwards they turned back, returning the way they'd come.

The Jew who'd been with them was the most affected of all by the sight. He couldn't rest until he'd stood before Chaim Mendel and said: "Do you have any idea who this guard of yours is? Go and investigate his actions at midnight!"

The next night Chaim Mendel himself went into the forest. When he saw the lofty service of R' Nota, he was beset by fear and trembling: Was this his watchman? This was a man of G-d — and this place the portal to Heaven!

He quietly left the place, lest the *tzaddik* spy out his scrutiny. When he returned he told his wife what he'd seen.

"If this is true," she said, "immediately exempt him from guard duty, and if you take my advice you'll stop him from teaching as well. Our children aren't going to become outstanding geniuses. This man, in contrast, is reaching for greatness, for miracles. If he can continue his service without interruption or bother, he will, in the future, certainly become one of the great men of the generation, and we are keeping him as a mere watchman or tutor! Why shouldn't we help him develop without anything to disturb him? We'll give him a small house with a bed and a table, a chair and a lamp, and there he can pore over his learning and serve G-d as much as he wishes!"

A woman has an extra share of insight; Chaim Mendel thought about it and accepted her suggestion. He immediately released R'

Nota from any obligation to him and took upon himself the burden of sustaining him for the next few years.

As the innkeeper's wife had predicted, so it was: R' Nota, without anything to disturb him, grew more and more elevated. Like the lovely fragrance of a spice box, his good name wafted outwards. From all directions Jews began to make their way him, to get blessings from his holy mouth and be caressed by his mighty spirit, which he shared generously. Finally, they figuratively grabbed him by the coattails and demanded of him: "Become our rebbe, our leader and guide."

At first R' Nota refused to listen to a single word on the subject, but the Jews wouldn't desist, continuing to badger him until he began to wonder himself: perhaps this was a sign from Above; perhaps Heaven wanted him to become a rebbe?

Because he couldn't figure out the answer himself, he traveled to ask the opinion of the holy rabbi, R' Mordechai of Neshchiz.

"Certainly, certainly," R' Mordechai answered vehemently. "The time has come for you to reveal yourself and take on the burden of guiding others."

R' Nota returned to his village and began to lead the people.

The number of his *Chassidim* grew and grew, until there were a great many of them. As his name grew and he became more widely known, the leaders of the community of Chelem prevailed upon him to come and live in their bustling city. For several years he did live there, and was recognized as one of the leaders of the generation, just as the innkeeper's wife had predicted.

Slowly, as R' Nota became greater and greater, his benefactor, Chaim Mendel, grew more and more impoverished, until finally he became a pauper. First he lost his inn and his forest; finally, he was down to nothing more than a loaf of bread.

His wife told him, "There's nothing left to lose. For several years we sustained the famous *Admor* of Chelem, now go to him and ask his mercy. Maybe when he sees his benefactor he will remember what you did for him in his youth."

Chaim Mendel traveled to Chelem for Shabbos.

Friday evening, when the former innkeeper went into the synagogue and shook the rebbe's hand, the rebbe didn't react at all. It was as if he didn't recognize him. Chaim Mendel was very upset by his lack of response. "How many years did he eat from my food; suddenly he doesn't know who I am?" The bitter thought raced through his mind, though he didn't reveal it to anyone. Then he regretted it — perhaps he'd been wrong.

But the same response came all that Shabbos, and at the conclusion of the *melaveh malkah* meal.

On Sunday, Chaim Mendel came to take his leave of the rebbe. And then, also, there was no special attention given, not even a spark of recognition. One more moment and he would be on the other side of the door, just another anonymous visitor.

The man's patience gave out, and he said to R' Nota, "I have a serious question to ask."

"Ask, my son, ask," the rebbe responded, his tone hinting that he had been waiting to hear what the man had to say.

"From the first day of *Selichos* we begin to beg for mercy, not in the merit of our own good deeds but in the merit of our forefathers. Every day of *Selichos* we say the same words: Remember for us the covenant of our fathers. We mention our holy forefathers, Avraham, Yitzchak, and Yaakov, again and again.

"Right before the Day of Judgment the *Selichos* are called *Zechor HaBris*, named for the poem, 'Remember the covenant of Avraham, and the binding of Yitzchak.'

"And so it goes for all the prayers of Rosh Hashanah and the Ten Days of Repentance. And when the holy day, the great and awesome Yom Kippur, arrives, a day of begging for forgiveness, we continually ask for mercy — in the merit of our forefathers.

"And now, before evening, during the climactic hour of the Days of Awe, *Chazal* arranged a special prayer service, said only one time during the year: *Neilah*. Completely different, completely unique.

"It would seem that we would not again mention the merit of our forefathers. Shouldn't we rather speak of something new, some merit that we haven't yet mentioned? But still, amazingly enough, what do we say there? 'Our father knew You from his youth.' We speak of the merit of Avraham, who recognized his Creator at the age of three."

"A good question," the rebbe agreed. "Do you have an answer?"

"Yes, I do," said Chaim Mendel. "Today the world is full of belief in G-d, but who was it who publicized G-d's presence in the world? Of course, it was our forefather Avraham. Before him the world was full of idols, humanity worshiped foolishness, bowed down before wood and stone. And then came Avraham and told all the world of G-d's Name.

"That is a very great merit, one that we have not yet mentioned, one we have not yet used in order to arouse mercy for us. The last weapon in our arsenal if, heaven forbid, we have no hope left. Gratitude! And so, as we pray before the moment when Heaven's gate will be shut, we discuss the unique merit of Avraham!"

Chaim Mendel's voice grew choked and a sob burst from his throat. "Holy rebbe, today you are famous; Jews from all over the land come to you and are helped. But where is the gratitude? Didn't I take care of you for several years? Didn't I make your name renowned at a time when none recognized your personality? Now I have reached bottom and have come to you to ask for help, and you act as if you don't know me? How can it be?"

R' Nottele's face glowed. "I've been waiting to hear that," he said happily. "Know, then, that at the time I came to you, a bitter decree of dreadful poverty had been made against you. Though I tried everything I could to have the decree lifted, nothing helped. I couldn't find anything to do for you but this: to wait for you to come with an honest, sincere complaint — 'Where is the gratitude?' Now that you have screamed out, your complaints have pierced the heavens and annulled the decree. From now on, you shall rise higher and higher."

Wonders for a Gentile

T HE THOUSANDS OF *CHASSIDIM* ESCORTING THE HOLY *Chozeh* of Lublin to his grandson's wedding stood open-mouthed, gaping at the shocking sight.

The crowd was on its way to the celebration, which for many days hence would be called "the great wedding of Zronovitza." The Rebbe of Lublin and his distinguished entourage were passing through the city of Vladislov and taking a short stop there to rest.

After they'd refreshed themselves, the huge convoy prepared to continue on its way. The participants included a wide array of impressive personalities, a cross-section of the *gedolei hador*, Chassidic rebbes, and the elite of the people. Now all were climbing into the carriages and waiting for the *Chozeh* to board his own vehicle.

One seat remained empty, that of one of the greatest of the *Chozeh's* students, a leader of a large congregation in his own right, but in the pandemonium of boarding no one noticed his absence.

And now the Rebbe of Lublin left the inn, approached his carriage, picked up his foot and leaned it on the step of the coach... and there he stood, one foot in the carriage and the other firmly on the ground...

For two and a half hours the *Chozeh* stood thus, as if frozen in action, one foot on the step and the other on the ground.

The *Chassidim* realized that this was no light matter. The veins throbbed in the Rebbe's temples and his shining eyes darted back and forth, watching. The *Chassidim* knew that the entire world was as clear to the *Chozeh* as the carriage in front of him, and his vision could see to the ends of the earth. But they had no idea where he was looking right now — the environment close by, or some place much farther. Was there some great event going on in the distance, thousands of miles from here — or was it nearby?

After two and a half hours a tiny figure could be seen approaching swiftly. As it grew closer, the assemblage could make out the familiar face of the *Chozeh's* great student, R' Dovid of Lelov.

He came towards the *Chozeh*, hoping to explain the reason for his delay, but the *Chozeh*, not letting him say a word, spoke first:

"R' Dovid, don't worry, we'll come to their aid!"

R' Dovid jumped into the coach and held a whispered exchange with the *Chozeh*, and then the entire convoy went on its way from Vladislov to Zronovitza. No one understood what had just happened, why the *Chozeh* had waited, watching so anxiously, what he meant by his words to R' Dovid, and what R' Dovid had been doing during the long hours.

A few days passed and the mystery was solved.

R' Dovid of Lelov had taken upon himself a fine custom: During his many travels from city to city, if he came to a village where his fellow Jews lived, he wouldn't just pass by. Instead, he would enter into the village and visit the Jewish residents to learn how they were faring.

R' Dovid had begun the custom after a trip that he'd taken some years before. He had traveled through a village where only one Jew lived, and when the man had seen R' Dovid pass his home, clearly not planning to come in, he raced out to him and screamed desperately, "Rebbe, stop!"

R' Dovid halted immediately, tensely awaiting the man's words.

"Can it be," the man asked, his voice breaking, "that a man will pass by the house of a Jew who lives all by himself among the gentiles, one lone lamb among 70 wolves, and he will not come in and find out how he is?"

R' Dovid used to analyze and learn from every event in his life; he routinely examined the meaning of each happening, trying to assess what his Creator wished him to learn from it. These words, said in innocence by a simple Jew, seemed to burn within him like a flame. From that time on he made it an unbreakable law: Whenever he visited a village or hamlet, he would find out where the Jews lived, go to their homes, ask about their welfare, learn of their physical and spiritual situations (in that order!), and do whatever he could to help them.

Like his colleagues, the students of the Rebbe of Lublin, R'
Dovid had set out on the journey to Vladislov, en route to
Zronovitza. In a tiny village behind Vladislov lived one Jew, who
rented a small inn from the local nobleman, the master of the village known as the *poritz,* and R' Dovid detoured in order to visit
him.

He was still some distance away when he heard a strange and
terrible thing: the sound of horses racing, mixed with bone-chill-
ing, broken screams.

R' Dovid rushed ahead; his heart told him that the Jew was in
trouble. But the scene that he saw before him was beyond anything
he could have imagined.

The carriage of the nobleman was racing through the street,
dragged by a pair of horses — and by their side, another pair — a
man and a woman.

The unfortunate couple had been tied by reins to the shaft of
the wagon, like horses. They could not, of course, keep up with the
pace of the swift four-footed animals. With their last remaining
strength they tried to lift their legs, their faces scarlet with mam-
moth effort that surpassed human endurance.

R' Dovid's kind heart all but burst: If he didn't do something
immediately, the two would die horribly before his eyes. He stood
before the carriage, a living barrier, and the surprised driver pulled
the reins hard, stopping the horses before they could stampede
over him.

The nobleman shook with rage at the interruption of his
enjoyment. "Why have you stopped the carriage?" he roared furiously.

The driver pointed to the man standing in the middle of the
road, refusing to budge.

R' Dovid didn't wait for another outburst; he approached the
carriage and began to speak earnestly with its occupant.

The nobleman was enchanted by the charm of this Jew, who
spoke the native tongue so fluently. His anger cooled down. Hardly
noticing, he became involved in the conversation and entirely forgot about the couple bound to the carriage.

"What is the story of these two?" R' Dovid ventured to ask, once he'd seen that the nobleman had accepted him graciously. The *poritz* opened his mouth and a flood of curses came flowing out. He told R' Dovid of the couple's unparalleled brazenness: this was the third year in a row that the man and his wife, who rented rights to run the local tavern, hadn't paid their annual fee to him. "I decided to teach them a bitter lesson," he burst into loud, fierce laughter, "so that everyone would see them and learn not to start up with a nobleman!"

"How much does their debt come to?" R' Dovid asked.

"One hundred and fifty rubles, in cash!" the *poritz* replied.

"I take the debt upon myself," R' Dovid declared. "Just free this pair, and stop torturing them."

"As you like, Jew; give me the goods and take them," the nobleman agreed.

"I don't have such a large sum with me," R' Dovid returned. "But I will sign a promissory note, and pay you the entire amount due on the date that you select."

The nobleman thought about it. "Who are you? How do I know if I can trust your signature? Maybe your note is nothing better than a scrap of paper."

"I am the Rabbi of Lelov."

The nobleman was satisfied. "Excellent." The carriage made its way slowly to his home and after the note was written up and signed by R' Dovid, the couple was unstrapped from their bonds and set free. The two sent silent looks of appreciation to their savior; they didn't know how to express their endless gratitude. It was clear that he had rescued them at the very last minute from a terrible fate.

The entire course of negotiations took two and a half hours, and only at its successful conclusion did R' Dovid make his way to Vladislov. The *Chozeh* of Lublin had known exactly what was transpiring, and he waited, one foot upraised on his carriage, until R' Dovid returned to him, promising his student he would help repay the huge debt.

Not far from the nobleman's house, in Vladislov itself, lived a Jewish wool merchant. The man had business ties with the *poritz*, a legal contract that gave him exclusive use of the nobleman's wool from his flocks of sheep. For his part, the merchant obligated himself not to look for any other supplier for his wool.

The agreement had stood the test of time, with the *poritz* supplying the merchant with all the wool he needed. The nobleman had deep confidence in the merchant's honesty and never haggled with him over the price. The merchant never bothered looking for another source or supplier.

Not long after R' Dovid had signed the note, the *poritz's* holdings were thrown into a ferment of activity. His workers labored from morning to night, shearing the sheep that were heavy with wool. When the shearing was over, two non-Jewish wool merchants stood before the nobleman.

"Sell us your wool," they said simply.

"I can't," the *poritz* refused them. "I have a contract granting exclusive rights to the Jewish merchant in Vladislov."

The two pretended this was news to them — though, in reality, their entire goal was to compete with the Jew.

"We're shocked," they said, as if they were offended, "that you're prepared to sell your merchandise to a stranger, a Jew, while to us, your fellow Christians, your flesh and blood, you are not?"

The nobleman wasn't impressed with their words and remained adamant.

"We have an offer for you that you can't refuse," the merchants said. "We'll add 150 rubles, in cash, over what the Jewish merchant would give you."

Such a generous offer couldn't be rejected out of hand; he sent a messenger with an urgent notice to his colleague. "The master wants to fulfill his contract with you, but he needs more money: do you agree to match the other merchants' offer and add 150 rubles?"

"I can't agree to that," the Jewish merchant said angrily. "I won't add a penny!"

And with that, he invalidated the agreement, leaving the *poritz* free to do what he wanted.

After they'd finished their business transaction, the merchants counted out the full amount into the nobleman s hands. The two sides celebrated their deal in the appropriate manner, and the merchants left with their load of wool.

"Wonderful! I've earned an extra 150 rubles today!" The nobleman walked through his home, his faced wreathed in smiles.

Suddenly he stopped short. "One hundred and fifty." The sum seemed familiar to him somehow. He jumped up as if stung, raced to his small metal safe, and pulled out a note. That's right: the amount written on it was exactly 150 rubles!

"The Rabbi of Lelov is surely a holy man," he muttered to himself, thunderstruck. "He ensured that I was paid back the amount of money in a hurry, up to the last penny."

With all his wickedness, the *poritz* couldn't close his eyes and heart to the open miracle. "The Rabbi of Lelov must be a wonder worker. Perhaps he can help my unfortunate son?"

In an instant the nobleman's servants were called to his palace, and instructed to pile high a collection of his best produce, as a tribute to the Rabbi of Lelov. The fruit of his abundant fields, his vegetables, ducks and clucking chickens were all placed in the large carriages.

When the convoy of laden carriages entered Lelov, the Jewish residents surrounded them, wondering if they were dreaming. They escorted the nobleman and his entourage to the home of R' Dovid.

Now the *poritz* stood before the impoverished house, not believing what he was seeing. He had thought this wonder worker surely lived in a palace.

"Holy rabbi," the *poritz* said, his voice shaking with emotion, as he stood before the rabbi, the note in his hand, "you have returned my debt in its entirety. I haven't lost even a penny. Here, then, is the note. Now that I know what powers you possess, I beg you: Save my son."

He turned around and gestured to a tall, burly young man standing behind him.

"This is my son, a young man in the flower of youth, but what a terrible fate," he said, weeping. "He is mute, silent as a fish. He has never said one word, not one word!"

R' Dovid got up from his chair, walked to a corner of the room, stretched out his hands, and spoke a few words.

Immediately, the mute began to speak like any normal man.

(From the *Sefer Kodesh Hilulim*, written by my uncle, the great Kabbalist R' Moshe Yair Weinstock, *zt"l*)

To Make a Stone Speak

IT WAS THE FIRST, AND PERHAPS ONLY, VISIT OF R' MOSHE Schreiber, the *Chasam Sofer,* to Posen. R' Akiva Eiger received his son-in-law's letter with profound joy. At that moment he decided to turn the rare visit into a kind of holiday for the town.

R' Akiva Eiger invited several *gedolei hador* who were in the region. At their head was his old friend, the fiery R' Yaakov Loberbaum of Lisa, author of the *Nesivos Mishpat.*

There was a great outpouring of feeling in the outskirts of Posen when the coach bearing the Rabbi of Pressburg entered the city limits. Everyone was there to greet their honored guest as he came to his father-in-law's home. When he descended from the carriage, his face glowed, reflecting the brilliance of the sun. The crowd, moved, gave voice to its amazement with the outcry: "Blessed is He Who apportioned of His wisdom to those who fear Him."

It was a scene that riveted the eyes: the two great men of the generation standing across from each other, facing each other, with G-d's Presence almost palpable, so to speak, between them.

R' Akiva Eiger then took his noted son-in-law to his *beis midrash*. There, awaiting him anxiously, were the rabbis who'd been invited as guests, great men of Torah, headed by the author of the *Nesivos Mishpat*. R' Akiva Eiger's students also sat among the congregation, though a portion of them had chosen to stand on the side and help serve the assemblage.

And the meal began.

After eating his bread, R' Yaakov Loberbaum stood up and began to speak. He had prepared a very deep Torah discourse in honor of the exalted visitor; an entire system of thought, well reasoned with unarguable logic.

An expectant hush fell as he started to speak. He began with a problem in a well-known *sugya*, solved it, brought in a proof, then dismissed it. And so he went, from *Gemara* to *Rif,* from *Rif* to *Rambam,* from *Rambam* to *Rashba*. The concepts grew, branched out, became more and more complex until, finally, R' Yaakov found a ford through the deep waters. From that huge pile of questions, problems, proofs, and counterproofs he managed, like a skilled jeweler cutting a diamond, to hone a new idea, one that sparkled and shone from every brilliant facet. He'd uncovered a deep well of thought, pure as a cold spring. The truth and ineffable logic gladdened the hearts of all who heard him.

And that, it seemed, was the end of the long and involved *pilpul* of the author of the *Nesivos*.

The guest of honor, R' Moshe Schreiber, then stood up and took the podium. "My teachers, my colleagues," he said, "I am too small to argue with the great men, but our Torah is true, and if the *pilpul* does not seem to be correct in my eyes, I must not keep silent, but say what I believe."

Much to the astonishment of all the students there, R' Moshe proceeded to repeat every single step taken by R' Yaakov of Lisa. He found tremendously difficult questions in his logic, and dug down to the foundations until not even one brick remained in the carefully constructed edifice of learning.

R' Moshe had just finished his own *pilpul* when R' Yaakov stood up a second time. The students watched as the two lions took each other on. R' Yaakov defended his logic with valor, refuting all of the great man's arguments, until he'd once again solved all the problems and had returned its former glory to the wonderful structure he'd struggled so hard to build.

The assemblage saw the argument coming to a close, but the *Chasam Sofer's* breadth of understanding was of an entirely different caliber: as far as he was concerned, that beautiful building that his friend R' Yaakov had labored so long to build was nothing more than a fairy castle built in the air.

R' Moshe explained his arguments clearly to the other guests, who listened to his words with eyes open in amazement. He ground all the closely reasoned proofs that R' Yaakov had brought into tiny pieces, piled a new heap of piercing questions upon them, covered them with a mound of proofs, until he'd undercut the wonderful building of R' Yaakov and brought it, collapsing, to the ground.

R' Yaakov of Lisa wasn't afraid, or cowed. This is the way of Torah learning — one contradicts, one builds. One raises problems, the other answers them. Scholars who study the Torah, becoming "enemies," refuse to move from the spot until they have again become reconciled.

Like a soldier going to battle, he once again prepared himself for war, polishing his armaments and plunging into the challenges posed by R' Moshe. He decimated these challenges, leaving no trace of them behind. His building was now a structure standing firmly on the ground.

The students exchanged laughing glances. Today they had truly witnessed the battle of Torah study. This time, they were certain, R' Moshe had nothing left to say — and the meal could go on peacefully.

But that's not how it went...

R' Moshe Schrieber didn't take a moment's rest. All his life he'd pursued truth, and it seemed, in his vast breadth of understanding, that the author of *Nesivos* had still not uncovered the absolute truth of Torah.

R' Yaakov had just sat down, having explained away all the problems, when R' Moshe jumped up, and for the third time proceeded to amaze all those in attendance. He dived into murky waters and uncovered hidden gems, proving in an almost wondrous way that R' Yaakov's words could not be accepted.

When he'd finished, the students again turned their gaze to R' Yaakov to see what he would say, but he sat, dumbfounded. There was no question: this time R' Moshe was victorious.

R' Yaakov's face had grown pale; he felt weak. Could it be that R' Moshe of Pressburg had been correct, and the mighty *pilpul* that he'd constructed was based on error?

R' Akiva Eiger felt the *Nesivos Mishpat's* chagrin. Knowing as he did how R' Yaakov's Torah was revered in the Heavenly Yeshivah, R' Akiva felt overcome by great fear. He was terribly afraid that R' Yaakov might feel just a bit upset, and R' Akiva's son-in-law might somehow be harmed.

R' Akiva Eiger called to one of the students who was helping serve the meal, a young man by the name of Yaakov-Yukav, "Tell me, what is your opinion: Who was correct in this great debate?"

Yaakov-Yukav grasped his apron with his greasy hands and said, "Who am I, with my limited understanding, to place myself between these two giants?"

R' Akiva Eiger wouldn't let him go; he repeated the question.

The student gathered together all his courage. "If you want my opinion, I believe that R' Yaakov of Lisa clearly won the argument."

"Why?"

All eyes were upon the student. Yaakov-Yukav closed his eyes for a minute, and then began a long explanation, one full of piercing logic, founded on clear principles of thought. And here, again, R' Yaakov's edifice was rebuilt, piece by piece, brick by brick. With elegance and precision Yaakov-Yukav explained away all the *Chasam Sofer's* challenges, word by word, concept by concept. Once again the *pilpul* of the *Nesivos* shone and sparkled like a newly-polished diamond.

The countenances of the two guests now underwent a strange

metamorphosis: R' Yaakov of Lisa beamed and laughed with joy at the sight of a student — a waiter! — rebuilding his argument. And R' Moshe Schreiber burst into tears.

A few students approached him and asked, "Can it be that you are weeping so bitterly because your argument was contradicted?"

R' Moshe stood up. "I'm not crying for my argument, but from deep emotion. Now I see, with my own eyes, the great holiness of my father-in-law, and I'm moved to tears.

"You must know, I haven't changed my mind," the *Chasam Sofer* said firmly. With the wave of a hand I could bring down this *pilpul* as well. I know that I am correct in this matter.

"But I am absolutely amazed by two things. This Yaakov-Yukav cannot be compared to R' Yaakov of Lisa; he doesn't reach his ankles in greatness. Could he possibly understand even a fraction of our argument? Secondly, even if we say that this student, this waiter, is a genius, he was hardly here, spending most of the time in the kitchen. He was constantly serving, carrying in food and placing it before the guests. How could he have known what to say, when the students sitting here, hearing every word, could hardly even repeat what we'd said, not to say comprehend them and build upon them?

"This must be," the *Chasam Sofer,* explained, "only because of the lofty holiness of my teacher, my father-in-law, who placed words in the student's mouth.

"And I am certain, gentlemen," R' Moshe's voice thundered, striking awe in the hearts of the many guests attending, "that if my father-in-law would approach a stone wall and command it to speak — even the silent stone would open its mouth and answer all the questions!

"Now you can understand why I wept: Now I have seen the incredible level of my father-in-law, and from the depths of feeling my eyes opened like two wellsprings of tears."

(I heard this from my father, my teacher, R' Shlomo Menachem Weinstock, *shlita*.)

Stuffed Chickens

THE HOME OF THE REVERED R' YITZCHAK SHOR, RABBI AND head of the *beis din* of Gvadzitz and author of the responsa *Ko'ach Shor,* always buzzed with the sound of visitors. R' Yitzchak taught Torah to great numbers, answered the public's questions, and his home was a magnet that drew everyone towards it. Some came to ask him halachic queries, others needed help clarifying complex financial controversies; still others looked to him for compromises in conflicts between business partners or for answers to all sorts of problems needing a rabbinical court.

As great as R' Yitzchak was in Torah, so he was lofty in holiness. He was removed from the vanities of the world, concerning himself only with Torah study and the service of G-d. Many turned to him for blessings, blessings that were particularly effective since his words were well received in the celestial spheres, and whatever he said came to pass!

One day the members of his household were shocked to find an unusual guest sitting in the living room and speaking earnestly to R' Yitzchak.

The guest was Dr. Mordechai Marcus Tzimbel, a Jewish attorney well known in Gvadzitz, who had both learned and strayed in his youth — learned a little and strayed far.

In the past he had been a top yeshivah student, but after his marriage, he had gone to the university in Lemberg to pursue his legal studies and there he had changed, abandoning the yoke of Torah and behaving like a gentile. Worse, he constantly searched for ways to strike at those who treasured their heritage, using the wisdom that he'd learned in his institute of higher learning.

For a long while Dr. Tzimbel had awaited the opportunity for a disputation with the rabbi of the city. A burning desire had entered him, a madness, almost an obsession: to be victorious in a debate with R' Yitzchak Shor, to prove to all the residents of the city that his wisdom was greater than the wisdom of the rabbi. And, incidentally, to instill awe in everyone: if the rabbi himself didn't know how to answer, what should the others say?

Dr. Tzimbel began to visit R' Yitzchak's home, waiting patiently until the rabbi would be free from his many duties and burdens, and then immediately entering into debate with him on questions of faith and religion.

R' Yitzchak answered his questions well, not avoiding any issues and not pushing away his bothersome questioner, even when fatigue threatened to overcome him. The members of the household and those close to the Rabbi burned with rage over the shameless apostate.

"Leave him alone," R' Yitzchak laughed. "Sometime in the future he will leave here with his head hanging down."

One day Dr. Tzimbel argued with the Rabbi over the meaning of the words, "No harm will befall the *tzaddik*" (*Mishlei* 12:21). He attacked the verse bluntly, claiming that it was absolutely impossible, from any angle. "What is this, *tzaddikim* have a greater protection than plain people?" He piled up a mound of logical arguments, declaring that there was no discrimination between people, everyone was equal, and so on.

R' Yitzchak answered him calmly, point by point. He proved that despite the fact that the power of choice is given equally to all mortals, still one can see with one's own senses how *Hakadosh Baruch Hu* guards His servants, the *tzaddikim,* those who do His will, helping them avoid all obstacles — even when they are unaware of it.

"No, the *tzaddik* does not come to harm, it's as simple as that!" R' Yitzchak concluded. Dr. Tzimbel, whose arguments had all been neatly countered, left the house in a fury.

"I'll show that Rabbi; he himself will fail in this," he muttered, walking swiftly towards the poultry market.

"What's happened to you, my good man; has the respected attorney turned into a butcher?" Dr. Tzimbel's wife asked the lawyer in surprise as he returned home, his face scarlet with exertion, three bound-up chickens in his hands.

"Make room for our honored guests," Tzimbel called out gaily. "They've got an important job to do."

He whispered something in his wife's ear, and she burst out laughing. "You're a genius!" she cried.

The lawyer and his wife began to fatten the chickens in a most unusual way. The wife bought lard from the gentile butcher nearby. Refusing them any other feed, she kept them on an exclusive diet of the pig fat. At first the chickens refused to touch the strange stuff and demanded, with loud clucks, the seeds and chicken feed to which they were accustomed, but when hunger got the better of them they began to tear away at pieces of the lard until, with no other choice, they got used to it. Slowly they grew larger on their diet of lard, until they were unusually fat.

"Now listen," Dr. Tzimbel ordered his faithful servant. "Go stand with the chickens close to the rabbi's house. If someone not from his household approaches you, ask for three times the normal price, so that he'll leave you alone. But when the rabbi's servant comes, or the rebbetzin, make it cheap, half the usual price, anything so that the chickens get to his house."

The faithful retainer didn't hesitate to fulfill his master's commands. Not an hour had passed and he returned, breathing heavily.

"I did it!" he declared happily. "I had just gotten out there with the chickens when the rebbetzin came out, looked around, and immediately noticed my wares. She came to me and said, 'I've never seen such fine birds. How much are they?' I gave her a very low price. The rebbetzin, her face glowing, murmured, 'I've gotten a great buy,' paid me for them, and took them home."

"Excellent, excellent!" The lawyer rubbed his hands in glee. "Now we just have to wait a few days. Then I'll prove to his excellency the rabbi, and to all the people in the city, which of the two of us was correct in our discussion of the verse, 'No harm will befall the *tzaddik*.'"

The lawyer and his servant burst into raucous laughter. "The Rabbi, our *tzaddik,* enjoying pig meat! What a great deed — he'll have to run far away from Gvadzitz, he'll be so embarrassed..."

The rebbetzin placed two of the chickens in the yard; the third, the finest and fattest of them, was slaughtered immediately. She cleaned it, removed the feathers, salted its meat, and turned it into a tasty dish for dinner. She placed it into a large earthenware pot and put it carefully down in a corner of the kitchen. When her husband was ready to take a rest from the rigors of his studies, they would sit down to eat.

It was the habit of the *av beis din* of Gvadvitz not to eat until he'd finished his entire schedule of learning. Much to the rebbetzin's distress, his studies that day took him much longer than usual. The Rebbetzin peeked covertly into his room and saw him lost in thought, pacing back and forth in the room, occasionally returning to look into the *Gemara*. She understood that the *sugya* of that day must be difficult and complex. She didn't want to disturb her husband and didn't call him. She and her children were satisfied with a dinner of bread and eggs.

That night the rabbi didn't go to bed at all. The difficulty in which he'd gotten entangled in his learning did not grow any clearer; he still hadn't explained the *sugya* to his satisfaction. When R' Yitzchak Shor said the words, "For they are our life" in *Maariv,* he was speaking the literal truth: all his life, all his being, was given over to the Torah, and if he couldn't understand something, or if the *sugya* didn't seem satisfactory to him — he found no rest, and would neither eat nor sleep until everything had been resolved.

The next morning the rebbetzin stooped over the pot in order to pick it up and warm it on the stove. She was still bent over when a cry escaped her lips.

"What's the matter?" asked the rabbi.

"Look." She pushed the pot in front of him. The rabbi peeked in, and a look of disgust covered his face.

The thin, delicate strands of a spider's web covered the top of the pot.

"I never saw such a thing," the rebbetzin whispered. "What can we do with the food?"

"The food is kosher," the rabbi gave his halachic decision, "even though a fine person is repelled by it. Leave it in a corner of the kitchen for a little while."

That day the rebbetzin cooked the second chicken, but the rabbi was called away for a *pidyon haben* at noon. That night he refused to eat a meat meal, declaring that he'd already had one at the celebration of the *pidyon haben*. The chicken was put off for another day.

The next morning the rebbetzin again opened the pot. She shuddered: the spider had again woven its web upon the delicious dish.

"What's going on here?" she wondered. "Something strange is happening..."

With the instructions of the rabbi, the second pot was also put down in the kitchen, next to the first spoiled dish. The *shochet* was called again, and the third chicken slaughtered. The rebbetzin prepared a fine meal, its aroma wafting through the house. The rebbetzin was full of hope: this time nothing would go wrong, and the dinner would be fit for royalty.

But her hopes were soon dashed...

"Who is at the door?" the rabbi asked.

"So-and-so and so-and-so, two of the prominent men of the city. They have a complex legal battle going on between them, involving a large sum," the rabbi's aide said.

"Let them come in."

The partners entered. The rabbi recognized the litigants. They were two of the richest men of Gvadzitz, owners of a large liquor factory. Even before they had opened their mouths he understood that this case he could not judge by himself.

"Go and call two judges, and on your way pick me up a nice

amount of snuff," he commanded his aide. But before the man had gotten far one of the litigants appeared at his side. He had snuck out of the rabbi's house secretly and now he had a deal to suggest to the aide: "Why work so hard? I'll buy the snuff, and you go call the judges. But so your master doesn't know about it, you give him the snuff."

The naive aide innocently fell into the snare. The wily partner bought the snuff and inside the container, beneath the fragrant tobacco, hid three gold coins.

The judgment began. It was, indeed, a complicated and difficult case that demanded deep concentration and close attention. R' Yitzchak used to take snuff at times like this, believing that inhaling the tobacco assisted him in concentration. Occasionally he would place his fingers into the round silver snuff box and put a little in his nostrils.

"That's strange," he whispered to the other judges after several hours of discussion that had gotten nowhere. "On the one hand it seems to me that the arguments of A are more just. On the other hand, my heart is pushing me more towards giving a favorable verdict for B, without any explanation or logic."

Finally he turned to the two litigants. "Go home," he said. "I will consider your judgment tonight, study it well, and tomorrow we will know."

That night again the Rabbi knew no sleep — and, needless to say, neither he nor his family sat down to a dinner of roast chicken. The others once again ate bread and eggs to their hearts content, and the Rabbi sat in his room all night long.

He referred to his many *sefarim,* occasionally putting a finger into the snuffbox and placing a bit of snuff in his nostrils, as an aid to concentration. Finally, at dawn, he put his hand into the box and felt the cool roundness of a gold coin between his fingers.

"What's this?" he thought, shocked, as he stared at the three gold coins. "Who put these here?"

The morning light grew brighter. When the sun's rays had penetrated into the house, the rabbi called to his assistant. "Tell me the truth," he said, his voice threatening, "and don't leave out a thing. Who bought the tobacco? How did these coins get into my snuffbox?"

The aide, confused and nervous, confessed everything.

The rabbi's eyes brightened now that the secret was revealed. "That is why I felt my verdict being pulled in his favor. It was because he'd hidden a bribe in my box," he cried, relieved.

And when the judgment resumed the rabbi shouted at the litigant, "You wicked man, admit it, you wanted to bribe me!" The man was led out. The case was now a clear one, and it didn't take long after that for the judges to find in favor of the other, ruling against the one who'd attempted the bribe.

At noon, when the *din Torah* had come to an end and the judges had returned home, the rebbetzin set the table for lunch, hoping to serve her husband a generous helping of roast chicken. She came to the kitchen to warm up the pot...

"No! Impossible!" Her shouts could be heard throughout the house. "This is beyond belief!"

"What's happened now?" Everyone raced to the kitchen.

They saw, for the third time, the same scene: The pot was covered with a spider's web so thick that they could not even see the chicken within.

"Tell me, rebbetzin," R' Yitzchak asked, "has this ever happened to you before?"

"Never!" the rebbetzin answered, her eyes flashing. "And certainly not three times in a row!"

"You can see, therefore, that this must have some kind of significance. Providence must have caused this for some unknown reason, so that we should not taste of these foods. We have to find out where they came from."

The rebbetzin told of the man who had stood in front of their yard at the beginning of the week holding three fat chickens, merchandise whose equal she'd never seen. Moreover, she'd only had to pay a few coins for them.

"This seems very suspicious," the rabbi answered. "Who is so foolish as to sell three valuable birds for a tenth of their value? Don't use any of these chickens; leave this one, also, in a corner of the kitchen, and we will see what happens."

That very day the mystery was solved. Dr. Marcus Tzimbel came to celebrate his victory.

"Ahha, Rabbiner," he chortled, "so no harm ever befalls the *tzaddik*? I know that you are a humble man, and you certainly wouldn't allow yourself to be called a *tzaddik*. But every child in Gvadvitz knows that Rabbi Shor is a great *tzaddik* and a holy man. And here we are, our revered *tzaddik* and his family have been enjoying pig meat all week! What do you say to that?"

R' Yitzchak stood up from his chair and gave the assimilated Jew a sharp look.

"What are you hinting at?" R' Yitzchak asked. "I have eaten pig meat? You are speaking like a fool!"

"The rabbi denies it?" The lawyer squawked like a raven. "Isn't it true that the rebbetzin bought three fatted chickens at the beginning of the week? The birds were cooked in your house, right? You ate them? Good. You've eaten pig meat. I myself fattened those birds; I and my wife with our own hands fed them pig fat for several months. What do you think of that?" he called out triumphantly to the rebbetzin. "How did you think those chickens got so fat? And now I'm going to let the news out in the city: The rabbi and his family ate pig meat for an entire week. We'll see what will happen to your fantasies, how you will explain the verse, 'No harm befalls a *tzaddik*.'"

The Rabbi answered serenely. "Slow down, don't be so pleased with yourself. It's true that the rebbetzin bought the chickens, true that she cooked them — and the pots will have to be kashered — but that we ate them? Why do you assume we did?"

"And what else?" Tzimbel cried out angrily. "Are they Chanukah candles — only for looking, but not for use? Don't try to fool me."

"Rebbetzin, please tell Dr. Tzimbel what happened this week to your meals," the rabbi said.

The rebbetzin, in a confident and joyous voice, told how Heaven had sent her a tiny protector in the form of a spider, to guard the holy table of the rabbi's house.

Tzimbel's face grew pale as death. "I don't believe it," he cried out weakly. "I never heard of a spider spinning a web on a pot of fresh food. And three times in a row... You're lying."

Without a word they took him to the kitchen and showed him the three pots.

"The rabbi has won," Dr. Tzimbel declared after he'd recovered his composure. "Now I have seen, with my own eyes, that Hashem protects His pious servants — and that no harm befalls a *tzaddik!*"

Postscript: In the *Sefer Da'as Torah* of the *Maharsham* of Brezhan (*Yoreh De'ah, Hilchos Treifos,* chapter 60, the end of paragraph 5) the following fact is cited: "Once a question was brought to the *gaon,* the *Maharshak* of Brod, regarding a goose that was so fat, everyone was astonished by it. It was discovered that someone had stuffed it with pig meat, and the goose was immediately declared prohibited."

What He Heard, What He Didn't Hear

HUNDREDS OF COWS GRAZED PLACIDLY IN THE FERTILE valley nestled between picturesque hills. The scenery was breathtaking, and the gentle breeze blowing through the verdant valley caressed Nachum's perspiring brow. He looked with dreamy eyes upon the river gurgling through, at the eddies of blue water flowing by, a harbinger of plenty. It had been a blessed year, that year in Rumania; the rains had come down in abundance, the cold was mighty and the chill had improved the quality of the crops. Yet Nachum was worried, terribly worried. Occasionally he would glance at the cows as if searching for one that might suddenly stumble and fall, dead, upon the ground.

Nachum was a cattle dealer, and for many years he'd been raising animals on his farm. His cows were the fattest in the region;

their milk was healthy and delicious. Nachum constantly upgraded the quality of his cows' nutrition in order to raise their value and fetch a high price for them.

Fortune shone upon him, and in the entire region it was known that one who wanted a prime cow, top-quality, must turn to Nachum, the Shtefenesht *Chassid* from Rumania. He was a simple man and an innocent one, who knew nothing more than *alef-beis,* but he was well-versed in the concept of *emunas chachamim.* From the time that the holy rebbe, R' Avraham Mattisyahu Friedman, was crowned as heir to his father, R' Menachem Nachum of Shtefenesht, Nachum had become his devoted *Chassid.* Occasionally he would travel to Shtefenesht with a request and a generous donation. The words of his Rebbe were like the words of the *Urim V'Tumim.* With the passing of days it became known that Nachum had learned to read between the lines, and to hear the Rebbe's words even when they came from utter silence and remained unsaid — and here is one such story:

That year an epidemic attacked the cattle of Rumania. It happened after the winter that had promised to bear such abundant fruit. The epidemic struck suddenly and left the cattle breeders helpless. Knowledge of medicine at that time was quite weak — and where more limited than in Rumania? — and, even more so, the study of veterinary medicine was almost non-existent.

The images were horrifying: animals dying by the thousands, with no way to stop the epidemic. None of Nachum's colleagues knew what to do. In the course of a few days, many became paupers, losing everything they owned. And then came Nachum's turn: He stood in the valley, hopeless, listening to the lowing of his beloved animals, his heart breaking. Here and there one of the cows would suddenly raise its neck upwards, give a terrible bleat of agony, and collapse onto the earth. The passing week had already left hundreds such corpses, and every moment he cast fearful glances at the herd. Whose turn would be next?

"No! I can't let this situation go on." A decision began to crystallize in his heart. "I began the week with 700 cows and I've only

400 left. If I stand here with my arms folded I'll lose everything and starve."

Nachum was a devout *Chassid,* and it had been many years since he'd ever done anything without consulting the Rebbe — how much more so when faced with such disaster.

There was nothing to do but travel to Shtefenesht, to the rebbe.

He boarded a train and left.

Nachum reached Shtefenesht before Shabbos, too late to see the rebbe. Nevertheless he tried his luck with the dedicated *gabbai.* "Please, help me! My animals are dying," he begged.

The *gabbai* agreed to go in and ask the rebbe if Nachum could enter, in light of his terrible problem. To his surprise, the rebbe replied with a definite, and uncharacteristic, negative answer.

"Just to say hello?" the *gabbai* ventured, but again the response was no.

Nachum spent his Shabbos in Shteftnesht, wondering how many of his cows were dying at that very moment.

Shabbos passed, and it was time for *seudah shelishis.* A group of *Chassidim* sat in the darkened *beis midrash* and sang *zemiros* with the Rebbe.

The rebbe sang the *zemer* of "*Baruch Hashem, Yom Yom.*" He reached the words "*nidachim kovetz.*"

Nachum was sitting quite far away, with 40 or perhaps 50 *Chassidim* between him and the Rebbe at the long table. It was hard for him to make out the rebbe's voice.

He made a strong effort to hear, concentrating on every word.

The Rebbe said, "*Nidachim kovetz.*"

"What was that?" Nachum said in astonishment. "He s talking to me!"

For he had heard the words "*nidachim kovetz*" as "*Nachum, koif vetz,*" — Nachum, buy wheat.

It was a clear, unambiguous instruction, a command that could not be ignored. The rebbe had answered him, though he hadn't even asked the question.

What had the rebbe said? It was simple: "Nachum, sell your flock before all your cows die, and with the money you get, buy wheat."

In other words, the rebbe had commanded him to change his occupation and become a dealer in wheat.

But — one might ask — Nachum hadn't managed to even ask the rebbe his question. How could the rebbe know what Nachum the cattle dealer wanted of him? How could he answer a question that had not been asked?

Another problem: The cattle dealer hadn't the faintest idea of how to buy or sell wheat. But that is the power, the beauty, of *emunas chachamim*. You don't ask questions; you just do it!

Nachum traveled home immediately after Shabbos, without mentioning a word of his dire situation to the rebbe. That week he sold the remaining cows, and with money, bought several tons of fine wheat. And thus Nachum, in the space of a day, changed from being a cattle dealer to being a seller of wheat.

Fortune once again beamed. Within a short while Nachum had become a rich man.

In his satisfaction he again traveled to the rebbe to thank him, telling him the whole story.

The rebbe said, "You must know that when you came to me before Shabbos I put you off, because I had no answer for you. I saw that devastating poverty had been decreed upon you — may we all be saved from it — and I couldn't do a thing for you.

"But you," the rebbe concluded, "with your honest belief, heard things that I never said, and in the merit of this simple belief you opened a new channel of prosperity and abundance that hadn't existed before. It was your own power that saved you, not mine! When you must be saved, even an error in hearing can help. Salvation can come from anywhere!"

(I heard this from the *gaon* R' Yitzchak Dovid Rotman, *shlita*).

Water on the Mountains

SILENTLY THE CARAVAN TRAVELED. A CHILD WHO CRIED WAS swiftly hushed. Even the animals carrying their burdens seemed to sense the seriousness of the moment and held their peace, making no noise. A deadly fear clutched at all hearts, the fear that any noise might thrust them into the hands of the Polish army. The faces of the men and women walking showed endless misery; their eyes reflected the agony of those whose lives have been shattered. No one who has not experienced this can ever comprehend it. These were people with no homes.

Their homes had not burned down, nor had they collapsed. These people were exiles; an entire community, hundreds of men and women, from an old and established large village. Its men and women had been banished on that day by the *poritz,* owner of the village, who, incited to anger by the anti-Semitic priests, had grown furious with them. For years the priests had been dripping poison into the *poritz,* until it had reached deep into his heart, and one day, for some perceived wrong, he had issued an immediate decree of banishment upon all the Jews of the village. Of course, their pleas all came to nothing; a large delegation headed by the town rabbi was sent away in shame by the *poritz's* servants, and almost fell prey to the man's hunting dogs.

Where could they go now? This was the question that hung like a dark cloud over the heads of the exiles. An answer was not long in coming: "We will go nowhere!" This was the decision reached by the heads of the group during the days of wandering. They decided not to burden any community, small or large, but rather to found a new city in Poland. And they carried out this plan. After several days of wandering, climbing up a track that could hardly be termed a road on the ridge of a mountain, they found themselves gazing at unbelievably beautiful scenery. Beneath them lay a fertile valley, dotted with the green and red patches of succulent fruit trees. A blessed silence foretold a serene life in this place; only the chirping of birds and the croaking of frogs broke the quiet. Without exchanging a word, the men unloaded the animals, each reading the others thoughts: *Here I shall settle...*

With the joy of action and diligent manual labor, the exiles began to conquer the emptiness, and after only a few days had passed, the first wooden houses stood upon the hill, at the edge of the mountain whose peak was hidden in fog. They worked for several weeks without stop, not complaining about the hardships — including, for example, the disturbing lack of water.

For, from the first day that they had arrived, they could not understand how the trees were laden with lush, ripe fruits, the entire mountain covered with an abundance of trees, in a place where not even the shadow of a spring could be seen. At first they assumed that the water source must be hidden, and if only they searched well they would find it. In the days that followed, several of them were sent to spy out water sources in the area. They climbed the mountain and descended into the valley, inspected crannies and investigated fissures, but much to their disappointment, could not find the least bit of moisture. The small amount of water that they'd carried with them ran out, and they still hadn't found a source.

"Soon we'll all die of thirst," the settlers thought, trembling. In order to avoid such a tragic fate, a few messengers were sent out on horseback to nearby Jewish settlements to bring back a supply of water. They did this several times, but realized that they couldn't maintain a settlement indefinitely without its own source of water. They hired experts, at great cost, to help them locate the water. These experts made certain to get paid in full before launching their search; they labored long and hard, checked and inspected, suggested drilling here and digging there. But all their suggestions resulted in nothing but more dry land; not one drop of water was uncovered.

Despair reigned. Without water, the settlement could not remain in existence! Would they be exiled once again?

During this time one of the *Chassidim* of R' Hirsch of Riminov happened upon the colony. He saw the anguish in the faces of the settlers and wanted to find out the reason behind it. He did not have long to wait: soon, he too felt the universal thirst. Water was carefully rationed, with each person receiving a miniscule allotment.

"Why don't you travel to nearby Riminov and tell the Rebbe?" he asked in wonder. It soon became clear, however, that the people did not know what he meant. They were not familiar with the concept of *tzaddikim* and *Chassidim,* and turned astonished eyes towards him. He told them about R' Hirsch of Riminov, the renowned *tzaddik* who had been orphaned as a young boy, whose father had been a simple tailor, and who had grown and risen until he became the heir of R' Menachem Mendel of Riminov. He told them of the wonders and miracles his rebbe had performed. But his fervent words didn't make much of an impression on the settlers, who were rather provincial and narrow-minded.

"You've invested so much money in the matter," the *Chassid* finally spoke in words they could understand. "Before you put in more rubles, why not send messengers to Riminov, to the rebbe? What do you have to lose?"

In the face of this logic, the last of the doubters grew silent. They immediately sent out a delegation of the notables of "New City," as they'd taken to calling their settlement, to Riminov. With bitter hearts they told R' Hirsch of their awful plight.

"Heaven has caused you to come here today," the rebbe told them joyously, his face shining. "Just now I have taken upon myself the debt of 300 *rendlech,* an enormous sum, for the purpose of freeing captives. If you can give me the money needed to save lives, your salvation shall come soon."

The members of the group exchanged disbelieving looks. "Does the rebbe think we're rich, and that huge sums such as three hundred *rendlech* are just jingling about in our purses? Besides, who can guarantee that we will find water if we give the rebbe the amount requested?"

"You are right," said R' Hirsch, "your words are just. Give me only half of the amount now, and as soon as the water begins to flow in your city, give me the other half."

They accepted the terms, traveled to New City, and with great effort, collected 150 *rendlech*. When they returned to Riminov with the money, the *tzaddik's* eyes lit up. "If you knew how happy you'd made your Father in Heaven, you would go out and march with tambourines through the city streets," he declared, his voice full of emotion. "May G-d be with you. There is a verse in *Tehillim*: in Psalm 104 David *HaMelech* says, 'On the mountains stands the water.' If so, go up to the summit of the mountain next to your city, dig there on the top, and you will undoubtedly find water with which to quench your city's thirst."

On their way back to New City the members of the delegation laughed, mocking the rebbe's suggestion without cease. So he knew a verse in *Tehillim*: Didn't they, too, know the same verse? And yet, when they came back to the city and told the others what the rebbe had said, the residents accepted his words with simple faith. A few experts went up, shovels in hand, and climbed to the top of the mountain. At the very summit they stopped, grabbed their equipment, and with a prayer on their lips began to hit the ground. Rocks and earth flew in all directions as they dug feverishly, rending the ground and scarring it.

"Do you smell it?" one of the men suddenly shouted to his comrades. "The smell of water is in the air!" A thin stream suddenly burst out of the earth; cold droplets sprayed upon the men's radiant faces. "On the mountains stands the water," one of the men repeated the rebbe's words in shock and wonder. The sound of flowing water, fresh water, suddenly filled the air, growing greater with each moment until it had become a mighty roar, a great spring flowing mightily in the channels and ravines. "It climbs the mountains and descends into the valleys," the workers muttered the words of David *HaMelech* over and over. "Who sends springs in the rivers, flowing between mountains..."

Like the workers of Yitzchak *Avinu* in days of old, the men descended the mountain crying, "We've found water!" Experts directed the water towards the city, and the Jews of New City were saved.

"And Yeshurun grew fat, and kicked..." When the water was found, the residents began to regret their hasty promise to pay 150 more *rendlech*. With little discussion it was decided that there was no need to pay the second half. The waters were flowing beautifully. And what had the *tzaddik* done, after all? He had just quoted one verse of *Tehillim*...

Two weeks had not yet passed when the letter came from Riminov: "You are obligated to pay the second half..."

They ignored the missive. A month later a messenger came from the rebbe, bearing a reminder and a warning: "If you don't pay what you've promised, the spring will dry up."

Some of the people were frightened by the threat, and wanted to hurry the group into paying what it had promised, but several of the community leaders arose and persuaded the residents with their thought-out arguments. The water was flowing in abundance; who was foolish enough to believe that a r3ebbe, at such a great distance, could command it to stop? The complainers grew silent.

On that very day, when the water carriers came to the well, they were paralyzed with shock and terror. The strong flow that had been surging out had diminished into a thin trickle. They returned to the city immediately and announced to the people that the rebbe's words had come true. But wickedness still prevailed: Even in the face of a fast-disappearing spring, the townspeople hardened their hearts and their miserliness grew greater. But after a few days the spring had dried up completely!

The city's residents waited one more day, two more days: Perhaps the spring would once again give its water. But the spring had turned to stone.

With hearts mourning their foolishness, the residents collected 150 *rendlech* and shamefacedly returned to the *tzaddik* of Riminov, prepared to receive a severe rebuke for their greed and stubbornness. But the *tzaddik* neither roared nor reprimanded. His face glowing, he explained to them, "The *mitzvah* of freeing captives is a great one, and whoever merits being a part of it brings upon himself prosperity and blessing. Because you didn't want to participate in the *mitzvah*, the blessing from Above was sealed off. When those conduits were blocked, the springs dried up of their own accord.

Now that you've returned and become a partner in this *mitzvah,* you will be able to draw water, rejoicing, from the wellsprings of salvation, and you can be sure that the spring shall never run dry again!"

(I heard this from R' Yitzchak Dovid Rotman, *shlita.*)

The Little Horse

T HE *TZADDIK* R' MOSHE LEIB OF SASSOV WAS A STUDENT OF the holy R' Michel of Zlatchow. R' Moshe Leib's father, R' Yaakov, was a great Torah scholar and an opponent of *Chassidus,* and did not look favorably upon his son's participation in that movement. Yet he didn't place obstacles in his path, seeing what great heights of spirituality his son was reaching in this way of serving G-d. R' Yaakov lived in Brody and R' Moshe Leib, who was intensely careful about the *mitzvah* of respecting his father, wanted to be as near him as possible in order to serve him constantly. Yet his longings for his rebbe, R' Michel Zlatchower, his teacher and guide in the service of Hashem, were no less strong. What did he do? He chose to live in the city of Sassov, located midway on the road between Brody and Zlatchow, and thus he could divide his time between his father's home, the house of his rebbe, and his own home where, it seemed, he spent the least amount of time.

But what should a person do if he always feels that he hasn't even crossed the threshold of respect for his father, and despite all his great efforts, feels constantly that he hasn't done enough? Particularly in the winter, when the roads were covered with a thick blanket of snow and the trip to Brody was not an easy task, R' Moshe Leib agonized over the fact that he was forced to stay home without the ability to properly serve his father. The anguish settled heavily in his heart and would give him no rest. As if of their own accord, his legs took him to the market plaza that served as a kind of "central bus station": Several wagon drivers stood, shivering with cold, looking anxiously for a traveler who would save them from the boredom of doing nothing.

Astonishingly, even in these frigid days there were travelers. R' Moshe Leib approached a wagon filling up with passengers. "Tell me, will you be in Brody?" he asked one of the men inside. "If so, please do me this tremendous favor, an unparalleled *mitzvah;* go to my father and tell him that his son, Moshe Leib, is alive and well, he and all his family."

The messenger, who was carried away by the fervor and emotion of the speaker, didn't ignore the plea. "Who knows how many years it is since the concerned father heard from his son and his family," he thought with a hint of self-satisfaction. "I will perform this great *mitzvah,* to calm him." The carriage had only stopped in Brody when he sprang out, like an arrow from a poised bow, to find the home of R' Yaakov.

In one breath, and with a great feeling of joy, he sent the heartfelt regards of the son. How shocked he was, then, to hear the laughing sigh of the father: "May my Moshe Leib be well and healthy, you're the seventh messenger today!"

The "messengers" substituted for him only during the cold season; other times he fulfilled the declaration of the Sages, "a *mitzvah* is greater done by him than by his messenger," and he wasn't satisfied with regards sent by others. Out of his great esteem for his father he would make the journey between Sassov and Brody many times.

The journey between Sassov and Brody is very long, and on a winding road that wends its way through thick forests. Most of the way there is no place to stop. There was one small station, well known among travelers, where everyone would rest. It was located in a small village by the name of Podhortza, mid-way on the route.

The kings of Poland had seen in this small village, located on one of the highest ridges, a first-class strategic possession, and as a result King Jan Sobieski had built a giant fortress there that commanded a view of the entire area. The Jews, though, did not see eye-to-eye with the king, and only two Jewish families lived there, one of them Chassidic.

One of the members of this family, R' Sender, owned the local inn. Every time R' Moshe Leib passed through the village he would make his way to R' Sender's, to rest a little beneath his roof. R' Sender was a very special man, a scholar and a man of refinement. No wonder, then, that in a short while the bonds of friendship grew strong between them. R' Moshe Leib became like a member of the household, closely involved in the lives of R' Sender and his family.

R' Sender thought very highly of this young man, who seemed in his eyes nothing less than an angel. He noticed that sometimes, during his many visits to Podhortza, R' Moshe Leib would sneak out of the inn and disappear. His curious host followed him once and found his guest wandering through the adjoining forest. "What can he be looking for, among the trees?" R' Sender wondered. He found the answer to his question almost immediately: R' Moshe Leib wrapped himself up in his *tallis* and *tefillin* and broke into prayers that he, R' Sender, had never before heard in his life. It seemed to R' Sender that the world had stopped its turning; the entire universe sang praise together with this praying angel. For the first time R' Sender truly understood the meaning of the words, "Then all the forests of the trees shall sing joyously." He was certain that even the trees were dancing, sharing the happiness of R' Moshe Leib.

At that time, when the young rebbe of Sassov was revealed to him in all his grandeur, R' Sender came to a clear decision, and from then on he followed him carefully, and asked his advice and guidance in everything.

During one of their conversations, R' Sender asked his guest from Sassov, "Have I told you yet about my wonder horse?"

"No," R' Moshe Leib replied, understanding quite well that he wasn't referring to the miracle of a swift race horse. "What are the wonders of your horse?"

"It happened two years ago," the innkeeper began.

That year R' Sender had traveled to the great fair in Leipzig. During the past cold season, several of his horses had frozen to death and, without any means of transport, he was trapped in his house the entire winter. With the coming of spring, R' Sender had hurried to Leipzig to buy some fine horses. In all the pandemonium of the fair he somehow found his friend Itzik, a well-known horse dealer. "What can you suggest for an old customer?" R' Sender smiled at Itzik as he was busily combing the mane of one of his huge horses. Itzik gave a surprised and happy shout at the sight of his old friend, who seemed to have sprouted from the earth. He quickly showed R' Sender the best of his merchandise, thoroughbred horses that stood straight and tall, as if aware of their worth. Occasionally they would give a shake of their brown bodies and snort from their wet nostrils. R' Sender had already worked out a deal on the price of two fine horses when his eye fell upon a small horse that stood, as though ashamed, hiding in a corner.

"What about that pony?" he asked Itzik, who replied, "No pony, but an old horse that for some reason never grew. I'm not even sure why I brought it here." R' Sender had already prepared to leave with his new pair, but something in the humble bearing of the little horse seemed to pull at him. He approached it and looked it over carefully. The little horse lifted its head and stared at R' Sender, its eyes beseeching. It seemed to R' Sender as if the animal were begging to be taken home.

Itzik looked at his friend in surprise. "You want it, this old nag?" he asked in wonder. "It's not good for anything!" he said, dismissing it. R' Sender waited for a minute, as if trying to make a decision, and Itzik added, "If you want, I'll throw it in for close to nothing."

When R' Sender returned to his home in Podhortza he found, to his shock, that the opposite of what he'd been told was true. The little horse soon revealed very special and unusual abilities. The tiny investment had been paid over many times. The two fine thoroughbreds that he'd brought from Leipzig proved their breeding and might only by the huge amounts of grain they downed. But the two gluttons couldn't compete with the powers that the tiny horse showed. For every chore that needed great strength, R' Sender would put rein and bridle on the little horse, which demonstrated its might again and again. From day to day it grew even stronger, and everyone spoke of this rare phenomenon.

Once, when a carriage got stuck in the mud and several horses working together failed to pull it out, R' Sender brought his little horse and, much to the astonishment of everyone there, it quickly hauled out the carriage as if it weighed almost nothing, without any special effort.

From that time on, the little horse became a gold mine for its owner. All the gentiles in the area who'd heard about the wonder horse wanted to hire it for the sowing season, the harvest. It was especially renowned for its ability to pull out wagons stuck in the mud, and R' Sender, who was blessed with a canny business sense, got top prices.

"The most amazing thing of all," R' Sender ended his story, "is that the little horse hardly eats a thing, just a little feed, and after that he's ready to work an entire day. Sometimes the strange thought hits me that he's trying to appease me, and I don't know why. The costs of his maintenance are negligible, and the income from him keeps going up more and more."

R' Moshe Leib heard the tale in silence, showing no reaction to the strange story. That night he skimmed through the old books in his host's home. From one of the books an ancient, yellowing piece of parchment fell to the ground. R' Moshe Leib bent down to retrieve it. The note spoke of a debt that a Polish Jew owed another Jew. R' Moshe Leib went to R' Sender and asked him to explain the note.

At first R' Sender couldn't figure it out. The note had been hidden among the old books he'd inherited from his father. His father had, in turn, inherited them from R' Sender's grandfather. Until this evening R' Sender hadn't paid any attention to any of the little papers in the books. After some examination, it appeared that the note referred to a debt reaching back two generations, a large debt that had been owed to R' Sender's father's father. Both the debtor and the lender, of course, were long since dead.

"Tell me," R' Moshe Leib turned to his host, "since you are by law the legal heir of your grandfather, are you prepared to forgive the debt with absolute sincerity?"

"What kind of a question is that?" the other replied heatedly. "In any case there's no way of ever collecting on it, so why not forgive him?"

"You are praiseworthy, for you have saved an unfortunate soul," R' Moshe Leib burst out. "And now let's go out and look at your little horse."

The two went out to the paddock in the courtyard. The puzzled villager saw, to his consternation, that the little horse was stretched out on the ground, dead. A shout of anguish burst out of his mouth for the loss of his beloved horse.

"You should know," the rebbe told him, "that if someone owes something and doesn't pay, he is forced to repay it from on High. This little horse," he said, pointing to the dead animal, "was a reincarnation of the soul of the man who had incurred the debt, and not repaid it. It was sent from the World of Truth in order to repay you, your grandfather's heir. That is why it worked so hard and cost you so little. Now, when you forgave him, the unfortunate soul found its *tikkun,* and in the merit of your mercy you shall see great blessings and success."

And indeed in the coming years R' Sender was known as one of the most prosperous men in the region.

"You Fold Up"

EVEN BEFORE HE'D TURNED 13, ANYONE WHO KNEW YOSEF Shtekstil knew that his fate was inevitable: Yossel Shtekstil would be a soldier. Whether he wanted it or not, Yossel would be drafted into the Tzar's army and would faithfully serve his master, Tzar Franz Josef, ruler of the Austro-Hungarian Empire.

It was actually when he was 12, a year before he was to become a man, that Yossel, an inveterate overachiever, began to mature. He grew quickly and soon was unusually tall. At the same time he put on weight and by the time he was 13 he looked like a full-grown adult in height and build. He also sprouted facial hair.

His father, R' Kalman Shtekstil, was one of the notables of the city of Lemberg, or Lvov, in Galicia. Torah and worldly greatness combined in his home; he was a scholar, well versed from youth in the tenets of *Chassidus,* and from the time he went into business after his marriage, the sunshine of fortune had beamed upon him and never set. This happy combination of merchant and philanthropist, *Chassid* and businessman who generously gave to the poor caused all to respect him greatly: some for his piety and learning, others for his wealth and generosity.

In honor of the bar mitzvah of his beloved son Yossel, R' Kalman prepared a meal fit for a king. Crowds of chefs and bakers toiled in his large kitchen for many days, preparing the meal in all its glory. On the day that Yossel took upon himself the yoke of *mitzvos,* the community of Lemberg converged upon R' Kalman's spacious villa for the festive meal.

Upon their arrival the invited guests stood open-mouthed. The variety and the abundance of foods and the elegant serving platters were enough to turn anyone's head. But more than that, anyone who didn't know the bar mitzvah boy was certain he was his older brother...

"We thought we're coming to a bar mitzvah meal, but it seems we're mistaken; it must be a wedding celebration. After all, the groom is standing in front of us," several of the guests joked upon seeing Yossel, the tall, bearded bar mitzvah boy.

Even the relatives who knew Yossel and were aware of his rapid growth in the past year could hardly believe what he looked like. Now that he had donned a suit and a *deshikel,* the cap worn by men in Poland and Galicia, the youth looked like a full-grown man.

In the following years Yossel immersed himself in his studies in a "*kloiz*," or small *beis midrash*, near Lemberg, in the company of dozens of young men who, like him, thirsted for Torah knowledge. They found what they were looking for from the mouths of several well-known scholars, headed by a well-known Talmudic genius. Yossel spent some years in diligent study, and reached great heights in scholarship; he was included among the brightest in the group, with a wonderful future before him. That is, if only he could manage to stay within the *kloiz*... But that was doubtful, and Yossel's spiritual future remained enveloped in a haze.

Actually, there really wasn't much doubt at all.

Anyone who knew Yossel was certain that he would be drafted into the Tzar's army. They didn't hide their opinion, and when Yossel would hear their words, he would sink into a deep, dark gloom.

"Yossel, Yossel, the doctors on the draft board would have to be blind as a day-old kitten in order not to see your potential," his friends would tell him, giving him an amicable slap on the shoulder — and it needed some doing, to reach his tall shoulder. "Just look at your height, your broad shoulders. Only a complete fool would give up a strongman like you, a man among men, perfect for the service of the Tzar. The draft board is searching everywhere for heroes like you, and they just have to take one look..."

Other friends, truer ones, out of honest concern for his future, came up with a variety of ideas of how he could escape the rigors of army service. These included concealing himself in some secret hideaway, giving himself a serious wound in one of his limbs, and pretending to be insane. On and on the discussions went.

These suggestions were all rejected for various good reasons. Both Yossel and his friends knew well that there wasn't much chance of his being able to go underground for many years, and if he would do so he would live in constant fear of informers. He also had no desire to stand before the army's medical committee, jump on a table and make noises like a rooster or a horse in order to persuade the members that he was mad.

One suggestion was never even made, even though Yossel's father could have surely seen it through. In an organized, efficient nation such as Austria, bribery was absolutely out of the question; Heaven protect the man who was found trying such a thing!

When Yossel approached draftable age, his father, R' Kalman, was seized by real terror. If he didn't do something, Yossel, his son and the light of his life, would be taken from his warm, loving family straight into the unyielding arms of the generals, those cruel and merciless soldiers!

All through Galicia one could hear terrible tales of strong young men taken forcibly into the army to meet a bitter fate. There was R' Anshel, a *Chassid* of Sanz, who every Friday would cast off his gun belt because it was *muktzeh* and stand in a corner of the barracks to *daven*. On Shabbos he would walk with his army comrades until he'd reached *techum Shabbos* and then come to a halt. For this he endured more than his share of floggings and punishments. Finally, he was examined by the army doctors, who found him sane. He was declared a rebel against the king, tortured, and finally died of his torments.

"I'm going to the rebbe," R' Kalman announced to his household one day. The family members didn't have to ask what rebbe he meant.

How did R' Yechezkel of Shinova, eldest son of R' Chaim of Sanz, put it?

"There are some *gedolei Torah* who reach incredible levels of sharpness or proficiency, and their *chiddushim* in Torah are works of art of *pilpul,* structures built piece by piece, soaring to the skies.

"There are *tzaddikim* who serve Hashem, who put all their energies into their service and their prayers, with their *tefillos* piercing the heavens.

"There are those who do wonderful deeds, all their lives pursuing charity, kindness, helping thousands.

"But where in the entire world can one find a person like my father, R' Chaim of Sanz, in which perfection in all these three areas — Torah, service of G-d, and lovingkindness — has been reached, and in such quantity that the human mind cannot fathom it?"

One of R' Chaim's duties in the realm of lovingkindness was praying that Torah students be exempt from the rigors of army service.

R' Kalman and his son, Yossel, stood before R' Chaim of Sanz. R' Kalman poured out the worries that were burdening him, weighing on his heart like a millstone.

"Rebbe, my trouble is a trouble indeed." R' Kalman pointed to his son, Yossel. "I am afraid that the members of the draft board will take one look at him, and draft him on the spot into the Tzar's army."

R' Chaim's pure and holy eyes ran over the young man, until they met Yossel's shining ones.

"A fine young man," he murmured in admiration. "Truly a Samson. What do you say: Don't you want to serve in the Tzar's army?"

Yossel felt his mind reel. A frightening suspicion filled his breast. Who knew what the rebbe's words were hinting at? He burst into tears.

"My soul longs for Torah," he said, his voice trembling, his entire body heaving with sobs.

"You don't want to serve in the army?" the Rebbe asked, as if surprised.

"Absolutely not," Yossel cried.

R' Chaim sank into a reverie, his face growing red with effort.

"*Men kneitsch't* — you fold up," he finally answered.

R' Kalman stood, puzzled. What kind of answer was this: words without meaning, incomprehensible. What should they fold, and how?

R' Kalman stood and repeated his words, from the beginning to their bitter conclusion. Who knows, perhaps the rebbe hadn't quite understood what he had said. But when he had finished and finally grown silent, the Rebbe again replied with the same strange words, "*Men kneitsch't.*"

R' Chaim held out his hand in a gesture of farewell. Father and son left the room, their hearts heavy.

All the others his age had already received their "*tzetlach,*" official notices from the army. Each had been given a day to stand before the draft board.

Only Yossel hadn't received a notice.

It was clear to all that the *tzetel* was on its way. It was just a question of time until it reached its destination. Why, after all, should he be different from his fellows?

A week passed, another week, a month and two months, and there was no sign of the notice.

R' Kalman trembled. Perhaps his beloved boy was under some kind of covert surveillance. Maybe they wanted to trap him in some dark alley, fearing that otherwise he would flee. The strange silence frightened him; not knowing what was going on ate into him like a hungry worm.

At R' Kalman's suggestion, Yossel went underground for some months in order to avoid possible ambush in one of the city's ill-lit streets. Afterwards, thinking again about the rebbe's strange words, R' Kalman came up with an explanation, and the unfortunate Yossel was commanded to walk around bent over, like a 100-year-old man.

"'You fold,' R' Kalman thought in a flash of genius. "The Rebbe wanted to say that you should fold yourself, walk around huddled up and bent!"

Yossel walked around like that for some days, until his muscles and spine groaned in protest and he finally straightened up again.

The terrifying *tzetel* never arrived. Yossel was as forgotten as the dead.

Three decades passed. R' Kalman had already gone to his reward, Yossel was a respected householder, himself father of a new generation. All his years he'd put his learning first, before his livelihood, and his spiritual stature far outstripped his material accomplishments.

In his later years Yossel decided to move to *Eretz Yisrael*. He went to the government office to arrange for a passport.

"Yosef Shtekstil of Lemberg." The bureaucrat looked through the papers for quite a long time. "There is no such name."

Yossel was taken aback. What did that mean, no such name? Didn't he exist, after all? Not long after his birth, Yossel's father, an upright and law-abiding man, had duly registered him in the population records.

"Check again," he urged the functionary. The man did his best, and even turned to his superior. Together they once again perused all the many files.

For several days Yossel jumped between one clerk and the next, one administrator and the other, until they all grew tired of this bothersome Jew who was forcing them to look for a name that did not exist.

"Your father never registered you," one of the top clerks growled at him. "Why are you complaining to us?"

Yossel wouldn't give up. "Have mercy on me," he begged a top official. "If you can't find my name on the list, that will be the end of my dream of moving to *Eretz Yisrael*."

Something stirred in the man's heart. "When were you born?" he asked.

Yossel told him.

The clerk wrinkled his brow in thought. "We can check the archives, in the old files of that year."

Yossel went down with him to the basement and helped him burrow in the yellowed files heavy with the dust of generations.

"Here is the registration book of births from your year," the clerk finally crowed in delight. "Maybe we'll find you here and finally know if you really were born, or are only a figment of our imagination."

He skimmed swiftly through the old pages until he reached Yossel's date of birth.

"Here," he muttered, "Edward Klempferer, Nicholas Johannes, Vitchich Mikolovski..." He turned the page. "Yaakov Weiss, Manfred Kontzki, Vladislav..."

"I guess you don't exist," he said, casting a mischievous look at Yossel. "Your name isn't here on the list."

Yossel felt on the verge of collapse. "Look again," he said weakly, though he himself had no great hope of success. The clerk again felt a wave of pity for this Jew and turned back to the page.

"Nicholas Johannes, Vitchich Mikolovski," he murmured again. "Wait!" he shouted. "Look!" He placed the file before Yossel's half-closed eyes.

The page was slightly folded on the bottom and the last line had been covered up. He straightened it carefully and read it aloud.

"Yosef Shtekstil."

"Do you understand?" the clerk said, his voice deep with excitement. "Your name was folded over! Somehow it got lost in the fold of the paper, and when they copied the names into the updated population registry it was omitted. I've never heard of such a thing happening before; it's the first time."

Yossel understood. Oh, how he understood. He understood many things: the power of a true *tzaddik,* the value of his every word. Two words had come from the mouth of the holy man of Sanz, and those words had folded over a population register hundreds of miles away, in Lemberg. A fateful folding that would change his future.

"*Men kneitsch't.* You fold..."

(I heard this from R' Gedalia Segal, *shlita.*)

Last Warning

WHEN R' YUDEL OF NEUSTADT REACHED HIS MIDDLE years he made a firm decision: to move to *Eretz Yisrael.* "I've already passed 50 years in this world. How long will I live in the land of the gentiles, where the very earth is impure?"

R' Yudel would conclude, "It is better for me to go up to our Holy Land. There, in the King's antechamber, I can delve into the Torah without interruption."

He prepared to carry out his intention. R' Yudel almost immediately began to pack his things. His wife, Bina, was a fine woman who was also prepared to undertake the move, despite the incredible hardships the journey entailed. Because she was a true helpmate, and since they had few possessions, she faithfully promised that from the moment she knew their departure date it would take her only a few days to be completely ready.

"And now I will be leaving the house for a few weeks," R' Yudel told her.

"Why?" Bina asked, startled.

"I am traveling to all the *tzaddikim* of our generation to ask for their blessing," he explained to his wife. "You can't imagine that I will go up to the Holy Land without asking for a farewell blessing."

So R' Yudel went to all the great men in his own area, and after a few days reached Premishlan and came to the home of R' Meir'el.

Unlike the other *tzaddikim,* who heard him out and then rained down upon him a flood of heartfelt blessings, R' Meir'el interrupted the excited *Chassid* in mid-sentence:

"You're traveling to *Eretz Yisrael*? You'll need a respectable sum for travel. Do you have any money?"

R' Yudel, ashamed, muttered out of the side of his mouth that he didn't have a ruble yet.

"Nu?"

R' Yudel explained, "I thought to go visit my friends and relatives and ask them to help..."

R' Meir'el looked at him with his clear eyes, eyes that saw with a prophet's vision, and asked, "And what about *bitul Torah,* what about prayers? A Jew, a scholar such as you, should go like a beggar from door to door? And who knows what they will give you?"

"So what should I do?"

"Take my advice," the *tzaddik* told him. "Meir'el doesn't permit you to waste your precious time. Stay here in my court, spend your time in learning and prayer as you usually do, and with G-d's help Meir'el will collect the sum you need for travel expenses."

R' Meir'el didn't have to work very hard to convince R' Yudel; he agreed with great pleasure to the surprising suggestion. Instead of wandering from house to house he would sit and learn, would pray and devote himself to G-d's service, while R' Meir'el would worry about all his concerns. Could there be anything better than this?

Four weeks had passed while R' Yudel stayed in Premishlan. Men came to the holy court and left. Several Jews with a look of great prosperity arrived for a visit. R' Yudel covertly watched them, sure that soon he would be summoned to the rebbe's chamber, but no call came. He sat all day in the *beis midrash,* deep in Torah and prayer, and each time he saw the rebbe he tried to catch his eye. R' Meir'el saw him, but did not say a word on the subject.

A faint worry began to stir in R' Yudel's heart: The rebbe was overworked, busy with G-d's service from morning to night. Jews came to him constantly. Perhaps he had forgotten the whole matter?

"Impossible," the *Chassidim* who lived in Premishlan constantly told him. "The rebbe isn't a regular person, who isn't careful with his words. If he said something, it's certain he will fulfill it. He's not talking about it? The time, obviously, has not yet come!"

After a few more weeks R' Yudel's patience ran out. Bina was probably worrying herself half to death, and so much time had been wasted for nothing. That evening, R' Yudel snuck into the rebbe's room, not asking permission from the *gabbai.*

When he walked into the room, R' Meir'el put out his hand, as if he'd never seen him before. "Hello, Reb Yid, where are you from and what would you like from me?"

"Woe is me," R' Yudel thought anxiously. "The rebbe has forgotten about me." Out of respect for the rebbe he didn't correct the error and instead repeated, word for word, what he'd said more than a month before.

"I've come to ask the rebbe's blessing; I'm going to *Eretz Yisrael.*"

"And where are you getting money for your expenses?" R' Meir'el, too, repeated what he'd said earlier.

"I'm planning on going to my relatives and friends," R' Yudel answered, again.

"And what about *bitul Torah*? What about prayers?" R' Meir'el's face suddenly wore a grave mien. "Didn't I tell you a month ago to sit with me and learn, and pray, and the money will be collected? You may ask, where will Meir'el get 400 rubles for travel expenses? I'll tell you: Meir'el has the trait of faith. He has faith in Hashem and is not at all concerned. The money will undoubtedly come; you just need a little patience!"

The door of the room suddenly opened. The *gabbai,* who didn't know of R' Yudel's presence, walked in. By his side stood an elegantly dressed Jew. One could clearly see that here was a rich man.

The *gabbai* hastily jumped back and the wealthy man, too, seeing that the rebbe was with someone, stood confused, not daring to come in. He waited for the Jew standing inside to get the hint and leave the room. However, the rebbe told R' Yudel not to go. At the same time, he gestured to the rich man to stay where he was.

His face coloring, the rich man stood by the door. Inside him a storm raged. He wanted to ask R' Meir'el what he would do with the *Gemara s* dictate: Rebbe honors the wealthy (*Eruvin* 86). Was this how the rebbe showed honor to a rich man such as he, letting him stand by the door, sharing the room with one of these beggars?

R' Meir'el took his eyes off the flushed face of the wealthy man near the doorway and turned to R' Yudel.

"R' Yudel, listen well to the story I'm about to tell you. It's an interesting tale. And you too, rich man standing by the doorway; I will ask that you listen with attention and interest, for you can derive an important lesson from it."

In a certain city lived a Jew blessed by G-d with all good things, with houses and fields, orchards and gardens, silver and gold. The man was a miser and, unfortunately, the more his wealth grew, the greater his stinginess grew as well. His house was closed before all the poor, and if in the past he would give a few pennies to *tzedakah,* as G-d granted him more wealth and honor he stopped giving completely. This is the way of the world: the poor man has a small, beggarly *yetzer hara,* evil inclination, while the rich man's *yetzer hara* is great, as befits a wealthy man. And so the rich man completely gave up the *mitzvah* of charity. He warned his servants as well, charging them not to allow anyone over the threshold, particularly if he was a beggar.

The servants, though, possessed more mercy than their master. "What do we do if a hungry man comes to the door, or someone who needs a few coins to sustain his starving family?"

"Throw them out to my neighbor!" came the cruel reply, straight from the man's closed heart.

This rich man indeed had one neighbor, a simple householder, a man of limited means with a heart of gold and an open hand, who gave most of his money away to charity.

The miser rejoiced in his generous neighbor, and if any beggar erred and came to his house, he was immediately sent to his poorer neighbor's home.

And so the years passed. The rich man became even more prosperous, his wealth growing as if mixed with yeast. No penny from his treasures ever passed to charity. In contrast, his neighbor, never blessed with an abundance of possessions, continued to give more and more to *tzedakah,* finally sustaining all the poor men his rich neighbor sent on to him.

The merciful angels created by such philanthropy went up to Heaven, together with the dreadful angels that came out of the tight fist of the miser, and stood together before the Heavenly Court. There was pandemonium in Heaven. The trait of judgment gave its strong, unyielding case: Could it be that the rich man, who had so much, and who gave so little — who gave nothing — gained, while his neighbor, who took bread from the mouths of his own family to give to the poor, should lose?

The Heavenly Court decided to change the situation: to give the wealth to the philanthropist and the poverty to the miser.

But it seemed that this miser had performed one *mitzvah* in his life, and the angel created from it came to speak well of him. "You can't just snatch his wealth away. You must give him one last chance. Give him a test. If he passes it, he deserves to retain his riches. And if, heaven forbid, he does not, let all his money be taken away and given to the better man."

The day was cold and stormy; the winds whistled and the grey skies gave off torrential rain. Not a living thing could be seen in the street. The biting chill, the raging winds, and the heavy downpour all combined to drive off even the hardiest of animals or humans.

The winter's bitterness could not be felt in the spacious palace of the rich man. The large fireplace was cheerful with burning branches that gave off a pleasant warmth throughout the room. Oil lamps illuminated with a bright light. The windows and shutters were well shut and one could hardly hear the wind's roar.

Ensconced in his armchair, the rich man was enjoying a book, along with a warm and steaming cup of tea on a tiny table next to him. Occasionally the man would stop reading for a moment, put the mug carefully to his lips, and take a small sip, murmuring, "Ahh! Nothing like a cup of tea."

His protuberant eyes under fleshy lids took in the warm room with satisfaction, trying to catch a glance from behind the thick curtains of the storm raging outside, to appreciate even more the light amidst the darkness.

The loud banging on the door suddenly disturbed the tranquility, breaking through the peaceful silence. The servant went to see who was knocking and opened the door just a crack to keep out the brutal wind.

The sight before him was terrifying: In the doorway stood

one of those awful paupers, his ragged clothes dripping water and his lips blue with cold. His teeth chattered, and it was only with great effort that he managed to make his request, just to come in for a few minutes, until the worst would be over, to warm up a bit.

The servant was perplexed. He knew full well that his master didn't like to take beggars into his house, and particularly beggars dripping water... And yet, even a heart of stone such as his master possessed would be forced to soften a little in view of this pitiful sight. He therefore let the pauper in and told him to wait by the door.

"Throw him out immediately!" the rich man screamed, his eyes growing even wider in his wrath. "He's bringing his filthy mud into my house! Get rid of him. These beggars are disgusting; give them a finger today and tomorrow they'll demand the entire hand! Go tell him that this is not a hotel."

Without a choice the servant sent the poor man out, into the cold, into the wind and the rain. For a long while they could hear his pleas by the door: "Good Jews, have mercy, have mercy; I'm freezing from this cold."

But the heart of stone did not soften...

The defending angel returned to the Heavenly Court, humiliated. His attempt had failed. The Court was about to take all the wealth from the rich man and transform him into a miserable pauper, a beggar knocking on every door.

"But Meir'el didn't agree." R' Meir'el of Premishlan turned to the rich man standing in his doorway. "Meir'el argued that one doesn't punish until one has first given a warning. A man must be given a final warning. So the Heavenly Court granted an extension to see if the man would heed Meir'el's warning.

"And now," the rebbe said to the rich man, whose face was white as death, "if he decides to change his ways and immediately gives 400 rubles to R' Yudel for his travel expenses to *Eretz Yisrael,* good. And if not..."

With a piercing cry the rich man fainted. The *gabbai* brought him back to consciousness with a liberal dose of cold water.

"Rebbe," the man cried, "every word you said was correct. Everything is true. I am the miserly rich man. I am the one whose heart was hardened on that freezing day. I accept upon myself to completely change my ways."

At the same time the man whipped out his wallet and placed 400 rubles on the *tzaddik's* desk.

R' Meir'el turned to R' Yudel:

"What are you waiting for? Take what belongs to you. You've seen that if Meir'el promises, Meir'el fulfills. I could, by the way, have gotten you money in a different way, but I wanted to help this man as well. This *mitzvah* that he is fulfilling for the first time through you will open the door to many others..."

The Wagons Will Be Burned by Fire

"The bow He will break,
and cut the spear;
the wagons He will burn in fire..."
(Tehillim 46)

"T HE WAGON WILL BE READY?"

"On the day agreed upon," promised the carpenter.

"Then it will be paid for, every last cent."

A number of the community leaders of Brod had a rather strange desire. All the affairs of the community, it seemed, were being taken care of with gratifying efficiency, and with no complaints. Only one thing needed improvement: The dead were being carried to the cemetery on a simple bier lifted upon men's shoulders, following the Jewish tradition throughout the ages. But this tradition had become obsolete, or at least so it seemed to these men, who envied the gentiles' impressive and cultured funeral rituals.

"What's good for the non-Jews is good for us too," they said to themselves, those foolish men who felt themselves so enlightened. They turned to a craftsman, a worker in wood, and commissioned from him a high wagon painted black and decorated with flowers. When the work was done, the wagon would be hitched to horses and from then on, funerals in the holy community of Brod would take place with all the pomp and ceremony of a gentile funeral.

The Sages said (*Bava Basra* 4): "A bad servant does first and asks permission afterwards." So did these enlightened ones behave. After they'd ordered the carriage they decided to go to the city's rabbi, the holy *gaon* R' Shlomo Kluger, and ask for his agreement, after the fact.

"What's the difference; why should it bother him if we carry the dead on shoulders or on a fine wagon? Certainly he will agree and not put obstacles in our path."

That was what they thought.

R' Shlomo Kluger heard their words and was horrified. "It will never happen!" he declared firmly.

"Why not?" the men demanded, obstinately adhering to their plan.

R' Shlomo, too, dug in his heels, quoting the famous words of R' Moshe Sofer: "That which is new is forbidden by the Torah in every place."

"Bringing a corpse on such a wagon is forbidden for several reasons," he continued to explain. "But even if we could find a way to permit it, because this is the custom of the non-Jews it is a Divine prohibition for us, as it says, 'You shall not walk in the ways of their statutes.'"

"But we've already ordered the carriage!" One of the men

blurted out the secret, much to the discomfort of the others. R' Shlomo, much moved, shouted angrily, "I will not permit such a thing!"

"Respected Rabbi," one of the men, a boorish and brazen one, said, "it's a shame for you to fight us. We are stronger than you and your rabbinate. Soon the carpenter will be finished and from that day on the dead will be brought to their resting place on a fancy carriage, with great pomp and ceremony."

If not for the seriousness of the situation R' Shlomo would have laughed at its absurdity, but it was not the time for laughter. A war against the tenets of Judaism had been declared, and R' Shlomo was determined to join the battle.

The community officials had hardly left their rabbi when the news went around the city: In the near future, at the very next funeral, there would be a surprise in store for the residents. Only a volunteer was missing, someone who would serve as the first corpse to merit a kingly burial...

The rumors came almost immediately to the notice of R' Shlomo, and his sharp response was not long in coming.

He refused to answer any rabbinical questions posed to him!

The rabbi of the city, who daily solved difficult and important problems, refused from that day on to hear any questions, and would continue to refuse until the rebels had recanted.

No one could remain indifferent to the rabbi's "strike action;" from the very first day the absence of his incisive reasoning and clear answers could be felt. The city slaughterhouse particularly felt the lack, for questions of *kashrus* came up there daily. The first cow had been slaughtered and already there was a question of a blemish in the lungs. They put it on the side, and immediately found another, even more difficult, question of *kashrus* on the second animal. And so on with the third, the fourth...

The *kashrus* experts threw up their hands: These types of questions were far beyond their ability to solve.

From that day onwards the people of Brod stopped buying

meat, and the stench of the slaughtered animals pervaded the atmosphere. The ones who normally received the payments for each slaughtered animal — the majority of them members of the group demanding wagon-borne funerals — suffered great financial loss, and their fury grew to boundless proportions.

Most of the city's residents sided unhesitatingly with the firm opinion of R' Shlomo Kluger, but there were some, men who were ready to cast off their beliefs and traditions, who incited the masses against the rabbi and his "old-fashioned" ideas. The atmosphere in the streets grew hotter and hotter. The ones who wanted change were firm, and the black wagon already stood, ready and waiting. On the other side stood the vast majority of the people of Brod, good Jews and G-d-fearing men, ready to step into the fray. Everyone waited for the first funeral. The tension grew and only a spark was needed to start a conflagration.

"From the day Brod was founded, there was never such a thing," declared the people.

For three solid weeks no Jew died in the city, a large and populous metropolis whose number of elderly and sick yielded — in normal times — a few deaths a day. The oldest among the people of Brod, who could remember a few exceptional days when there were no deaths among the Jews, could not point to such a phenomenon: three weeks in a row!

From the day the carriage stood ready to take the corpses, the Angel of Death seemed to have announced a boycott of the great city of Brod.

With no reason for existence, as there were no bodies to be transported, the elegant hearse stood forlorn and unused. The ones who'd brought the conflict, who'd fanned the flames of controversy and civil war, threw up their hands helplessly. The white-hot atmosphere cooled down a little.

After three weeks a loud voice made the announcement: So-and-so has died.

The townspeople of Brod emphatically demanded that the

rabbi of the city come and take part in the funeral, which would, naturally, include a non-Jewish ceremony with the accompaniment of the fine carriage. The communal workers managed to slander their more religious fellows to the authorities, claiming that the religious were planning to lynch the ones who'd changed the tradition. The police sent large forces to secure the funeral route.

R' Shlomo Kluger, with no choice, went to accompany the carriage. With him, walking bitterly and broken, were the majority of Brod's religious Jews, who suddenly noticed that the rabbi was walking barefoot.

Soberly and quietly the funeral procession walked to the cemetery. The reformers couldn't contain their joy and openly celebrated their victory — a victory that didn't last very long.

When the carriage reached the open grave, the corpse was carried off the carriage. Suddenly the people gave a shudder of revulsion, as it became clear that the shrouds were red with blood. The dead man, it was discovered after some investigation, had been shaken from side to side in the jolting carriage, and his flesh had been so damaged that it had begun to bleed.

The dead man's family, who had never been totally comfortable with the new decrees, complained openly about the shocking desecration that had taken place. Immediately after the funeral, the furious mob made their way to the courtyard of the synagogue. From there they marched to the city hospital, where the embattled carriage stood.

The guards at the hospital, taken aback by the sight of the approaching mob, quickly shut the gates before it. No use: before such a throng, even heavy metal bars were powerless. They broke under the pressure of furious hands, burst open like the thinnest of wood.

The crowd began to take out its anger on the carriage. The people climbed upon it, brandishing hatchets and axes, and wrathfully took it apart. The sound of hammers and picks could be heard from far, far away.

And suddenly the police came, clubs in hand.

The frightened mob dispersed to all sides, but some, less quick than the others, were caught by the enraged police and beaten mercilessly. After the fray, R' Shlomo Kluger himself received a notice to prepare for the arrival of a state commission of inquiry from Zlatchow. The conclusion was almost foregone: the respected rabbi was in grave danger of being thrown into the municipal prison!

"I'm not afraid at all," the rabbi told his followers, "because I am innocent. If they sentence me to prison? This, too, is for the best. At least I'll finally have the time to write down my *chiddushei Torah,* a task that has been put off again and again..."

On the day the delegation arrived from Zlatchow, the people of the city were terrified. Only the rabbi counseled, "Do not be afraid." After *Shacharis* he went, under heavy guard and escorted by thousands of Brod residents, to the courthouse where the investigation was to take place.

For three hours the Rabbi underwent piercing interrogation, answering mildly and with wisdom and cleverness, in clear and pleasant language. Every sentence was beautifully crafted. The members of the committee, judges who were specialists in their field, could not but wonder at the depth of understanding of the Rabbi, at his wisdom, and his thought. His vindication was inevitable.

When he left the courthouse, the crowd that had awaited their Rabbi for three tense hours greeted him with cries of joy. And when the second part of the decree became known, in which the Jews of Brod were expressly forbidden to use wagons to bring their corpses for burial, and were forced to carry them only on shoulders — the reformers turned pale, and the religious Jews of Brod sighed in relief.

The Prison Sentence

THE *BEIS MIDRASH* OF THE REBBE OF MUNKATCH, R' CHAIM Elazar Shapira, author of the *Minchas Elazar*, was jammed with people. It was the holiday of Rosh Hashanah, and the fear of judgment was palpable in the room. A profound and expectant awe hovered on the people's faces. During this interval in the prayers the people were waiting for the rebbe to arrive for the shofar blasts. No one wasted time, now: Some recited *Tehillim* with intensity and devotion; others put their fervor into Talmud study. There were also those who stood quietly, lost in thoughts of repentance.

Suddenly a deep hush cut through the confusion, a silence that announced the arrival of the rebbe to the *beis midrash*. Almost entirely wrapped in his *tallis*, the rebbe stood by the *bimah*, and only those next to him could see his face, pale with fear.

"The Rebbe, may he be well, wishes to speak," announced the *gabbai* in a thunderous voice.

"My teachers and rabbis," the Rebbe began, "*Klal Yisrael* finds itself in deep distress. Spring has passed, summer is over, and we have not seen salvation. The son of David hasn't come yet, and our troubles grow worse with each passing day."

In the corners of the *beis midrash* the sound of weeping could already be heard. Some of the more sensitive among the congregation quickly pulled handkerchiefs out of their pockets and dabbed at their eyelids. Many felt a stab of pleasurable anticipation for a powerful speech that would liberate all those feelings dammed up in their hearts and allow a sweet and cathartic bout of weeping that would wash away all the agony of the past year.

"Not a day passes that is not more cursed than the day before," the rebbe continued, his voice edged with sobs. "And if we don't repent with full hearts and return to our Father in Heaven, who knows what will happen?"

The rebbe's voice struck awe into the listeners' hearts. The congregants cast fearful eyes upon the *tallis*-clad figure, and he continued to speak.

"The ones who came before us were truly like angels. Listen to an amazing story that I will share with you today, a story of the holy R' Mordechai of Chernobyl, may his merit protect us."

And the rebbe told this tale:

The holy rabbi, R' Menachem Nachum, the *maggid* of Chernobyl and author of the *Me'or Einayim*, was one of the generation's pre-eminent distributors of charity. He would dedicate his days and his nights to wandering the roads in order to collect money for the poor. He was completely oblivious to his waning strength, to his health, and, of course, to his honor. These were as nothing to him, no more important than the peel of a garlic bulb, against his lofty goal, a goal that seemed to hover before him day and night: to take care of the poor, the sick, the orphan, and the widow.

There was still another *mitzvah* that he was willing to give his life for, and that was the *mitzvah* of redeeming captives; to rescue from prison those unfortunates who'd fallen into the traps of schemers, to assist those who'd become entangled in the snares of debt, or to help those innkeepers who rented their businesses from gentile noblemen at huge cost. These innkeepers were obligated to pay their fees at the end of the year, and if times were hard and they couldn't repay, they were cast into the hands of the nobleman, for good or for ill. At the blink of his wicked eye they could be flung into the darkness of a dungeon. R' Menachem Nachum sacrificed his all for these people. If he heard of a Jew cast into prison he wouldn't rest until he had collected a ransom for him, whatever the master demanded, and only after seeing the prisoner released would R' Menachem Nachum return to his home.

When R' Menachem Nachum, the *maggid* of Chernobyl, returned his soul to G-d, his son, R' Mordechai, took his place, both as rav and *maggid* of the city, and as the one who distributed the *tzedakah* funds. He also took upon himself to sustain the 36 hidden *tzaddikim* of the generation, a holy mission that he accepted after the death of the Saba-Kadisha of Shpoli, who had supported them before.

R' Mordechai particularly evinced the deepest feelings for the *mitzvah* to which his father had shown such dedication; that of redeeming captives. For this there was no day or night; he would take to the roads at any hour in order to redeem someone imprisoned by a *poritz* or any other cruel malefactor.

A troop of gendarmes surrounded R' Mordechai's home in the middle of the night. After they'd banged heavily on the door, they burst their way in like a horde of demons.

"Are you Rabbiner Mordechai?" the commanding officer demanded. When he received a positive answer he growled, "You're under arrest for rebellion against the king!"

The rebbe's hands were immediately manacled and in a short time R' Mordechai had been flung into prison, in the company of thugs and underworld figures.

The city of Chernobyl was in a ferment. The news of R' Mordechai's imprisonment had spread swiftly, and the faces of the Jews were dark with misery after the terrible tidings reached them.

A delegation of honored rabbis and community activists that met on that very day with the regional ruler in an attempt to liberate the rebbe found itself facing a brick wall of obstinate, inexplicable refusal. Terrible slander had been spread against the rebbe, and the evil judge who was hearing the matter jumped eagerly upon it; the men's pleas were to no avail. The activists then turned to that tried and true solution, bribery; when the money found its way into the hands of the greedy rulers, the *maggid's* prison conditions improved a little. From the horrible hole he'd been sharing with the dregs of mankind he was transferred to a relatively more comfortable cell and given permission to bring in his *tallis*, *tefillin*, and kosher food.

On Thursday, a few men close to R' Mordechai, who'd been given permission to visit him, felt that something was different. A cloud darkened that holy face. "Without *tzedakah* my life is no life," the *maggid* sighed. "Every Thursday I normally give out charity to the city's poor, so that they'll have something to buy their Shabbos needs with, but now that I'm under lock and key, who will care for them?"

That day the activists used their influence on the king's ministers, asking for permission for the rebbe to return to his daily tasks. And from then on, every Thursday, all the poor of the city would gather together in the yard of the prison, and the rebbe distributed the money to them from the tiny window cut into the door of his cell, each receiving what he was used to. For the impoverished women he would leave the money on the sill, and they would come and take it.

The sight of a woman standing near the window broke through the rebbe's reverie. As usual, he took out a coin and began to lay it on the sill, when the woman spoke. "I don't need money; I've come to ask you a question."

R' Mordechai awaited a question about whether or not a chicken was kosher, or if a blood spot invalidated an egg, or a similar query, but much to his surprise the woman began by quoting straight from a passage of *Gemara* (*Bava Kama* 50):

"The story is told of the daughter of Nechunia the Digger of Wells, who fell into a deep well. They came and told R' Chanina ben Dosa. He told them, 'She's already come out of the well.' They asked her, 'Who took you out?' She said, 'A male ewe [belonging to Yitzchak *Avinu,* which was slaughtered in his stead: *Rashi*] came, and an old man [Avraham *Avinu*] was leading it, and he took me out.' They asked R' Chanina, 'Are you a prophet, then?' He answered, 'I am no prophet, nor the son of a prophet, but I said this to myself: Shall the thing which a man took pains with — shall his children stumble on that very same thing? Should the daughter of Nechunia the Digger of Wells — whose very name testifies that he dug wells so that the people coming up to Jerusalem shouldn't suffer from thirst — Impossible!'

"Holy Rebbe, I, too, ask," the woman continued. "Your father took such pains with the *mitzvah* of redeeming captives; shall his son be held captive? You, especially, his son who has continued on his father's path — you languish in prison?"

R' Mordechai grew lost in thought, in his shock hardly noticing that the woman was addressing him directly to his face, something none of the Jews of Chernobyl dared to do. He delved into her words and finally said, "I, too, find this affair astonishing, and I don't know the answer."

"If so, I will tell you," the strange woman said — and R' Mordechai felt the power and truth of her words — "that this has happened because you have sacrificed for this *mitzvah*. Heaven wanted you to feel on your own flesh the bitter taste of captivity, to know just how a man thrown into prison feels, how terrible it is for him. From now on you will understand even more how much you must toil and work for this *mitzvah* of redeeming captives. Now that you have felt on your own body the misfortunes of those who sit in the darkness, it is time for you to go free, and so I give you this blessing: May you soon be released!"

When the woman had grown silent, her image seemed to simply melt away and disappear. On that very day the warden of the prison was given the orders to release R' Mordechai, without any accompanying explanation.

The *maggid* was very curious as to the identity of the learned woman who had spoken to him directly and who had brought about his release so quickly. He found no rest, praying incessantly, until Heaven finally revealed to him that it was Rachel *Imeinu* herself, who had come to ascertain the welfare of her beloved son — and for that reason she addressed him directly, for a mother may do so, no matter how great her son is. She had come, also, to awaken Heaven's mercy upon him through the *Gemara*. And, indeed, her blessing came through immediately.

"*Oy gevalt*, Master of the Universe," the rebbe of Munkatch cried out, and the entire community sobbed with him, "Rachel, Rachel, Rachel *Imeinu*. How many thousands of Jews work constantly, morning and night, to redeem captives, and yet the nation of Israel still finds itself in captivity, in the hands of a cruel nation. Please, awaken Heaven's mercy for your sons, and let the words of the verse come true: And they shall return from the land of their enemy. "

One Thousand Napoleons and a Visiting Card

"I WANT A QUARTER OF A LOAF OF BREAD."

"Just a quarter of a loaf?"

"That's right. And also give me..." the customer bent forward and whispered something into the salesman's ear. He quickly cut a slab from one of the loaves of bread arranged neatly in a pile on the table in front of him. Then he casually slipped several gold coins beneath the counter, into the waiting hand of the customer. The bills handed to the salesman in exchange for the glittering coins told the tale of underground currency purchases, forbidden by law, but still common, far from the curious eyes of the secret police.

The "bread salesman," a young Talmud student and Jerusalem resident by the name of R' Yosef Dovid Brandwein, glanced carefully from side to side. It seemed to him that no one who was interested in such illegal activities was watching. But he was wrong, as he would soon learn.

These were the days of the First World War. In Israel the Ottoman Empire had ruled for centuries, a despotic and absolute rule. But suddenly wide cracks could be seen in the walls of the Turkish regime. The British army had conquered Egypt and from there had placed a siege on *Eretz Yisrael* in an effort to wrest the country from Turkish hands. The Turks fought fiercely and yet continually retreated from one position to the next. Military strategists could clearly foresee the fall of the Turkish army, while diplomats knew that the end of Ottoman sovereignty over Palestine was approaching.

The increasingly impoverished treasury of the Ottoman Empire could not possibly sustain the enormous expenses of its huge army. Thus both the Jewish and Arab residents of the land, against their will, became the primary supporters of the Turkish troops. The Turks stole in any way they could, forcibly appropriated wheat, produce, and beasts of burden, and kidnapped men to work for the army.

The pitiful economic condition of Jerusalem's Jews grew even worse when the Turkish government announced the newest emergency regulation: All residents were obligated to bring all the money in their possession to the government treasuries. In exchange for the coins and the authentic currency, the citizens were given Turkish notes of little or no value.

This was a decree that no one could live with. Until now it was accepted that every coin, gold or silver, was worth its face value. Changing these coins for notes was nothing more than appropriating the entire wealth of the citizens for the benefit of the Turkish war machine, whose days were clearly numbered.

The people went underground for anything related to financial matters. Outside they showed admirable obedience, going in great numbers to the central treasury office to change their coins for notes. But the public preferred to keep a very close eye on the greatest portion of its fortune. The concealment industry sprang up within days: the "liras" and gold "napoleons" were hidden in every possible place — in wells, beneath floor tiles, in sewers or earthenware jugs.

The people continued to do their real business in hard coins and not valueless notes. Arab moneychangers sprang up on every corner and street. The black market flourished and grew.

The government reacted quickly. Shem Bey, the Turkish ruler of Jerusalem, announced that anyone found taking part in black market business would be hung. The threat didn't deter the city's moneychangers, who continued their business, until a legion of Turkish gendarmes swooped down on the streets of the Old City and caught 12 Arab moneychangers in the act. They were taken without benefit of trial to be executed in the square near the Jaffa Gate.

Fear and terror fell upon the city's residents.

R' Yosef Dovid Brandwein was a young student, and the burden of sustaining his household fell upon him. During the war years all of Jerusalem hungered for bread, and men didn't shy away from any means of livelihood. Young Yosef Dovid found himself making connections with the owners of a Jerusalem bakery. He offered to sell bread in the Arab neighborhoods at a salary of two loaves of bread per day.

At least his family wouldn't starve.

In this way the young man became quite comfortable in the Arab neighborhoods of Jerusalem, familiar with the inhabitants, and up to date on all that went on.

One day, while he was walking through an Arab neighborhood, a surprising incident occurred. Three Turkish officers wandering through the area followed him for a short while and then called him into a quiet corner.

"Come here," they gestured with their fingers.

Yosef Dovid was nervous; this could only mean bad news. "What do you want?" he asked, his voice trembling.

When he heard the answer he could hardly believe it. Because his job took him in and out of the Arab areas, the three wanted him to change notes into gold coins for them!

The Turkish soldiers themselves knew the true worth of their notes. They wanted real money, not paper good only for scribbling.

R' Yosef Dovid heard their words and his heart beat wildly. For a moment he was certain these officers meant to entrap him. He looked covertly at their eyes, but their faces were serious. No, this was no snare. He agreed to the strange request, and within days he had become an agent, the connection between the Turkish soldiers and the Arab citizenry. The two groups distrusted each other, but both relied upon this Chassidic Jew, whose countenance testified to his integrity and honesty.

From a small-time, itinerant moneychanger, one who gave gold coins with his bread, his business grew, until he opened his own "bakery," on Jews Street. The main portion of the business took place not on top of the counter, but beneath it...

The moneychanger's commission was five percent of the transaction. Yosef Dovid's family knew prosperity at last, at the same time that many others in the city were almost dead with hunger.

Yosef Dovid was tranquilly walking up the steps of the Old City's market when he heard an emotional shout. "Yosef Dovid!"

An acquaintance ran towards him, panic clearly written on his face. "You shouldn't know such troubles: A secret policeman was in your store looking for you. He left you an urgent message, to go and present yourself at the home of Shem Bey!"

The young man grew pale as death. If the dreaded ruler of Jerusalem, Shem Bey, was looking for him, his secret must have been uncovered. The noose was tightening around his neck.

"Let me go speak to my wife," he thought despairingly. Perhaps she could find some clever way to save him from the death sentence.

His family awaited him mournfully; the bitter news had reached them a short while before. "Flee the city," his wife sobbed. "Quickly, run for your life," his father-in-law pleaded. "Go underground until everything dies down," the others begged.

Yosef Dovid disagreed. "I must appear before Shem Bey, as commanded. I can't run away; the Pasha's soldiers are all over the country: where can I run? Besides, if they find that I've run away, I'll make matters that much worse."

Finally, after a short time, Yosef Dovid left the house, escorted by his wife and father-in-law.

Where do Jerusalemites go for advice in such a time? It was simple: to the holy rebbe, R' Dovid — Duvid'l — Biderman. Even those not close to him would do so; how much more so R' Yosef Dovid Brandwein, who was one of R' Dovid's devoted *Chassidim*.

Just stepping over the threshold of the home of the *tzaddik* made their hearts feel lighter. The floodgates of tears, shut tight until now, were released and opened. More than the rabbi of Jerusalem's residents, R' Duvid'l was like a father and mother to the city's inhabitants. In his shadow, Jerusalemites felt as secure as a beloved child in his merciful mother's presence.

Tzaddikim tend to hide their lofty stature within one particular trait, one that overshadows and conceals all the rest. R' Dovid secreted his elevated level, his mysterious understanding of higher worlds, his deep comprehension of both revealed and hidden knowledge, the holy spirit that sat upon him day and night, his prayers and blessings that never went unanswered, his wisdom, deep as that of King Shlomo. R' Dovid hid all this within the enormous, unbounded love that he held for all Jews.

Only R' Yosef Dovid managed to speak normally as he stood before the *tzaddik;* his wife and father-in-law merely cried, their words lost in their sobs.

R' Duvid'l's glance, warm and loving, fell upon his young *Chassid.* "What was your first instinct? What did you think you should do when you heard that Shem Bey was searching for you?"

"To go before him," the *Chassid* answered.

"Do so," the Rebbe agreed, adding, "and I have one request of you. When you return from the Bey come to me and tell me what he wanted from you."

This was a lantern in the darkness swirling around Yosef Dovid's head: If R' Duvid'l had said that he should come to him upon his return, it appeared that the Gates of Mercy had not yet been sealed. He, Yosef Dovid, was destined to return...

From the rebbe's house Yosef Dovid's feet took him, almost against his will, to the home of the ruler. The young *Chassid* was lost in thought, wondering about the rebbe's words, trying to figure out what the Bey could want from him, if not to place him on the scaffold.

Two mustached figures, standing erect, their rifles at the ready, stood before the ruler's door and would not let him pass. "What do you want, Jew?"

"The Bey invited me to his home."

"What?" the two roared. "Insolent Jew, how dare you say such lies! The master of the city and its ruler would lower himself to invite a Jew to his house?"

Yosef Dovid would have been thrilled to return to his own home. Here was a perfect excuse, all ready for him. He could tell the Bey he'd fulfilled his orders and come, but the sentries wouldn't permit him to enter. However, he knew full well that the Bey wouldn't accept such excuses, and the sentries would no doubt deny the story.

What should he do?

An idea flashed through his mind. He pulled a pad of paper and a pencil out of his pocket and pretended to write down a complaint on the guards' behavior. "I'll tell the Bey how you conducted yourselves," he muttered, pointing a threatening finger at them.

The maneuver was successful. The sentries, frightened by the Jew writing down their names, allowed Yosef Dovid to enter.

Much to his surprise, the Bey invited him to sit down on a comfortable chair. He spoke to him politely and pleasantly, telling the shocked young Jew all about his, Yosef Dovid's, life: his childhood, his studies in *cheder*, his marriage, his employment through the years and, of course, his last business, that of the under-the-counter, illegal moneychanger.

The Bey knew all; the Turkish secret police had done their work well.

"So you see," the Bey concluded, "your life is in my hands."

Yosef Dovid seemed to curl up in fright. The Bey hadn't summoned him here for a pleasant chat. What could he want?

The Bey approached a closet and pulled a huge bag out of it. He opened it wide.

Glittering gold coins seemed to illuminate the room like a blinding flash of lightning. The sound of their clinking filled the air.

"I have 1,000 napoleons here," he said, preening like a peacock before the astonished eyes of the young moneychanger. "I want to change them for notes for a specific time for a reason I cannot reveal. According to the information I have from the secret police, there is no more honest moneychanger than you. I trust that on the day specified you will return the coins to me."

"The fish smells the worst from the head," thought Yosef Dovid as he walked home, guarding the bag of 1,000 napoleons as if they were his own. "The Ottoman Empire is rotten from top to bottom."

After a short time he returned to the Bey's home, a wad of notes folded in his purse.

"Tell me what you want for your commission," the Bey said, his voice purring with satisfaction. "Five percent? Take 50 golden napoleons from the pile I gave you."

"Heaven forbid," Yosef Dovid protested. "I don't want a single coin." The mouse that managed to escape from the lion's mouth doesn't ask for a prize; enough that he got his head safely out of the beast's jaws...

"All right," the Bey said contentedly. "Let me give you something, at least." He took a visiting card of his, scribbled a few words on it, and handed it to the Jew. "If you ever need me you can get to me, at any time you want, using this card."

From the Bey's home, Yosef Dovid went to the rebbe. His dancing heart seemed to carry him there on winged feet. Who would have believed it: an hour ago the scaffold loomed before him, and now he was one of the Bey's close friends.

R' Dovid gazed at the visiting card. "I'd like to leave this in my house. We will have need of it."

"Gladly," R' Yosef Dovid agreed. "But I'm afraid that the rebbe's house, resembling a busy market, might not be the best place to protect something as valuable as this visiting card. Perhaps it's better to leave it in my house."

This time R' Dovid agreed with the young man. It was true: the rebbe's home was always filled with guests, with the homeless and the hungry. Who could be sure that if one of them might not want to pocket the valuable card?

No more than a few days passed and the Rebbe's foresight was once again revealed to the people of Jerusalem.

On Shabbos, at dawn, there was an urgent knock on Yosef Dovid's window.

"Who's there?" he cried, jumping out of his bed.

"Yitzchak Grish," a voice replied. "The rebbe needs you urgently at his house."

Yosef Dovid swiftly donned his Shabbos garb and accompanied the Rebbe's *gabbai*, R' Yitzchak Glickson-Grish. When they arrived at the rebbe's, Yosef Dovid learned of the events that had brought this early-morning summons.

The Turkish encampment was retreating before the conquering British army. The Turks had built a front-line position in Beer Sheva, and after their army had taken heavy losses they were hard put to complete the line. In the middle of the night the Turks had pulled hundreds of yeshivah students out of their Jerusalem homes, drafting the elite of the yeshivah world. They'd been hauled up on trucks and, with dawn, were destined to be taken to Beer Sheva, to serve as human cannon fodder on behalf of the dwindling army of the Turkish Pasha.

R' Dovid's home was the center and heart of Jerusalem, and with dawn's first light, all the rabbis of the holy city converged upon it for an emergency meeting.

"Do you have the Bey's visiting card?" the rebbe asked. R' Yosef Dovid nodded his assent.

"Go immediately to the home of the Bey. Take the card with you, and do what you can to annul the decree," the rebbe commanded. Yosef Dovid hurried out, without saying a word. He didn't even ask what he should tell the Bey, or what he could say to persuade him.

"What do you want of me?" The Bey rubbed the last vestiges of sleep from his eyes. "I hope you have a good reason to wake me so early in the morning."

"I have come to tell you that serious damage is about to be done to the Ottoman army," Yosef Dovid said, his voice cracking with emotion.

"Serious damage to the army?" the Bey asked, shocked. "How?"

"They've conscripted all the sick and weak men in Jerusalem tonight," Yosef Dovid explained. "These are young men who've never seen a rifle in their lives. Can they serve as soldiers in the Pasha's army? Just at the sight of approaching English soldiers they'll run away like deer in a field, and they'll make your veteran soldiers terrified too!"

"Jew, you may be right. I haven't seen these soldiers yet," the Bey said. He hadn't thought about the situation in quite this way.

Much to Yosef Dovid's surprise, the Bey put on his overcoat and walked swiftly to the area where the yeshivah boys had been gathered. He walked from one to the next, examining their physiques.

"He's absolutely right," he roared, his face darkening with rage. "Whom have they drafted here — chickens? Dismiss them immediately," he barked in a loud voice.

The yeshivah students were immediately released, much to the relief of all Jerusalem. Only one, a heavyset, burly young man, was kept on, and the Bey promised not to send him to Beer Sheva, but instead, to assign him as an assistant to a local doctor; the Turkish soldier currently serving there would be sent to the battlefield in his place.

The rebbe commanded that the Bey's visiting card be placed in a safe place, but miraculously, almost immediately afterwards, it simply disappeared. Yosef Dovid knew exactly where he'd concealed it, and was certain no one had taken it — and yet it was gone.

The card had done its job.

Who Told the Rebbe?

"THERE WILL YET BE HEARD IN THE CITIES OF YEHUDAH and the outskirts of Jerusalem..." The clang of a fragile ceramic plate being broken on a stone floor accompanied the sound of singing that wafted out of the arched window and into the crowded neighborhood. The two sounds announced yet another match being woven together, another *shidduch* in Jerusalem's impoverished Old City. In those days, 190 years ago, no grand sum was needed to bring a girl under the *chuppah*; however, with the rampant poverty that abounded, even the modest amount for a dowry and for clothing for the bride and groom was out of the reach of many of the inhabitants.

On the day after the engagement, the father of a bride went out to the city streets. For many hours he wandered in an aimless ramble, like one who was drunk. He wondered if his friends would question his sanity. What would they do if he revealed to them his troubled thoughts? Instead of feeling thrilled, a terrible worry pressed down upon him. He continued his wanderings, not knowing what to do next.

A pat on the shoulder broke through his dark thoughts. "What's the matter, my friend?" a pleasant voice asked. He turned around and saw the *Chassid* R' Nachman Yosef Wilhelm, one of the luminaries of Jerusalem, standing near him and smiling cheerfully. "I heard that your daughter is engaged."

"That's true."

"That's a good reason to rejoice, not to wander through the city streets with a mournful face."

"You're absolutely right," the bride's father said. "But what can I do? My pockets are empty. If I merited it, angels from on high would come down to meet me and send me a treasure of silver and gold. But I don't deserve such a thing, so my purse is bare. I don't have a single coin to help cover the expenses of the marriage."

"Remove all worry from your heart," R' Nachman Yosef waved away all the man's concerns with a gesture of the hand. "Have you forgotten that I am responsible for the *tzedakah*? Your worries are mine; from today on I'll collect funds for you."

The man's face lightened, and he left his good friend with a much better feeling, never suspecting that R' Nachman Yosef had told him that only to calm him, without having a clue as to where he would find even one *majida*, one Turkish lira, to give...

The house of the rebbe of Lelov, R' Duvid'l Biderman, in old Jerusalem, was the central address for all the important issues of the city that needed to be dealt with. Both communal and personal matters were discussed at his table and many of the city's most difficult problems were solved there. It was not surprising, then, that after a few hours, when R' Nachman Yosef began to fully feel the pressure of the burden he'd taken upon himself, he left his own home and headed towards the rebbe's. The rebbe had often held out his loving hand for the needs of a bride or the support of a poor family — and who, in Jerusalem of those times, was not poor? The holy rebbe was a dependable fount of charity. Many wealthy men in the diaspora, and the people who managed the yeshivos abroad, saw in him a faithful and honest treasurer and entrusted large sums to him for distribution as he saw fit.

R' Dovid would, of course, see to it that the money reached the proper destination. And though the rule is, "The poor of your town (i.e. those closest to you) have precedence," the rebbe was scrupulously careful not to allow his own family members to benefit from the funds, though they, too, lived in grinding poverty. Not a penny of charity money was ever used by the rebbe or his family; indeed, he warned them sternly that such money was fire, and they must not touch it at all.

R' Dovid possessed a soft and merciful heart; he never refused a call for help. Therefore, R' Nachman Yosef was particularly taken aback when this time the rebbe shook his head with a negative answer, and refused to give him even a single coin for this new cause. "I give only to one who does not have; this man has much."

R' Nachman Yosef couldn't understand what he meant. "I just

spoke to him. He's not doing well: his daughter was just become engaged and he has nothing. I promised him I'd collect the money."

R' Dovid was adamant. "You needn't collect for him; he has more than enough to marry his daughter off honorably. He can even give to others..."

Now R' Nachman Yosef understood what the rebbe was hinting at. He stood silent, paralyzed. R' Dovid bid him farewell and the distributor of *tzedakah* left the house, his head throbbing. He felt betrayed. Had his friend, the father of the bride, fooled him when he'd claimed he had nothing? Yet hadn't his eyes shown true anxiety, the anxiety of a poor man? Why had he done this? Didn't he know that the *tzedakah* funds were very limited, and were only to be used for someone in dire need?

Lost in thought, R' Nachman Yosef wandered through the narrow streets. It was a rainy and cold winter's day, with lightning cutting through the sky and thunder rumbling above. His feet stepped through the ankle-deep water. Dripping wet he returned home, resolving to have it out with his friend, a rich man disguised as a pauper.

That very evening the father of the bride came to R' Nachman Yosef's house and, without knowing it, stopped that worthy *Chassid* from suspecting an innocent man. In great astonishment, R' Nachman Yosef heard his story — and, incidentally, learned from him just how far-reaching was the rebbe's vision.

"After I spoke with you I wanted to go home," his friend began. "But before that I went to the marketplace to buy something.

"The skies were dreary; I had noticed it before, but I had no idea what kind of storm was coming. Suddenly there was a clap of thunder and the skies just opened. Rain poured down."

R' Nachman Yosef nodded his head in comprehension; he, too, had been stuck in the street during the worst of the storm. His friend continued.

"I looked for a way to get home before I would be completely drenched, but the rain was strong and I couldn't move. I stood under an awning and waited for the worst to be over.

"Water was gushing down the narrow street in a powerful stream, pulling with it everything in its path. With nothing to do I aimlessly watched the flow and everything that was being dragged along with it: fruits that had fallen off stands, small branches and twigs, torn bits of paper, straw baskets.

"Suddenly I noticed a cloth bundle that had also been dragged down towards the street. You could see it was heavy: even in the streaming water it wasn't being pulled easily.

"My curiosity was aroused. What could be in the bundle? I bent down and pulled it out of the powerful flow. I looked around, but no one was near, and with trembling fingers I opened the wet knots.

"There were gold coins sparkling before my eyes — many, many coins..."

"I looked around again, but there wasn't a living being to be seen in the dark alley.

"I wondered what I should do now. Who could the bundle belong to? Maybe a Jew had fallen down and dropped it, in which case I was obligated in the *mitzvah* of returning lost objects.

"I waited a bit. When the rain abated somewhat I started to walk up the street, looking for anything out of the ordinary. I soon found what I was searching for; the sound of raised voices reached my ears. Several Arabs were standing around and speaking excitedly. I went over to them and asked them what had happened.

"I knew one of them, and he told me that not long before the rain had started, a beefy monk, one no one there had ever seen before, appeared and asked to buy some expensive spices for his religious rituals. He'd stood around arguing with the spice seller until they'd agreed on a price, and then he pulled out a bundle of coins. Suddenly a loaded camel appeared — no one had any idea where it had come from — and in trying to pass, bumped heavily into the monk's hand. The bundle flew out of the grasp of the shocked monk straight into the streaming water and, before he managed to bend down and retrieve it, it disappeared with the flow down the street.

"The monk raised a cry, 'My money, my money, all my money

was in that bundle!' All the Arabs tried to find it, assuming that he would give a fine reward to the one who located it, but none of them were successful. A few moments later a wagon driver came and sped away with the monk as a passenger, on his way to leave on a boat. Then I arrived.

"I said nothing to the Arab. I rushed home, knowing that this was a legitimate find — a large sum that would enable me to give charity to many others...

"So I came just to thank you for your good intentions," the friend ended. "But since Hashem has sent me the money I have no need for your help. And here is a donation; you can give it to someone who really needs it."

R' Nachman Yosef was deeply moved. "Your good fortune doesn't surprise me," he said.

"Why not?" his friend asked in astonishment.

"Because I heard about it from our holy rebbe, even before it happened," R' Nachman Yosef replied. "Though I wonder: If your riches are such a closely held secret — who told our Rebbe?"

"I Shall Give You a New Heart"

H E STOOD ON THE OTHER SIDE OF THE DOOR AND WEPT out loud. Within the hospitel room his wife had been suffering through terrible pains of childbirth for hour after hour, and the end of the ordeal was nowhere in sight. R' Shmuel stood, a *sefer Tehillim* in his hand, and poured his heart out to his Creator.

He listened with mounting tension to a sudden uproar within the room. And then a thin, weak wail announced the birth of his son.

The midwife held the newborn upside down and lightly tapped on his back in order to help the infant's breathing.

"Why is he so blue?" the new mother asked.

"That's what all newborns look like after birth," the midwife explained confidently.

But to her great anxiety, even after being properly cared for, the baby kept his bluish tint. The midwife, an expert in her field, seemed not to pay attention, in order not to frighten the mother, but quietly she called in some of the best doctors to examine the baby. The infant was given a careful examination, and the doctors decided to report their grave findings directly to the father.

"Mr. Green," one of the doctors said, his face solemn, "I've got to tell you the truth. Your baby is suffering from a critical problem in his heart. His days are numbered."

R' Shmuel grabbed at the edge of the table; the room seemed to swim around him, the walls danced wildly.

"What are you talking about?" he asked weakly.

The doctor stood up from his chair and pulled out a medical chart. "This is a healthy heart," he said, pointing to a colored diagram, as if giving a lecture before a class. "When this area is damaged," he continued, pointing again, "when there is a defect such as your son has..."

"My son has a heart defect?"

R' Shmuel felt as if he, himself, had a hole in his heart. "Are you sure? Is that a final diagnosis?" he asked weakly.

The doctor's face reddened. A patient dared question his professional opinion? "You may take your son to another doctor and consult with as many specialists as you care to," he said stiffly.

R' Shmuel paid little attention to the doctor whose ego he'd bruised. If they hadn't been speaking of his son perhaps he would have noticed it. But when the life of his son, his own flesh and blood, was hanging in the balance, would he care about such nonsense?

That very day he had his infant transferred to a prestigious hospital in New York. The baby was examined by the top specialists in the field, but to his sorrow the diagnosis remained unchanged. All the doctors confirmed it: The baby had a serious problem in his heart.

From then on, the treatments sent the entire family careening between hope and despair. The tiny body was given high doses of medications. There was talk of open heart surgery as a last resort, a very risky last resort.

R' Shmuel sat on a bus, returning from the distant hospital, a sad and silent despair in his heart.

If you wonder if R' Shmuel was a man of little faith, one who believed and yet didn't believe, that was not the case at all! A powerful belief in Hashem and in Torah leaders who represent Him surged within him. He was closely tied to his rebbe, the *Admor* R' Mordechai Shlomo of Boyan, who lived in New York but whose court extended to Israel. Immediately after his son's birth R' Shmuel had entered the rebbe's sanctum and wept before him, and the rebbe had faithfully promised him that salvation would come. But that salvation seemed far away, without a trace of it on the horizon.

R' Shmuel's eyes darted back and forth among the passengers, like one seeking a life preserver from the sea of troubles overwhelming him. In the back of the bus he suddenly spotted his friend, R' Yitzchak Stern, a formidable scholar and noted genius as well as a famed *rosh yeshivah* in *Eretz Yisrael*. Now he, too, was spending time in this distant city.

"R' Yitzchak, what are you doing here?" he said, his eyes lighting up.

"And you?"

R' Shmuel gave a sigh that came straight from the heart.

"If a man has a worry in his heart, let him discuss it," R' Yitzchak encouraged him.

"Well put. A worry in the heart," R' Shmuel's voice grew almost defiant. "My worry is in the defective heart of my baby son. I'm just coming back from another failed attempt to cure him, and I have no more strength even to suffer."

"Can this be you?" R' Yitzchak gave him a look of disbelief. "Is this how a believing Jew speaks?"

"Of course I'm awaiting Hashem's help," R' Shmuel sighed, "but it seems that I have sinned, and I don't deserve salvation."

"Have you been to the rebbe?"

"Of course. On the very day the problem was discovered."

"And where is your faith in the *chachamim*? Maybe in your distress you've forgotten how effective the rebbe's blessings are?"

R' Yitzchak glanced around the bus before continuing. "Listen, my friend, to an amazing story that happened to me not long ago."

"As you know, I am here for the purpose of collecting funds for my yeshivah in Yerushalayim. Though the Jews are good people who help me, still there are great humiliations and little profit. Our brothers, the Sephardim, say in *Birkas HaMazon,* 'Please do not make me have need of man's gifts, for their gifts are small and their humiliation great.' Oh, how right they are!

"But one of the advantages of raising funds is that I found myself free for many hours a day to learn in the *beis midrash*. I will never forget the scene. Into the *beis midrash*, full of his own self-importance, came a priest of the city. He had to speak to someone, one of the regular congregants, and could find no other place to come than the *beis midrash*. On his chest he sported a large golden cross.

"A cross in the *beis midrash*!

"What can I say; I'm a resident of the Holy Land, and I have never grown used to such symbols of impurity. I felt myself shaking and trembling. I ran over to the audacious priest, and pushed him out, shouting at him all the while. Several residents tried to calm down the offended priest.

"The affair took just a few seconds, but it was destined to haunt me for much longer. It was as if a dybbuk had entered within me. To my great chagrin I simply couldn't remove the image of that symbol from my memory. From that moment on it was ingrained in my head, constantly before my eyes. It confused my thoughts and disturbed my senses. I couldn't concentrate on either learning or prayer. As if to taunt me, that symbol stood constantly before my eyes.

"And what does a *Chassid* do in times of trouble?" R' Yitzchak's voice took on a singsong. "He turns to his rebbe! When I realized what a problem I had, I raced to the courtyard of the rebbe. I arrived there just at the moment when he was saying farewell to a large group of *Chassidim*. The Rebbe was giving out his coins to the *Chassidim*."

R' Shmuel nodded his understanding. He knew well the Rebbe's tradition of giving out coins to serve as a kind of protection. On each coin, originating in one of the countries of western Europe, was the shape of a cross.

"As always, the rebbe had given his assistant the coins some time before. The assistant would spend many hours with a small hammer, carefully pounding out the image of the cross on each round coin, so that the *Chassidim* would receive them already kosher.

"But when the rebbe saw me, before I could say a word, he looked at the *gabbai* and said, 'Give R' Yitzchak a coin not yet hammered out, and let him destroy the symbol with his own hands.'

"After I, myself, had destroyed the cross, the nightmare that had gripped me simply disappeared."

"That's really what happened?" R' Shmuel asked, his mind in torment.

"Absolutely," R' Yitzchak answered. "The rebbe put a new heart into me. Now you're putting all your faith in doctors?"

That evening R' Shmuel came to the rebbe's home. He was clutching a precious bundle to his chest.

"The rebbe doesn't feel well," the *gabbai* informed him. "He can see no one today."

"A king can break rules," R' Shmuel thought to himself, "and I am the king of suffering." Still holding the package in his hand, he found a way to avoid the *gabbai* and was soon speaking to the rebbetzin.

"I have no more strength," he stammered brokenly. "We've passed through the seven levels of hell with this son, and we have no hope left. I need to see the rebbe.

"If not for me — then at least for the sake of this innocent infant." With that he lay the well-swaddled baby next to the rebbetzin.

The rebbetzin picked up the baby and hugged him close. "Come with me," she whispered, "but don't let the *gabbai* hear us..."

They quietly entered the room. The rebbe was at his table, his face pale.

"This baby is R' Shmuel's son. His heart is defective and the doctors have given up hope," she said mournfully.

The Rebbe put on his glasses, stared at the infant's face, looked at his alert eyes. The baby, for his part, stared curiously at the glowing face of the rebbe, and made happy noises.

"I don't understand what the fuss is about," the rebbe said calmly. "I see a healthy child. He doesn't look sick at all."

"You've been saved!" the rebbetzin whispered to R' Shmuel. "Now get out quickly. Take your child — you've gotten what you came for."

With a heart that was singing R' Shmuel told his wife what the rebbe had said.

"We've come for the examination scheduled for today."

Because Jews have an obligation of *hishtadlus*, of making their own effort, R' Shmuel and his wife came to the hospital — though in their hearts they believed there was no need.

The nurse went into the office and returned after some delay. Her face showed her consternation.

"I can't find the patient's file."

Several doctors and other staff members joined the search.

"How can it have disappeared?" the ward clerk shouted angrily. "The file weighs more than the child!"

But the file was gone!

The doctors discussed the problem among themselves and finally came to a conclusion.

"Your son has been hospitalized for a serious problem. We won't bother with bureaucracy: we will simply run new tests on him."

"One of two possibilities," the specialist told the parents, after a lengthy examination. "Either you're making fools of us and have brought us another child, one completely healthy, who has never been ill... Or," he continued, a mischievous spark in his eyes, "perhaps you can tell us who is this wonder rabbi who has given your child a new heart?"

Innocent!

THE METERS ATTACHED TO THE FAUCETS AT THE END OF THE pipes turned swiftly, indicating with enviable accuracy the amount of liquid passing through them.

But it was complete fantasy.

George Tolkien, manager of the liquor processing plant, was very pleased with himself. He had an entire chain of factories spread all through Rumania, and the profits were unusually high — thanks to Yosef Berger, that diligent Jewish worker. In addition to his usual job, Yosef Berger had a particular specialty in the factory, and it was because of him that the profits were much higher than average.

Every plant manager wants to increase output and maximize profits. Occasionally the manager allows himself to daydream about profits without the burden of taxation.

George Tolkien was no exception.

His Jewish worker, Berger, had chanced upon a means of moving the indicators on the meters back, so that they would not report true figures. Naively he told his boss about it; that was his big mistake. Tolkien smelled money, a lot of money, and forced the Jew to translate his knowledge into action and eventually to improve upon the method and add new innovations to it. Berger found himself in an inescapable trap set for him by his crafty employer. Tolkien demanded forged figures from him, threatening to turn him over to the police. The terrified Berger became, against his will, the greatest tax evader in Rumania. The meters in Tolkien's factories reported half the true output, sometimes even less. The tax inspectors never suspected the huge hoax and charged him excise taxes based on the meters. George Tolkien rejoiced.

Yosef Berger was kept incredibly busy. He traveled from branch to branch and tampered with the meters. And the meters showed only a small part of the alcohol flowing through the pipes...

More than 60 employees in Tolkien's network of plants were privy to the secret. They cooperated and their income went higher and higher.

No one is protected forever. One of Tolkien's assistants decided to open a plant of his own. He copied all the techniques that he'd learned from his employer and didn't stop, obviously, at the best technique of all, moving the meters. But one thing he didn't learn: not to get caught. At the moment when he was concentrating on adjusting the meters backwards he didn't notice two tax inspectors standing at his side, watching his impressive display open-mouthed.

At his interrogation in the police station the man broke down and confessed all he knew, incriminating his former employer. Tolkien, for his part, washed his hands of the affair; he claimed that he knew nothing about it. He paid bribes to the proper authorities, and placed the entire blame on Yosef Berger and his assistants.

The tax laws of Rumania are severe; economic infractions are considered grave crimes. The worker who broke those laws could expect horrible tortures and an extended prison sentence. On the day that the news that they were being sought by the authorities came to the ears of the workers, they fled to Hungary, but in accordance with the extradition treaty between Hungary and Rumania, the escapees were soon returned.

Only wise Yosef Berger remained within the borders of Rumania. He found a hiding place and let the word go out that soon he would flee to *Eretz Yisrael*.

His imprisoned colleagues considered their options. Yosef, it seemed, was free in any case; Palestine had no extradition treaty with Rumania. Why not put all the blame on him?

That was how Yosef became the chief villain in the meter-adjustment scandal that rocked the entire nation. The prosecution unveiled an indictment for a million-dollar fraud; Rumania was in a ferment. The government put a 25,000 *leu* reward on his head; copies of his photograph were distributed to every policeman in the land and prominently displayed at border crossings beneath the banner headlines: Wanted!

His mother's house in the city of Dergamersht was placed under 24-hour observation and all incoming and outgoing mail passed the careful scrutiny of the censor.

Overnight, Yosef Berger had become Rumania's public enemy number one; every Rumanian policeman longed to be the one to capture him. The high reward was a grave temptation to all.

If the policemen of the city of Grosverdein had known the identity of the stranger who walked by the police station, wrapped in a coat, his head covered by a scarf, they would have fainted. Yosef Berger was a courageous man. He wandered from place to place, passing beneath the very noses of the policemen. His mother had — under police coercion — sent him a request to appear in the court of Klausenberg. Though the invitation had reached him, the detectives watching the messenger came up with nothing. Yosef simply changed his disguise and identity, again and again, and slipped like an eel through their hands.

Eighteen months had passed, and the police hadn't managed to lay their hands upon him. Yosef Berger had made a fool of the entire police department.

At the beginning of the month of Sivan, Yosef came to his aunt's house in Grosverdein. He *davened* in the *beis midrash* of the Vizhnitz *Chassidim,* confident that no one would identify him in his disguise. He was almost correct, but there was one exception: a *Chassid* who almost passed out at the sight of him. It was an old friend of his father's who'd known Yosef since his childhood. The old *Chassid* winked at him and, at the end of *davening*, pulled him out to the courtyard.

"Yosef, what are you doing here? The police are all after you!"

"You're telling me?" Yosef sighed, pouring out all his troubles and fears. As he spoke his voice broke; he was soon in tears.

"I'm tired of living!" he bawled like a child. "Since the police have come after me there's no day and no night. I can't spend more than two nights in any one place. I'm constantly looking over my shoulder, terrified. Every time a policeman passes me, my heart starts beating wildly. I can't take it any more!"

"And what does the rebbe say?" his friend asked him.

"The rebbe?" Yosef shrugged his shoulders. "Why should I ask him? If he tells me to give myself up to the police, I won't do it. And if he advises me to continue to stay in hiding, I'm doing that in any case..."

"Fool!" His friend nodded his head. "A Jewish Sage is so close to you and you don't use the opportunity?"

Yosef said nothing.

The two continued walking through the large courtyard, speaking pleasantly to each other. Yosef didn't suspect a thing. When their stroll took them past the rebbe's room, the wise friend suddenly opened the door and thrust Yosef, startled, inside.

"*Rabbeinu*!" The *Chassid* turned humbly to the rebbe — that is, the *Admor* R' Yisrael of Vizhnitz. "I beg you to listen to this Jew" — here he pointed to Yosef Berger, standing with his head bowed — "his soul is bitter and his heart, broken."

Before Yosef could utter a word of protest the *Chassid* had turned around and closed the door behind him, standing in front of it like an alert watchman to ensure that no one disturb the fateful conversation going on within.

For more than an hour Yosef poured his bitter heart out to R' Yisrael. The rebbe listened to his painful story and reflected on the difficult tale.

This was a man who, against his will, had become a criminal, a fugitive from justice, a man who could expect a lengthy jail term, perhaps even life imprisonment. It was even possible that he'd crossed a red line: The government of Rumania would not soon forgive the double humiliation — the large-scale fraud in the factories and their inability to lay their hands on one measly criminal — and the death sentence itself seemed to hover over his head. Every policeman was equipped with a copy of his photograph; his face was one of the best-known in the country.

The rebbe's heart was torn with anguish and pity for the unfortunate Jewish soul who had drawn such a terrible lot.

"What I can advise you," the rebbe said to Yosef, who was awaiting his words anxiously, "is to give yourself up."

That was what he, Yosef, had been afraid of! "What?" he cried, terrified, "The rebbe is commanding me to put my neck in a noose? I can't, rebbe," he cried, eyes gushing rivers of tears. "The minute I appear in a police station they'll throw me in jail and I'll be lost forever.

"Truthfully, I'm not at all afraid of sitting in prison," Yosef continued. "But my mother is a widow, my two orphaned sisters are of marriageable age, and everything depends on me. If I give myself up, who will support them? Besides, if my mother hears of what has happened to me, her heart will break."

All the while the rebbe sat, looking at him with eyes both wise and merciful, saying nothing. Yosef understood the extended silence as the rebbe's way of avoiding an argument. Obviously, the rebbe was steadfast in his opinion.

"Rebbe," he cried, his heart sore and bleeding, "if that is your desire, I bend my will before yours. Tomorrow morning I will go to the nearest police station."

"Let me explain something to you," the rebbe began to speak in a soft, friendly tone, without a hint of condescension, as if he and Yosef were old childhood friends.

"You think that I fly around the heavens and I heard from behind the celestial veil what it is you should do? Absolutely not. I have considered every aspect of the affair on the scale of logic and I repeat to you, you have no other choice but to give yourself up.

"Look for yourself," the rebbe explained. "How much longer can you go on living like this, like an animal at bay? One day you'll forget to be careful and they will catch you. Then you'll be thrown into jail; you won't be able to avoid it. But if you give yourself up, perhaps you can lodge an appeal, defend yourself, and be found innocent. Why, then, should you suffer the tortures of exile? There is no greater joy than an end to doubt."

Yosef stood up, encouraged. For the first time a spark of optimism flashed through him. The rebbe was speaking of appeals, of the possibility of vindication! Perhaps it could happen...

"Good, tomorrow morning I will go to the police station," he said, accepting the inevitable.

"Were you summoned to the police station in Grosverdein?" the rebbe asked, surprised.

"No."

"So then where was it that you were supposed to go?" the rebbe asked.

Yosef remembered that in his pocket lay a summons to the court in Kloiz — known as Klausenberg to its Jewish inhabitants.

"So travel immediately to Klausenberg and stand before the tribunal there. May Hashem grant you success," the rebbe said decisively.

Yosef stood up, his knees trembling, feeling like one with a death sentence hanging over his head, like a man voluntarily walking up to the scaffold for execution. The rebbe gazed upon him warmly and gave him still another blessing:

"Don't be afraid. Go, and Hashem will help you."

That very day Yosef left for Klausenberg.

When he left the room of R' Yisrael of Vizhnitz, Yosef was like a new man. Or, to be more precise, like the man he had once been. Before this he was terrified of any uniformed person, hiding behind dozens of assumed identities and countless disguises. Now, all fears had vanished as if by magic. He was at peace with his decision to give himself up; no one frightened him now.

Yet with all this, when Yosef descended from the train at the Klausenberg station he was certain he could not take more than a few steps before one of the nation's secret police would lay a hand upon him.

He knew all these detectives personally; a year and a half ago he'd tucked many crisp wads of bills into their pockets as hush money. But the bribe money had lost its effectiveness on the day the government announced a 25,000 *leu* reward on his head.

The detectives saw him; that he could tell. And yet none raised a finger at the sight of this criminal, despite the fact that a huge treasure awaited anyone who captured him.

" 'We were as dreamers,' " Yosef murmured to himself, astonished. "But maybe it's a trap." The thought flitted through his mind, but he discarded it. Such subtleties did not fit in with the feeble minds of the Rumanian police.

He flagged down a taxi and drove to the home of one of his friends, who was shocked at the sight of him.

"What are you doing here? Why aren't you disguised?"

"I am presenting myself to the tribunal in the morning."

The friend grew terribly agitated; he was certain that Yosef had been struck by madness. "With open eyes and a clear mind you're going into the lion's den?"

"It will be all right. Don't worry," Yosef said with feigned indifference. But he wondered how everything could be "all right," there before the tribunal...

The tribunal of Klausenberg was the nerve center of the justice system in the entire region. In addition to the district court, the huge building also housed the investigation division of the police and a prison for criminals. It was a somber and fear-inspiring building, and even completely honest men who'd never broken a law passed it with a shiver. The investigators there knew how to squeeze information from those being interrogated; the horrifying screams that could be heard from the windows of the building kept the local residents up for many a night.

No wonder, then, that the closer Yosef got to the bleak, grey-faced building, the faster his heart thumped, and the more his blood surged through his brain, beating endlessly in his ears like a tom-tom.

When he crossed the threshold into the building, his face was grey as the walls; a cold sweat stood upon his forehead. He waited for them to fall upon him, like the Talmudic two men who "grab a *tallis*"... He, Yosef, was worth a lot of money, and his face was as familiar to the residents of Rumania as that of King Karol. Who was so foolish as to give up such a fabulous sum?

To the undiscerning eye Yosef wore a mantle of contentment and serenity, walking directly to the office of Peter Tzumkut, head of the investigation division, a senior officer whose very name was enough to freeze one's heart.

When Yosef passed his summons into the hands of the investigator he continued to maintain his composure.

Tzumkut looked over the familiar words carefully. "One minute. Let me try to understand," he said. "This is dated a year and a half ago."

"That's right," Yosef said, his face a frozen mask. "But I couldn't get here until now."

The officer picked up his head and stared at Yosef's face. His jaw dropped in surprise; he cleared his throat nervously.

"Impossible! You're not Yosef Berger, the fugitive?"

"Exactly." Yosef nodded his assent.

"Who brought you here?" Tzumkut seemed about to explode.

"I came by myself," Yosef answered evenly.

"Listen here," the officer had risen from his chair, his eyes protruding in rabid anger. "Have you **decided** to make fools of the entire Rumanian police force? To come here on your own and give yourself up, after we've been chasing after you for a year and a half? No! That's not the way it goes! Until I see you in handcuffs, being led away from your mother's home in Dergamersht — I refuse to accept you. You won't make us into a laughingstock! Get out of here!" the officer screamed in fury, pushing Yosef out the door. "Go to Dergamersht and give yourself up there!"

Yosef left the tribunal the way he'd come. His friend and host, who never dreamed he'd see him again as a free man, stood shocked by the sight of him.

"You've come out of the lion's den safely?"

."I don't understand a thing," Yosef answered. "It's like some hidden hand is protecting me. Everyone knows who I am, I've given up my disguise, and yet no one is trying to get near me to see if it's the fugitive Yosef Berger or not... Have they taken away the reward money for my capture?"

"Are you kidding?" his host laughed. "You're still worth 25,000 *leu.*"

"That's why I don't like this," Yosef said. "I'm afraid that someone is plotting to throw me into a bottomless pit. Can you get me a good lawyer?"

Yosef consulted with the attorney who came to his host's house. The expert heard the strange story and gave the matter some thought before speaking.

"I also smell something wrong. You were standing right by Tzumkut and he threw you out? Impossible. I'm going to speak to Tzumkut. The trip to Dergamersht is nothing but a trap."

During the long and arduous meeting between the lawyer and the investigator, after many pleas and demands, the officer was finally forced to put Yosef into the tribunal prison and make kosher meals available to him.

Yosef sat in prison, leaned against the bare concrete walls and wondered at himself, at what had made him agree to such foolishness. How had his friend put it? "With open eyes and a clear mind you're going into the lion's den?"

The heavy iron door squeaked on its rusty hinges. The investigating officer walked in and gave him a look fraught with meaning.

"So what do you say, Mr. Berger?" Tzumkut turned to him, his voice tinged with amusement and contempt. "How many years are you going to get? Twenty? Thirty?"

Yosef shrugged his shoulders and remained silent.

The officer softened his tone. "I thought of putting you in prison until the end of the trial. But I see that you're an honest man; you gave yourself up willingly. So I'll make a deal with you: you can go home, and come to me every day for the next three months, until we've gone over your entire file and prepared the case."

Yosef had just left the tribunal when a leaden hand fell upon him. "It was a trap," the painful thought hit him.

"Yosef Berger!" the unfamiliar detective exulted, trying to push him onto the rocky ground of the courtyard. "I'm bringing you in to Peter Tzumkut, and collecting my reward."

"Slow down," Yosef extricated himself from the iron grip. "I've just come from there."

He waved a certificate freeing him, signed by the chief investigator, before the eyes of the detective. The man's face fell in disappointment: 25,000 *leu*, gone in a moment.

For three months, Yosef was interrogated daily. He denied all connection to the fraud and claimed that he was completely innocent.

"We have iron-clad proof against you; why deny your connection with it?" the interrogator warned him. "Just sign this document and you'll be set free, just like the others. But if you continue to deny it, you may spend the rest of your life in prison."

Yosef didn't believe a word of it, despite the friendly voice telling him these things. He knew the interrogation methods of the police and realized that if the investigator did have real proof, he wouldn't have any need for a confession.

"I have nothing to confess," he repeated. "I don't know why they are keeping me here, and why I have to keep coming for these tiring interrogations."

"Where were you in the year 1929?" the interrogator asked. (The main part of the fraud was perpetrated in that year.)

Yosef, without hesitation or fear, replied that during that year he had been struck with pneumonia, and had, at the suggestion of a well-known professor, traveled to the Tatar Mountains in Czechoslovakia to recover.

What bothered Tzumkut the most was the fact that Yosef had all the necessary papers to prove his contentions. They were all carefully scrutinized and found to be authentic.

What Tzumkut didn't know was that Yosef had, indeed, been ill and was on the verge of traveling to the Tatar Mountains, but instead had recovered immediately before setting off on the journey.

The interrogators worked tirelessly, searched everywhere, and finally found evidence against him: a truck driver testified how he'd given Yosef a ride, together with a load of liquor, the year that the fraud had taken place.

The interrogators felt the testimony was incriminating, but Yosef, confronting the truck driver, tore apart his declaration and found numerous contradictions within it.

It was one of the most complicated trials in the history of Rumania, the worst fraud ever perpetrated, worth tens of millions of dollars. It ran for 70 consecutive days — excluding weekends — and 150 witnesses took the stand to give testimony.

No one could understand how, among all those who knew Yosef, not one could be found who would testify that he'd seen Yosef turn the meters back.

The trial that opened with such fanfare closed with hardly a sound. Every one of the accused men were found guilty, some for more serious offenses and some for less, though when the verdicts were issued the punishments were light.

The only one that the judges declared "not guilty" was ... Yosef Berger.

(From the book *Kedosh Yisrael*)

A Blank Piece of Paper

"AND I ALSO REQUEST THAT AFTER 120 YEARS, I BE brought to Yerushalayim for burial on Har HaZeisim. And if it is not possible to bring me to Yerushalayim, then let me be brought to Tzefas or Teveryah." Thus wrote the rebbe, R' Yisrael of Hausiaten, in his last will and testament. The date of the will was 23 Nisan 5699 (1939), ten years before his death. The words were amazingly prophetic: when they were written, the road to Har HaZeisim was completely accessible. Who would have thought that Har HaZeisim and the cemetery built upon it were destined to fall into Jordanian hands some nine years later? Though no man knows the day of his death, it seemed that someone told R' Yisrael of Hausiaten in Nisan, 5699 (1939) — when he was already over 80 years old — that he would live for close to a decade longer, until the 29th of Kislev, 5709 (1948), half a year after the road to Har HaZeisim was closed...

And when R' Yisrael was taken to the Heavenly Yeshivah, two words in his declaration came clear: "or Teveryah."

For it was on a Friday, a wintry Friday, when the days are short. There wasn't much time, and to reach far-off Tzefas was clearly an impossibility.

The heads of the Chassidic community and the rebbe's relatives discussed the matter, and decided there was no choice but to bring the coffin to Teveryah.

Heartbroken and mourning, the *Chassidim* traveled towards Teveryah. In their sorrow and confusion they paid no attention to the simple fact that because of the shortness of the day they would not be able to return home, and would spend Shabbos in the city on the shores of the Kinneret. A few resourceful ones remembered to take Shabbos clothing; most did not. In any case, the funeral cortege reached Teveryah as Shabbos was fast approaching. The men of the *chevrah kaddisha* worked more swiftly than usual as they placed the pure body into the holy soil, not far from the graves of the *Baal Shem Tov's* students, in the area where many of the city's great *Chassidim* lay, as well as the community's rabbi, R' Moshe Kliers, *zt"l*. The gravediggers hurried, lest the sun set and the Shabbos Queen descend upon them.

When all was done, the *Chassidim* attending the funeral turned anxious eyes to the sun making its way towards the horizon, and immediately began rushing towards the city.

"Where are we running?" one of them, breathing heavily, asked the others. "We have no idea where to go."

"And anyway," another broke in, "why should we run? There are dozens of us here. Who could possibly put us all up without advance notice?"

"Let's go to the Polaniah Hotel," a third suggested. "It's not far from here, almost next to the cemetery." (In later days, it would be called the Aviv Hotel.) "The owner is a *heimishe Yid*, a man like us. We'll certainly be able to find a place suitable for spending Shabbos, at a reasonable price."

They discussed it and agreed, and soon the group of guests, like a swarm of bees, were buzzing around Mr. Eisenberg, owner of the hotel.

"What's going on? Why have you all come together at such a late hour?" Mr. Eisenberg asked in wonder. "You all want to spend Shabbos here, and none of you made advance reservations? And why are you covered in dust, and where are your Shabbos clothes?"

"We've just come from a funeral," one of them said evasively, as if hoping that this information would suffice. However, the words simply fanned the curiosity of the hotelier.

"Who was it who died?" he asked, interested.

"One of the great rebbes, but I rather doubt you've heard of him."

"So who was it?"

"The rebbe of Hausiaten, who lived in Tel Aviv," the *Chassid* said in a whisper.

Much to their surprise the face of the innkeeper darkened. He grabbed his head in his hands and began to wail bitterly.

"Woe is me, *gevalt*, the holy grandfather of Hausiaten has died and was buried here in Teveryah, and I knew nothing of it!"

The guest stared at him in surprise. The hotelier didn't look like a *Chassid;* why this screaming and moaning?

"You knew the holy rebbe?" one of them asked in wonder.

"Me?" Mr. Eisenberg groaned in a voice that broke. "Me?"

For a few minutes the man sobbed quietly for his great loss, with the group of guests staring at him, dumbfounded. Afterwards he stood, lost in thought, and it could clearly be seen that he was far, far away. The guests waited anxiously for him to break the silence.

Finally, he seemed to rouse himself. "Gentlemen, Shabbos is Shabbos. We may not mourn on Shabbos. With G-d's help, I will tell you a fascinating tale when Shabbos is over, a story of the holy rebbe whom you have just brought to rest."

Somehow Shabbos passed. Immediately after *havdalah* the guests sat surrounding their host and impatiently urged him, "Tell us the tale."

And the hotelkeeper willingly granted their request.

As he did every year, R' Moshe the merchant prepared to travel to the great fair in Leipzig. He'd been collecting a good supply of merchandise, as well as a large sum of money that would stand him in good stead in the hubbub and turmoil of business enterprise. Who knew — sometimes one could make as much in those few days as during the course of the entire year.

As he did every year, R' Moshe also prepared to visit the court of the holy rebbe of Hausiaten on his way to the fair. Each year, before attending the fair, he would take a long detour for the sole purpose of getting a blessing for his business from the *tzaddik,* R' Yisrael, son of the holy R' Mordechai Faivish of Hausiaten and grandson of the Saba Kaddisha, Rabbeinu Yisrael of Ruzhin.

R' Moshe had long since learned that there was no comparison at all between a trip to the fair after a visit to Hausiaten, to one without a stop at the house of the *tzaddik.*

R' Moshe bid farewell to his family, kissed the *mezuzah*, and went off to the marketplace. Several wagon drivers stood there, yawning from boredom. R' Moshe chose the fastest of them to bring him to the train station in the adjoining city.

The horse began walking at a sedate pace, as one that has all the time in the world. R' Moshe pulled a gold watch out of his coat pocket and glanced at it impatiently. "Give this lazy horse a bit of a switch with your whip," he called nervously to the wagoner. "At this rate I'll get to Leipzig a week after the fair is over!"

A few smacks of the whip let the sleepy horse know that it was better to gallop than let its owner hit it again. R' Moshe made the train and traveled to Hausiaten, his heart singing.

But had he known what was going on at that moment inside the walls of his home so far away, it is highly doubtful he would have continued humming that joyous melody…

A few hours after the wagon driver had left the marketplace a tearful woman appeared, asking if R' Moshe was still there.

"R' Moshe the merchant?" the drivers asked. "He left here a long time ago, on his way to the railroad station."

The woman didn't hesitate. "Take me there, as quickly as you can," she begged one of the drivers. "Maybe I'll manage to catch up to my husband before the train leaves."

A gleaming coin that appeared in her hand persuaded the wagon driver more than any other words could have. He whipped his horse, which began galloping wildly on the road towards the next city. But much to her consternation, she found that the train had departed some hours before.

R' Moshe sat down to write his *kvittel* (request), his heart full of awe and fear. He carefully chose a smooth, white sheet of unlined paper, as is customary among *Chassidim,* and wrote down his name and that of his wife. Beneath he added the names of his children, beginning with the eldest and ending with the youngest.

At the end of the list R' Moshe added his yearly request: a plea for a blessing for success in the fair to which he was traveling.

When he'd finished, he looked over the message. It took up a little less than half the paper. An exacting man such as R' Moshe would never allow such waste! He folded the paper in two, exactly in the center, and carefully tore it into two equal parts. The top part, the one with the writing upon it, he placed in his right-hand pocket; the second half, completely blank, was put in his pocket on the left side. Order, always!

The *Admor* R' Yisrael of Hausiaten, glanced quickly at the paper. He held out a hand, soft as silk, and shook hands with his faithful *Chassid.*

"Hashem should see to it that there should be a speedy recovery and good news soon."

R' Moshe couldn't believe what he was hearing. Who'd been speaking of recovery and sickness? In his *kvittel* he hadn't made a single mention of health matters.

"Rebbe, I want a blessing for success in the fair," he said courteously.

The rebbe again stared at the paper. "A speedy recovery and good news soon."

The merchant was perplexed. It seemed as if there were two deaf people carrying on a conversation here; he was asking for a blessing for commercial success and the rebbe was obstinately blessing him with a speedy recovery. To the best of R' Moshe's knowledge, no one in his house was sick.

After the rebbe repeated the same blessing a third time, R' Moshe left the room, like one struck by lightning. Hardly noticing what he was doing, he jammed his hand into his right-hand pocket — and immediately pulled it out, as if stung by a scorpion.

The *kvittel* was still there!

Further inspection showed him that his left-hand pocket was empty. Obviously, he'd gotten confused. R' Moshe, the man who loved order so much, had made a mistake and given the rebbe the wrong *kvittel* — a blank piece of paper!

And the rebbe had "read" the blank piece of paper, and blessed him with a "speedy recovery."

"I don't understand a thing," he thought with growing confusion.

There was no choice. The Leipzig clock was ticking without cease. He traveled to the fair to do his yearly business, but his mind wasn't on it. Some of his deals were successful, as usual, others less so. But R' Moshe wasn't interested in his merchandise; the rebbe's hint had made him very uneasy.

Two weeks later R' Moshe returned home laden with all kinds of treats, his moneybag heavy with crackling crisp bills, fewer than usual but still a respectable sum. However, much to his surprise, the family members didn't ask him how he'd fared. Instead, they all surrounded him with their own piece of news:

"Blessed is the one who heals the sick — your son is well!"

"What are you talking about?" their father cried.

And the family told him.

R' Moshe had been mistaken when he thought that all his family members were well when he left them. A few hours earlier one of his younger sons had contracted a serious childhood disease. Just when his father was leaving the house, the youngster's temperature began to soar, but still it wasn't clear that anything was terribly wrong. Not long after the father's departure, though, the boy began to shiver uncontrollably. His fever was very high, his entire body was covered with red patches, and his throat was so sore he almost suffocated.

Terrified and panicky, his mother raced out to the doctor, who immediately diagnosed a severe case of scarlet fever, an illness that could be fatal.

The anxious mother heard that her son's life was in danger and immediately raced to the marketplace in order to stop her husband before he left on his journey. But she was too late. Despondently, she returned home to her sick child. The situation grew worse from hour to hour. At one point it looked as if all hope was lost, and the boy was about to die!

Suddenly, without any medical reason, the course of the illness turned around. The boy regained consciousness and asked for a drink of water. From that moment, his condition improved from day to day until he could finally stand on his own feet, healthy and well.

R' Moshe and his family worked out the time, the day, and the hour, when the lad's condition began to improve. Excitedly they realized it was the moment when R' Yisrael had "read" the blank *kvittel* and blessed R' Moshe with a speedy recovery and good news!

The rebbe had, indeed, "read" the *kvittel*, read it better than the father, who had written the other one.

Mr. Eisenberg grew silent and all the guests stood around him, open-mouthed at this additional testimony to the greatness of the rebbe who had just passed on.

"Do you know who this youngster was, and how I know the story?" the hotelkeeper asked his guests. "That child is — me. And you ask me if I knew the rebbe?"

The Man in the Fortieth Bed

I N THE LARGE ROOM IN MOUNT SINAI HOSPITAL'S INTERNAL Medicine ward in Manhattan lay 40 sick men. Among them was a patient with a remarkable countenance, a long white beard, and a face that glowed like the sun. His eyes were closed and he looked almost unconscious. The day before he had undergone a serious operation and his condition had not yet stabilized. The doctors were uncertain if he would live.

Next to the bed sat his oldest son who, not long ago, had left *Eretz Yisrael* to help his father in this difficult time. Now he gave a worried glance at the sick man, trying to see if there was any improvement in his condition.

He noticed some kind of commotion in the distance. For a moment he tried unsuccessfully to figure out what the sound was; afterwards he sat, lost in a sea of memories.

R' Moshe Yair Weinstock came to America, completely unknown.

In his hometown of Yerushalayim there was no one who didn't know him; for many years his reputation as a great kabbalist had accompanied him. The humble man had, against his will, been revealed many times in all his greatness and all appreciated who he was. When he reached America for a stay of a few months, which lengthened into two years, he hoped for anonymity. He lived in a humble lodging in one of New York's Jewish neighborhoods, locked in his room all day with his books and his writings.

And yet, his desire was not granted him. Like some tantalizing aroma that wafts its way out of a gourmet kitchen and cannot be concealed, so his good name preceded him. He was soon recognized among the masses as one who had delved into deep secrets. The entire Talmud, *Bavli* and *Yerushalmi,* well known *midrashim* and those hardly studied, the *Zohar* and the wisdom of Kabbalah were all well known to him. Slowly his house began to draw to it all those looking for wisdom or fear of G-d.

A few days earlier his son, R' Yosef Menachem, had met a Jewish scholar with a worldwide reputation in the hallway of the hospital. The scholar asked him his name.

"Are you related to the kabbalist?"

When told that R' Moshe Yair was indeed his father, the scholar was overwhelmed. "Where has he disappeared to? I've been looking for him for weeks."

The son, R' Yosef Menachem, looked curiously at the scholar's clean-shaven face.

"What do you have to do with my father?" he asked, with a touch of surprise.

"Oh, a lot. I call his house almost every day. I'm an expert in Jewish matters and I'm often confronted with questions about various Jewish subjects. Before I found your father, I would have to put in long hours of research in the library in order to find satisfactory answers. Since I've met R' Moshe Yair, any question that is sent to me, be it on *Chassidus* or research, the wisdom of the medieval Jews or any other topic, I just phone him up and ask him, or come to his house, and get a detailed answer immediately!"

A sarcastic question lay on the tip of R' Yosef Menachem's tongue — "And do you give the source of information a small percentage of the fat fees you pick up for your research?" — but he held his peace and instead brought the professor to his father's bedside.

When the professor saw the serious condition of R' Moshe Yair, he almost jumped away. But R' Moshe Yair weakly waved him back. On a scrap of paper he wrote a note to him.

"Do you have any questions for me?"

The professor reluctantly put 20 different questions to him, questions on all different aspects of Judaism and Jewish wisdom. R' Moshe Yair pulled the pen from his hand, and with feverish haste began scribbling on a piece of paper. Within minutes the professor had received detailed answers to all 20 questions!

White as the sheet on the hospital bed before him, the professor thanked the sick man and tiptoed away. He couldn't know that R' Moshe Yair had been writing in this manner since childhood, jotting down his *Chiddushim* with frantic haste. The ink had hardly dried on the first rows of print when he was finishing the last letters on the page.

Two days after his operation, when they'd removed his vocal cords and left him without the power of speech, even before he'd recovered, he had gestured that he wanted a pen and paper.

"Father, the doctors say you should wait a week or two..."

One stern glance sufficed; the writing implements were brought to him.

"I shall never forget the sight," the *Admor* of Boston, R' Moishele Horowitz, *zt"l*, said years later. "I expected to find someone seriously ill, almost critical... When I entered his room I saw, to my shock, R' Moshe Yair sitting on his bed, his eyes burning, a pen in his hand and a piece of paper in the other hand, writing down *chiddushei Torah* with incredible swiftness!"

The noise grew nearer and louder; there was a sudden bustle of activity in the hallway. The sick man opened his eyes and looked at his son. He turned up his hands in a question. Someone in the room walked outside and returned almost immediately.

"There's a large group of priests coming to visit the sick."

R' Moshe Yair paled, and with quick gestures pointed to pen and paper. "Take me out of this room immediately," he wrote.

A few nurses walked into the room, nervous and busy, and quickly tried to clean up the huge area, moving from bed to bed. They carefully scrutinized the entry hall.

In one corner of the room a patient waved to the nurse. "I want to rest; what's all the excitement?"

"We're fortunate enough to get a visit from such noted guests and you want to send them away?" the nurse hissed at him. "A group of high-ranking priests from one of the most important monasteries has taken the trouble of coming to visit. They don't miss a single bed, and visit each and every patient. Would you want to miss that?"

The sick man grew silent. A good Catholic, this visit could only give him deep satisfaction. Eagerly he looked at the doorway, awaiting his guests.

R' Moshe Yair again wrote urgently, "I asked you to take me out of here immediately!"

R' Yosef Menachem read the note and his heart sank. He tried to imagine the scene: His father could not even take a single step. His condition was serious. To roll out the heavy bed by himself was impossible. Only the medical or nursing staff was permitted to do so; indeed, only they knew how to transfer a bed from one room to the other. He, R' Yosef Menachem, would go to one of the nurses and ask to move his father to another room and the nurse — naturally, a good Catholic — would ask why. And what would he tell her?

"My father is a holy Jew, who cannot take the impurity of priests..."

He could imagine the scandal. All the hospital would be agog. The story might get into the newspapers, with unimaginable consequences. The more he thought about it, the more impossible it seemed.

"Abba, I can't do it."

R' Moshe Yair once again took up the pen.

"Have mercy on me and my health; I cannot bear the priests with their impure crosses."

R' Yosef Menachem looked around him in despair. Perhaps he would see someone he knew, someone who could help him wheel his father out quietly, without making an unnecessary stir.

At that moment, the delegation of priests entered the room, all decked out in their black robes with crosses gleaming on their chests. They began to make their way from patient to patient, from bed to bed...

"We're too late," the son thought despondently. "What will Abba do when the priests come to him? Will he pretend to be asleep?"

When he watched them, though, he saw that even the sleeping were not exempt. Everyone, but everyone, had to know of their great kindness: they'd come down from their lofty monastery and to visit the hospital!

R' Moshe Yair closed his eyes, lost in thought.

"Like that time, during *seudah shelishis*," his son murmured, and his mind flew back to distant Yerushalayim, to the Beit Varsha neighborhood.

The family had gathered for *seudah shelishis* at their grandfather's house. The house was bathed in the dim light of dusk. One after the other, the Shabbos *zemiros* were sung. Soon, Shabbos would be over.

R' Moshe Yair sat at the head of the table, his eyes shut and his face radiant.

"In ten minutes Shabbos will be out," one of those present thought to himself while singing. "In ten minutes the gates of

Gehinnom will be opened and the wicked thrust within them after their Shabbos rest. Among them undoubtedly is so-and-so, who so upset Abba and caused him so much heartbreak..."

The thought was still flitting around in his head when R' Moshe Yair's hand gently landed on his arm.

"During *seudah shelishis*, one may not think such thoughts..."

R' Moshe Yair opened his eyes and once again wrote a note:

"You don't have to do anything; they will not be able to come to me."

And so it was: The priests walked through the large chamber, visited each patient, not missing one — Jew and non-Jew alike. They stopped at thirty-nine beds — and when they reached R' Moshe Yair they simply passed him right by, as if he was not there!

(I heard this from R' Moshe Yair Weinstock's son, R' Yosef Menachem *shlita*.)

R' Yosef Menachem adds: My father, *zt"l*, was known as a man of many accomplishments, in many different areas. As a young man he put his hand to poetry, writing holy verses with such deep sensitivity that people familiar with the genre were amazed. When he had collected a number of such poems he published a book, small in size but great in quality, called "*Mas'es Moshe*," and printed a limited number of copies. I was a young man then, bar mitzvah age. One day I was surprised to see an unexpected guest in the house: a bare-headed man who shut himself in with Abba in his office and spoke privately to him for about half an hour. I asked Abba who the man was, but he refused to tell me. Only after a long time, when I had begged and begged him, did he tell me that in Tel Aviv a group had organized a literary convention with the participation of the best of Israel's authors and poets. In the course of the convention someone had approached a man considered the "national poet," and greatest of the poets of that era (the year was 5693 [1933]), and showed him the book *Mas'es Moshe*. This man read through it and studied some of the poems in depth. He then shouted, "We're sitting here in Tel Aviv making conventions, and in Yerushalayim lives a poet who stands far above us. I've never seen such poetry!"

After a few days the man sent a special messenger to my father with an unbelievable offer: the Hebrew Writers Organization would support him and his family and take care of all their needs in the coming years, on the condition that R' Moshe Yair would give them his poems and exclusive rights to publish his works!

"And what did you say to him?" I asked.

My father was shocked by the question. "Of course I refused. Would I sell myself to such people?"

More than 20 years passed. One day my father asked me, "Do you remember what I told you about that poet and his messenger?"

I answered yes.

"You should know," my father said, "that from that day forward I was not able to write poetry. From the day that I was told that that man was impressed by my work, the pen was taken from my hand. My fountain of poetry ran dry, I was so upset. Woe to me, that such a man enjoyed my poems, that people who rebel against G-d should be touched by them to the point that they would support me and my family! Although that particular secular poet died only a year after the convention, and the whole matter was dropped, I lost any interest in writing poetry.

"Today," my father revealed to me, "the power of poetry has returned to me; the fountain has begun to flow once again. Today a new spirit came down upon me and I wrote a poem."

(This is the well-known poem, *The song of the shepherd,* which struck a chord among many and served as the opening for his second collection of poetry, *The Harp of David.*)

What more need be said?

The Story of a Bottle of Wine

I N THE FOLLOWING TALE THE BOTTLE OF WINE DOES-
n't seem to play a very important part, and doesn't even
turn up until the end of the story. Despite this, I have chosen to give it this title, because when all is said and done, the
wine bottle is at the center of the tale, not in its own right but
because of what lay behind it...

Akiva Tzirkin* felt discriminated against from the time he was a child. It seemed to him that his older brothers were much more successful than he; compared to them he had been meted out a scanty ration of talent. Not only that, but his brothers always seemed to use their time well, and were never found without a *sefer* in hand, even during *bein hazemanim*, while he was always to be found in the playground or just wasting time chatting.

His father and mother could never understand this kind of behavior. "Akiva, why are you wasting your time?" Abba would growl at him. "Kivaleh, what's going to become of you?" his mother would sigh. The two of them always made him uncomfortable: whenever he was summoned to his parents' room for a talk, it seemed to him that they were comparing him to his older brothers and finding him completely useless compared to them.

"Look where he is and where they are," his father once said. "Yes, and they are successful and talented and he is not," his mother added. Akiva burned with shame and tears coursed down his face. There was no one to tell him that Abba and Ima were just comparing the new electrician in the neighborhood with his two predecessors... Akiva just knew that they were talking about him: If they were putting someone down, it must be him!

---

* All names have been changed.

A small bubble of bitterness, jealousy, and anger began to form in his heart. If his parents had given up on him — why should he try? Before this he had tried to prove that he, too, was worth something, that they shouldn't dismiss him as a failure, but now he knew that nothing would help. With his own ears he had heard his father say of him yesterday, "He's simply a dwarf!" (Actually, Abba was speaking of the new Arab worker in the neighborhood grocery, whose height was about three feet, but Akiva only heard that one sentence.) "If so, why should I make an effort?" Akiva thought wrathfully. "I'm a dwarf. A nothing. A big zero. And you hate me because I'm not as gifted as my big brothers. I'll teach you a lesson, a bitter lesson!"

In his anger he began to hang around with a tough crowd in the neighborhood, with whom he quickly slid, very far down. In a sharp twist Akiva changed from being a fine boy, one who kept all the *mitzvos*, to someone empty and dangerous. In order not to call attention to himself he didn't change his exterior appearance at all. His two curly *peyos* swung jauntily at his side, his round Yerushalmi hat was firmly placed on his head (at, it must be admitted, a slightly different angle), the long coat grew no shorter, not even by an inch. Yet in the darkness, Akiva behaved like any other who'd thrown off the yoke of observance, until he finally desecrated Shabbos.

But you can't fool parents; they always know. "What's happened to you, Kivaleh?" his mother wailed. "My dear Akiva, what is bothering you?" his father tried to get him to speak, but Akiva kept a stony face. "What have I done? Nothing! Everything is the same; why are you worried?" But deep in his heart he enjoyed the love being showered upon him. Finally he was getting some of the attention that he'd never enjoyed when he'd behaved himself; finally he was finding out that Abba and Ima loved him anyway, that they cared about him.

If the truth be told, after he'd gotten what he wanted — a good dose of attention and appreciation — he could have turned back and cut off contact with his wicked friends. But suddenly Akiva was learning two rules of life: It is easier to ruin than to fix; and it is hard to get away from bad friends.

Akiva did try to pull away from his new crowd, but the rebels closed in on him from all sides: just a short trip, a group vacation to some doubtful places, somewhere his parents would never allow him to go...

He didn't know how to get himself out of the mud, and he fell deeper and deeper into the mire. His angry parents tried everything: When they saw that the pleasant method didn't work, they turned to the stick: shouts and warnings and, finally, blows. The entire family rose up against him, issuing dire threats.

It was actually the "stick" that made Akiva feel more comfortable. Again he could justify his anger and his former despair. He managed far better with the blows and screams than with the pats and kind words. When they showed him love he grew confused: "What? They care for me, even though I'm not Yossi the *masmid* or Avremi the genius?"

He went from bad to worse. In practice he was completely secular, a secular Jew in the garb of a *Charedi,* with *peyos*, hat, and suit: a Purim costume every day. Yet that gave the parents a tiny measure of comfort: If Akiva had not yet shed the outer covering there was still a spark of hope. He hadn't completely burned his bridges behind him.

On the edge of despair, Mrs. Tzirkin heard about R' Mendel Fuchsman, a dedicated leader who was devoting his whole heart to helping these "children at risk."

"My Akiva is, in practice, a complete *goy*, a *goy* with *tzitzis* and a *kippah*," she poured out her bitterness to him. "Maybe you can do something before we have to sit *shivah* for him?"

R' Fuchsman was a young man, but he had already worked with a great many such young people, and he had seen many tough cases.

"Mrs. Tzirkin, I'm ready to do whatever I can for you," he said to her with a charming smile. "It seems to me that the best thing would be for him to spend Shabbos with me in Meiron. I want to speak to him privately, without anyone else around."

On that next Friday R' Fuchsman picked up Akiva in a taxi traveling to Meiron. The ice was soon broken and the two were talking like old friends. But not a word was said about the reason for the trip.

They lodged in a small apartment in one of the houses in Moshav Meiron. R' Fuchsman didn't want anyone to be with them during the meals. He had arranged for excellent food and the tantalizing fragrance of Shabbos dinner wafted through the room.

With the coming of Shabbos, the two of them walked together up the road towards the tomb of Rabbi Shimon bar Yochai. R' Fuchsman was buoyed by Akiva's joyous mood; a happy spirit is a necessity before a good heart-to-heart talk. R' Fuchsman had gone through many such discussions, and he was well prepared with arguments and persuasive points. He knew how to turn around hearts, and had much experience in doing so.

Inside the tomb, the sound of the prayers rose. Within Akiva's soul, so tortured by doubts and poisoned by bitterness that knew no outlet, something began to stir. Suddenly he found himself racing out of the tomb and standing on the long porch facing the darkened shapes of the forest. He broke out into the famous Shlomo Carlebach melody for "*Havu LaHashem bnei elim*," his voice full of emotion.

R' Fuchsman learned two important points that evening. One: Akiva Tzirkin was an emotional person, and two: He liked Carlebach *nigunim*.

After prayers they went down to their lodgings in the moshav. They chatted of this and that, small talk that gave no sign of the terrible events to come.

Akiva was in good humor, and his *peyos* were dancing in the light breeze. His hand found its way to his pocket, and casually he pulled out a cigarette. Before R' Fuchsman could say a word, Akiva had lit it up and was contentedly inhaling its scent, as if nothing had happened.

R' Fuchsman was suddenly thrust into a maelstrom of emotion. He'd never felt so betrayed, so cast down. How could it be: You were just *davening Maariv* of Shabbos with such loftiness of spirit, singing songs of the soul, and suddenly, in such a sharp turnaround — you light a cigarette?

"You lowlife," he longed to shout at the young man serenely smoking before him, watching him with alert eyes as if to see how he, R' Fuchsman, would react to this arrogant provocation.

A thousand harsh words stood on the tip of his tongue; all the harsh warnings of *Parashos Bechukosai* and *Ki Savo* were ready, together with a flood of rebuke.

He didn't say a word.

There was a long silence, a silence perhaps harsher and more piercing than any words he could have uttered. His hands trembled like one who is ill. How he wanted to slap this brazen rebel, a good hard blow that would send him flying from Meiron to his home in Yerushalayim.

He did nothing.

Only one prayer rose in his broken heart: *Master of the Universe, don't let Your great Name be desecrated, keep everyone else away from us, so that no man should see this shameful thing.*

Please, don't let anyone see two young religious men walking on the road, right by the tomb of the holy Rabbi Shimon bar Yochai, one of them smoking on Shabbos and the second walking unconcernedly next to him, without making a protest. Clearly, people will think that he must agree with this behavior!

His prayer was answered. No one saw Akiva Tzirkin in his degradation, no one passed them until his Shabbos cigarette had burned itself away. Just then several moshav members appeared; R' Fuchsman had no idea where they'd been until then.

They entered the room. The Shabbos candles were burning in their candlesticks. A lovely orange flame danced before them; a thin thread of smoke rose up from the fire. R' Fuchsman steeled himself and walked over to the table, although his heart still hadn't recovered from the turmoil he'd been cast into by that one cigarette.

They began to sing "*Shalom Aleichem.*" As if he hadn't just desecrated the Shabbos a few minutes earlier, Akiva sang with great enthusiasm. "*Barchuni l'shalom...*" *Miserable hypocrite,* R' Fuchsman wanted to shout at him, but he sealed up his lips with a lock of steel.

On the table a bottle of red wine reflected the candlelight.

"Oh, no!" he suddenly thought. "Here in the room with me is a person who desecrates Shabbos in public. If he touches the wine it will be *yayin nesech*!"

With a hurried motion, so that the young man shouldn't see him, R' Fuchsman grabbed the bottle and placed it under the table.

They continued to sing. Before *Kiddush* he bent over and pulled the bottle out from its hiding place. He poured it into the cup and said *Kiddush*.

They ate *challah* and fish.

R' Fuchsman began singing *zemiros*. Akiva hesitantly joined in. Slowly they turned to the poignant Carlebach *nigunim*. The young man was now completely carried away, his eyes shut, his fist hitting the table lightly in time with the melody.

To be honest, R' Fuchsman himself was flying on the wings of song into another world, until he suddenly realized that he was singing a solo. Akiva's voice broke, a choked wail came from his throat, a wail that somehow turned into a flood of tears.

Akiva cried and cried, completely out of control. His body swayed back and forth with the sobs.

R' Fuchsman remained silent.

When the boy had finally calmed down he said, his eyes downcast, "From the time that I can remember they were always screaming at me. Everyone was better than I was: my brothers, my friends, everyone... Nothing bothers me anymore, not screams, not blows. I was going to cross the line soon. I was tired of this double life. When Ima asked me to go with you to Meiron, I agreed. What did I care; why refuse a trip to the Galil, an adventure?

"But something has changed," the boy confessed. "That's why I tested you tonight. I wanted to see what you would say if I would be obnoxious enough to light a cigarette. You were silent — and you got me with your silence. I saw how the blood came to your face, and I was sure that you would explode, like all of them. But you didn't, you bit your lips and made a fist, but you didn't say a word. I felt that you understood me more than anyone else who was always pushing me away.

"And when you took the wine away from the table — I saw how you tried to sneak it away — you tried to hide it. And I know you tried to hide it. You did it quickly, and I realized why. But you did-n't want me to know, you didn't want me to be embarrassed...

"At that moment I felt how low I really was.

"So bad? Am I, Akiva Tzirkin, considered a *goy*? Do I make wine undrinkable, turn it into *yayin nesech*?"

"So you see," R' Fuchsman explains, "I had prepared speeches and speeches, a treasure house full of rebuke and censure, while still in Yerushalayim. But it was the silence, the words not said, that spoke to the heart of this boy, who turned himself around that Shabbos. Today he is a fine, upstanding young man, completely ob-servant. It was actually that swift movement, the one I tried to hide, the one I hadn't planned, that made the difference. Can you find a better meaning for the prayer, 'You give Your hand to sinners'? You, just You, the merciful Father in Heaven. We try, we speak, but oc-casionally You open our eyes to see that You are the One Who does it all!"

(I heard this from my friend, R' Tzvi Kup, who is involved in *kiruv rechokim*.)

The Boy From Holland

T HE SOUND OF SCREAMING COULD BE HEARD ALL THROUGH the house. "I can't take your behavior anymore," Mr. Epstein shouted at his son Pinny, as he rained blows down on him. The boy began to wail and rushed out of the room, his father's raised voice following him. "I'm losing my patience; if you don't improve I'll throw you out of the house!"

Pinny was a young man with troubles aplenty. His father, Wolf

Epstein, was a respected member of the Amsterdam Jewish community. As a youngster, Pinny was a bright and merry child, with two laughing eyes that held true Jewish charm. His teachers in the local Talmud Torah would sigh when they had to report on his behavior to his parents. "A talented and bright boy with a great future, if only he would want to." They would repeat, with another sigh, "If only he would want to..."

Pinny didn't want to.

Pinny spent all his days in the Talmud Torah playing silly games or getting into mischief. He liked to spend his free time with a gang of rowdy young thugs from the neighborhood. He would disappear from his house for hours and when he returned couldn't come up with a plausible or acceptable explanation for his absence. Every time Pinny would come back from spending time with his friends, Wolf would feel the blood rush to his temples, and sense that his heart was about to burst. In addition, Pinny resembled in many of his traits the infamous *ben sorrer u'moreh*, and was something of a glutton. Some of his teachers suggested that his brain be taught via his mouth: Keep him from any junk food for a day or two to teach him a much-needed lesson. Wolf listened to the advice, and tried it several times, but somehow, in miraculous manner, it was just on those days that the best of the foodstuffs disappeared...

Pinny's bar mitzvah was celebrated with great pomp in Amsterdam's finest hall, which Wolf could well afford. A hidden hope in Wolf's heart whispered that perhaps his beloved son would feel grateful for all he'd done for him and would turn onto the proper path. But as the days passed Wolf found himself more and more disappointed. If in the past, while still a youngster in school, Pinny had found youngsters whose behavior was questionable, now that he was growing older he began to hang around with gangs of bullies and hoodlums whose dark deeds had even awakened the interest of the police.

Finally Wolf decided: "No more." He had been told some time before of a house in far-off Yerushalayim that was like no other. The heads of the household, a husband and wife, gave of themselves entirely to others. Rumor had it that the mentally ill returned to sanity after being in the hands of R' Freund, and youngsters who had strayed off the right path returned back with the help of the man who knew how to find something precious left in a pile of garbage.

The next day Wolf and Pinny flew to Yerushalayim. "You should know," the father warned his son, "you come back to my house only as an observant Jew!"

From the airport they traveled directly to Yerushalayim. The cab wandered through the streets until it came to a stop. A house covered with Jerusalem stone, its walls grey with age, seemed to welcome them with the words, "This is the place."

Wolf asked no questions. Feeling suddenly ashamed, he didn't even knock. Instead, he asked a passerby if this was the Freund house. Upon hearing that it was, he immediately left Pinny there on the sidewalk, standing alone with his luggage in the courtyard of a strange house, while he, Wolf, drove off.

The rebbetzin came out into the yard, her warm heart seeming to radiate from her cheerful face. Her alert glance immediately took in the young man standing there, abashed. She wanted to ask him his name, but he stood, completely silent. Instead, she walked into the house, awaiting the right time. After about an hour she went back into the yard, saw him standing in the same position, half dejected, half defiant, refusing to answer anyone who tried to speak with him.

Something inside her whispered, "Not yet. Wait a little and then you'll be able to crack this nut." As always, she obeyed her instincts, and again returned inside.

When she came out a third time the young man was still standing, frozen, like a statue someone had sculpted and discarded.

"Who are you?" she asked him, her face welcoming.

Silence.

She didn't let up. "How did you get here?"

"My father brought me here from Amsterdam this morning." Pinny's lips trembled. "He left me here, said that someone would take care of me, and went back to Holland." Now it all came out in a rush, like a wall suddenly collapsing. He burst into tears.

"Why are you crying?" she said, like a loving mother. "Your father was right. Come into the house and Asher and I will take care of you." She took his two suitcases and entered the house with him.

For the first days Pinny moved around like a sleepwalker. The warmth and love showered upon him by complete strangers confused him completely. He suspected some dark plot — they wanted to win his heart by some pretense that would soon explode, and this kindness would be followed by harshness and stern discipline. But after a short time he realized that these people couldn't possibly pretend anything. They tried to understand him, made no demands, and spoiled him like an only child. He tried to repay them with pleasant behavior; he made an effort to improve. But a leopard cannot change his spots — not quickly, anyway. He soon returned to his rebelliousness, his gluttony, stuffing himself like a hungry beast. He would spend entire days wandering around doing nothing, not lifting a finger even when the house — which was always full of guests — needed his help. *Davening,* too, became a burden: He would wind the straps of *tefillin* around his bloated fingers in great haste, rush through the words, and finish up *Shacharis* in minutes. He would disappear from the house for hours, coming back only to eat, leaving again immediately afterwards. Ugly rumors flew about his new friends. But here, in this house, they knew how to deal with problems like these...

On that Friday, Pinny awoke, surly and ill-tempered. All day he walked around with a sour face. He didn't know what to do with himself, he felt so bitter and angry. The house was full of people. The needy were there to get their "Shabbos packages": fruits, vegetables, fish, and meat changed hands, and the heart that gave rejoiced, as it says, "More than the calf wants to nurse, the cow wants to give milk..."

All the excitement took place around him, but he closed himself to it, not letting all this kindness make even a small dent in him.

One could see the figure of the rebbitzin flying through the rooms. She'd been working for Shabbos since the Sunday before. If she found some interesting foodstuff, she would announce, "This is for Shabbos." If something better turned up the next day, then it was reserved for Shabbos. Now, with the approach of the Shabbos

Queen, she was busy with the preparations of *Erev Shabbos*. Straightening the tablecloths placed on all the tables, ironing out a barely-perceptible wrinkle; checking that all the dishes were clean; peeking into the pots standing on the stove. Many guests — as every Shabbos — would be eating all through the night. Guests who, if they didn't eat here, would go hungry. Guests whom no one else would be willing to entertain.

Candlelighting time approached. The rebbetzin wanted to go to the candlesticks, to light the wicks in their olive oil. But somehow her legs took her, almost against her will, to Pinny's room. A voice inside told her to go see what he was doing.

He was lying on his bed, his eyes glazed. "Pinny, Shabbos," she whispered, a whisper that came from the depths of a soul that was already imbued with the radiance of the special day.

Pinny pretended to be sleeping and didn't bother answering. "Don't you want to get dressed for Shabbos?" she asked in a gentle voice.

"No," he burst out angrily. "I don't want to."

"Calm down. So you won't," she answered quietly. "I under-stand you; you must be going through some sort of crisis. Still, Shabbos will not look away; you must give it something. Let me polish your shoes for you in honor of Shabbos."

Awkwardly Pinny raised his feet and kicked off his shoes. Not a word passed her lips in the face of such errant insolence. She brought the shoe polish and a brush and stood there, generously smearing on the polish, shining the shoes to a gleaming sheen. But it wasn't enough; she brushed them and brushed them until they sparkled. "*Nu,* Pinny, now you can look at yourself in the mirror," she laughed happily. Quietly she put down the shoes and left the room.

She had hardly closed the door when Pinny leaped out of bed as if stung, his eyes filling. The sight of her humble figure as she polished those shoes sent shivers all through his body. Something moved in his heart, that stone heart. "What does she owe me?" he found himself asking, a question with no answer. "They suddenly bring a boy from Holland to her house, a wild and troubled boy, and she works for him as if he were her only child." In a frenzy he donned his Shabbos clothes and raced outside; to show, to prove, that he was no stranger here. For him, too, it was Shabbos.

The Rebbetzin sat in her room, surrounded by her daughters and guests. Her face glowed with the light of Shabbos. When she saw Pinny she knew that on this day the turnabout had begun. Pinny the "*goy*" had been buried beneath the weight of a layer of shoe polish. The glow of the candles met Pinny with a welcome, "Good Shabbos; today you have become a man."

> May this story be a memorial for the soul of my righteous grandmother, the Rebbetzin Tzviya Freund, *a"h,* whose home was a home of *chesed.*All her life she took care of people who had no home of their own, fed the poor, gave drink to the thirsty, and let everyone feel that they were at home. She fostered unfortunate children for long periods of time and made "*menschen*" of them while they were in her home. They learned from her exemplary character, nobility of soul, and goodness of heart. Just as she was an example to all of lovingkindness, she was also an exemplar of a personality that can influence another without a word. She never scolded or rebuked, never shouted, but anyone near her was changed. This story was one of thousands that actually happened, with only the identifying details changed.